GREECE
and ROME
Builders of
Our World

RIGHT: ASTRIDE A DOLPHIN, MYTHICAL HERO TARAS CLUTCHES TRIDENT AND WINE CUP;
2,300-YEAR-OLD COIN FROM TARAS (TARENTUM), A GREEK COLONY IN ITALY.
OVERLEAF: ACHILLES VANQUISHES PENTHESILEA, QUEEN OF AMAZONS, AT TROY;
6TH-CENTURY B.C. ATHENIAN VASE PAINTING IN THE BRITISH MUSEUM, LONDON

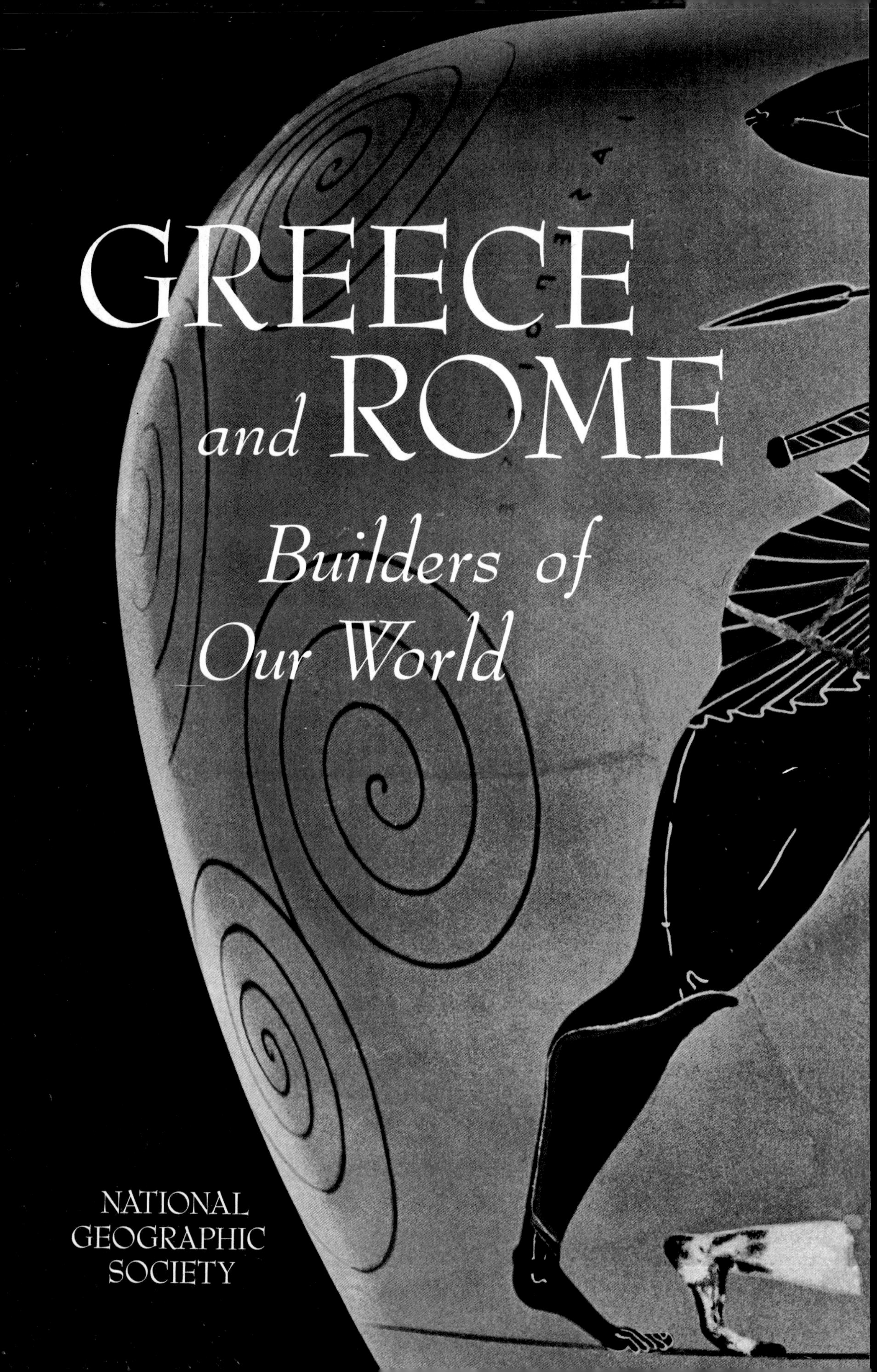

GREECE
and ROME
Builders of
Our World

NATIONAL
GEOGRAPHIC
SOCIETY

A VOLUME IN THE STORY OF MAN LIBRARY
PREPARED BY
NATIONAL GEOGRAPHIC BOOK SERVICE

PUBLISHED BY THE NATIONAL GEOGRAPHIC SOCIETY
MELVIN M. PAYNE, CHAIRMAN OF THE BOARD
ROBERT E. DOYLE, PRESIDENT
MELVILLE BELL GROSVENOR, Editor-in-Chief
GILBERT M. GROSVENOR, Editor

Foreword by
MELVILLE BELL GROSVENOR

Editorial consultant
PAUL MacKENDRICK
Professor of Classics, University of Wisconsin;
Visiting Fellow-Elect, Churchill College, Cambridge;
author of The Mute Stones Speak, The Greek Stones
Speak, The Roman Mind at Work; co-author of
Classics in Translation, The Ancient World

Special Essays by Dr. MacKendrick and
EMILY VERMEULE
Professor of Greek and Classical Archeology,
Harvard University; an excavator of the Minoan island
of Thera; author of Greece in the Bronze Age

EMELINE RICHARDSON
Professor of Classical Archeology, University
of North Carolina; an excavator of Cosa;
author of The Etruscans

GILBERT CHARLES-PICARD
Professor of Roman Archeology, the Sorbonne;
former Director of Antiquities in Tunisia; an excavator
of Carthage; author of Carthage; co-author of
Daily Life in Carthage at the Time of Hannibal

PIERRE GRIMAL
Professor of Latin Literature, the Sorbonne;
author of The Civilization of Rome,
In Search of Ancient Italy

Chapters by
ERNLE BRADFORD, author of Ulysses Found;
LEONARD COTTRELL, author of The Bull of Minos,
Lost Worlds, Realms of Gold; and TOM ALLEN,
JOHN J. PUTMAN, HELEN and FRANK SCHREIDER, and
MERLE SEVERY of the National Geographic staff

Staff for this Book

MERLE SEVERY
Editor and Art Director

SEYMOUR L. FISHBEIN,
EDWARDS PARK
Associate Editors

CHARLES O. HYMAN
Designer

ANNE DIRKES KOBOR
Picture Editor

THOMAS B. ALLEN,
ROSS BENNETT,
JOHN J. PUTMAN,
BERRY L. REECE, JR.,
DAVID F. ROBINSON
Editor-Writers

JAMES P. KELLY,
WERNER L. WEBER
Production Managers

WILLIAM W. SMITH,
JAMES R. WHITNEY
Engraving and Printing

JEAN F. LEICH, SUSAN SIDMAN,
ELIZABETH DONLEY, MARY HOOVER,
JENNIFER URQUHART, Editorial Research
MARIANNE HURLBURT,
SARA DE VENGOECHEA, Picture Research
EDWARD MARTIN WILSON, Design
WILHELM R. SAAKE, Production
ESTELLE SADUSK,
BARBARA STEWART, Assistants
ANDREW POGGENPOHL, Art
JOHN D. GARST, ANN RUHNKA, Maps
WERNER JANNEY, Style
DOROTHY M. CORSON,
JOLENE McCOY, Index
W. E. ROSCHER, European Representative

Sunset silhouettes marble maidens of the
Erechtheum atop the Acropolis in Athens;
Mario de Biasi from Mondadori Press

First two printings 325,000 copies
This edition 135,000 copies

ISBN NO. 87044-071-3
LIBRARY OF CONGRESS CATALOG CARD NO. 68-54521

Paintings by
PETER V. BIANCHI, LOUIS S. GLANZMAN,
H. M. HERGET, BIRNEY LETTICK, TOM LOVELL,
ROBERT C. MAGIS, *and others*

Photographs by
WALTER MEAYERS EDWARDS, ALBERT MOLDVAY, WINFIELD
PARKS, JOHN J. PUTMAN, HELEN and FRANK SCHREIDER,
and MERLE SEVERY *of the National Geographic staff;*
FARRELL GREHAN, PHILLIP HARRINGTON, MICHAEL KUH,
DAN McCOY, W. ROBERT MOORE, ADAM WOOLFITT, *and others*

541 Illustrations,
440 in full color, 16 maps

Foreword

Our CHART merely noted the spot as "ruins." But what magic ruins these were! For this dot on my map was Troy. The very name conjured up heroic deeds of Achilles and Hector; the legendary beauty of Helen that "launch'd a thousand ships" when its prince, Paris, stole her from Sparta; the golden treasure that emerged from the dust in one of archeology's greatest adventures.

The deck of the ketch *Yankee* heaved under my feet to the surge of Homer's "sea deep-thundering." Our sails swelled to the same winds that bore Agamemnon's fleet across the Aegean from Greece. From our deck we studied the sunny Turkish coastline where the vengeful Greeks landed for the ten-year siege.

Suddenly, 30 centuries of myth and history came alive. Jason and his fabled Argonauts passed here in quest of the Golden Fleece. Xerxes, King of Persia, flung a bridge of boats across the Hellespont and marched the hordes of Asia against the handfuls of Greece. Alexander the Great crossed here to invade Asia and conquer the greatest empire the world had yet known.

Twenty-two centuries later came a retired German merchant, Homer in hand, to fulfill a boyhood dream.

Our ketch anchored at the bustling port of Çanakkale, and as I sped in a car over a modern highway I mused on the fabulous life of that merchant, Heinrich Schliemann—a rags-to-riches story that culminated in his discovery under a mound named Hissarlik of the city many scholars had dismissed as fable.

TROVA—TROY. The sign jolted me out of my daydream. "Will we see the wooden horse?" my 12-year-old Sara asked. She had just studied about Greece in school, and her presence gave my wife and me a fresh perspective. The "windy plains of Troy" failed to produce any sign of a Trojan horse. The best I could find was a small wooden one in the souvenir shop. Yet Sara found far more.

"This south side of the city was not so steep," our guide Huseyin recited. "So the Trojans might have brought the big wooden horse in here, with Odysseus and other Greek heroes inside. On the west, Schliemann found 'Priam's treasure.'" The gold of Troy! "It came from that trench, beside the fig tree," he added.

Riffling through our *Iliad*, we read aloud of the epic duel when Achilles chased Hector "along by the watching point and the windy fig tree always away from under the wall...." Sara listened closely, then ran over to spread her hands along the selfsame wall. With her fingertips—here and elsewhere on our journey through the Mediterranean world—she met the builders of our civilization. And what treasures they bequeathed to us!

Greek inventiveness transmuted the Phoenician *aleph* and *beth* into the *alpha* and *beta* that gave us our alphabet. Here arose the concepts of law and government that rule our lives, thoughts that enrich our minds, beliefs that inspire our souls.

A HUMBLE HELEN *graces a Hellenic harvest. Timeless tableaux greet modern eyes in lands where Greek heroes reaped glory and Rome sowed the peace of empire.*

FARRELL GREHAN

Here began our literature, sports, medicine; the street plans of our cities, the architecture of our public buildings; the logic, geometry, engineering, and science that have transformed our world.

I made a pilgrimage to Delphi, where Apollo had settled at the "navel of the earth" to guide mortal men through his Oracle. I pondered its maxims, *Know thyself* and *Nothing in excess,* and gazed on Mount Parnassus, haunt of the Muses — majestic reminder that our poetry and song, drama and art were born in Greece. Climbing to the topmost row of the theater at Epidaurus, a perfect fan of stone spreading on a Peloponnesian mountainside, I recalled how *Oedipus Rex, Orestes,* and other Greek dramas probe the dark subconscious to illumine the human character.

Strolling the Acropolis by moonlight, we marveled at the Parthenon, serene though scarred by time and man's wars. In southern France we studied soaring arches of the Pont du Gard, a Roman aqueduct that once slaked the thirst of Nîmes. And I reflected that our concepts of what is beautiful and what is useful came from Greece and Rome.

In Bodrum, Turkey, where Crusader knights built a castle from stones of the original Mausoleum, we examined treasures from the sea that Dr. George F. Bass and his University of Pennsylvania Museum team have recovered from ancient wrecks. The National Geographic Society has helped sponsor his work for many seasons. Here we held earthenware plates and cups used by the sailors for their food and drink, the swords they fought with, axes, copper bullion, even stone anchors that took us back to Homeric times. How close we felt to Odysseus — that "much-enduring" wanderer whose homeward voyage from Troy spanned years of adventure in a realm of nymphs and monsters.

To give readers the same rich experience, Book Service Chief Merle Severy and I planned *Greece and Rome: Builders of Our World.* We sought to weave the story of the ancient world around its towering figures. Such an approach proved enormously popular in a companion volume, *Everyday Life in Bible Times* (now with more than 625,000 copies in print). In that book we witnessed the dawn of civilization along the Nile and the Tigris and Euphrates, the emerging life of the Old Testament, and the birth of Christianity. In this volume we see the flowering of Greek and Roman genius, enriching the march of civilization.

We sent National Geographic writers and photographers to the ends of the ancient world, tracing the footsteps of Odysseus, Pericles, Alexander, Hannibal, and Caesar. We commissioned artists to re-create Greek and Roman daily

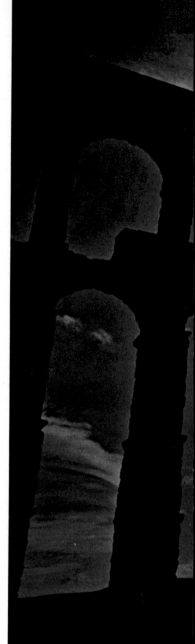

DAN McCOY, BLACK STAR

STONES WITHOUT MORTAR *soar into Spain's sky, still bearing water to Segovia 19 centuries after Romans raised the aqueduct. Rising 93 feet, spanning half a mile, the twin-tiered arches were devised by engineers who knew no peers until modern times. Roads, walls, aqueducts veined the empire. What ancients wrought and thought shapes our world today: All that stands is Roman, says an adage; all that moves is Greek.*

life. We turned to distinguished scholars to write special essays. Dr. Paul MacKendrick, Professor of Classics at the University of Wisconsin, shared his great knowledge as consultant during the long months of preparation. Final proofs followed him to the American Academy in Rome, where he was then a trustee.

As I reviewed the zestful text, I was struck by how much we owe the ancients in philosophy and science, in everyday customs and speech. Our Founding Fathers took over the Greek and Roman inventions of democracy and republic. They proudly placed on the Great Seal of the United States the eagle of Zeus, holding his thunderbolts and the olive branch of peace, together with the Latin phrase: *E Pluribus Unum* (Out of Many, One). Indeed, in so many ways, we are all Greeks and Romans. Let us voyage into the ancient world to find how that came to be . . .

Melville Bell Grosvenor

CONTENTS

To the strident sound of war trumpet, horns, and hydraulic organ, gladiators perform a dance of death in this

Unraveling the Mystery of the Etruscans 250

The World of Hannibal 275

In the Footsteps of Hannibal:
THROUGH THE ALPS TO THE GATES OF ROME 294

The World of Caesar 337

In the Footsteps of Caesar:
CONQUEROR'S PATH TO MIGHTY EMPIRE 372

2d-century Roman mosaic from a villa near Leptis Magna, preserved in the Museum of Antiquities in Tripoli, Libya.

Quest for Our

By Merle Severy

Golden Heritage

"Men exist for the sake of one another," wrote Marcus Aurelius, Roman emperor, Stoic philosopher, warrior despite himself. His once-gilded bronze, from the 2d century A.D., stands amid Michelangelo's Piazza del Campidoglio in Rome. Photograph by Adam Woolfitt

IT WAS A MIRACLE that the great horse with fiery nostrils escaped—to bear its imperial rider down the centuries. All other Roman equestrian bronzes fed the fury of barbarians and fanatics, the crucibles of metal-hungry generations.

Piety preserved this magnificent statue, now on the Capitoline, most sacred of Rome's seven hills. Christians thought the rider was Constantine the Great, first Roman emperor to embrace the faith. How ironic, I mused, that they mistakenly immortalized a pagan predecessor, Marcus Aurelius. His officials had dutifully persecuted members of a Palestinian sect who preached that Rome would be "thrown down with violence" and "burned with fire."

Today we honor both—the sainted Constantine although he put to death wife and son, the pagan Marcus Aurelius because he was humane and left us his *Meditations* on the dignity of man.

Each age has found new values in its quest for Greece and Rome. Invading Vandals and Goths took land and booty. The medieval church borrowed Rome's language, organization, and concept of universal empire. For a thousand years monarchs clung to a Holy Roman Empire that, Voltaire reminds us, was "neither holy, nor Roman, nor an empire."

Renaissance men proclaimed the rebirth of Greece and Rome, drank deeply at the wellsprings of their art, and enriched us with masterpieces. The American and the French revolutions flamed with ideals of the Roman Republic and Athenian democracy. Our forefathers looked at their bold new world through Rome-colored glasses. The Roman patriot became the ideal citizen, the Roman tribune the guardian of man's rights, the Roman general the most valiant of leaders. Rome's laws and monuments were a vision of grandeur.

13

The Greek War of Independence in which Lord Byron gave his life fanned feverish enthusiasm for the glory of Greece. Athens, citadel of freedom and culture, flowered anew in men's minds. Sparta's stand at Thermopylae stiffened many an upper lip. Boys' schools prided themselves on Spartan discipline, discomfort, and will to win. Had not the "Iron Duke" of Wellington proclaimed that "the Battle of Waterloo was won on the playing fields of Eton"?

We still find fascination in antiquity's heroes: Odysseus, Pericles, Alexander, Hannibal, Caesar; its heroines: Helen of Troy, Cleopatra. . . . As we learn more, we idealize less, but become increasingly aware of our debt to Greece and Rome.

I SENSED ROME'S POWER, the reach of her empire, atop Hadrian's Wall that once spanned Britain; at Palmyra, amid Syrian sands; at throbbing Vindobona—Vienna—on the Danube; at Volubilis, Thugga, and Leptis Magna, spreading grids of silent streets under the North African sky. Nowhere did I feel the pulse of Roman life stronger than in the shadow of Mount Vesuvius at Pompeii.

Cross the threshold of a Pompeian house, and 19 centuries drop away. In the peaceful court, fountain and foliage delight the eye. In rooms alive with murals detailing the labors of Hercules, the loves of Venus, voices seem to echo. How easy to conjure a family from its portraits, to surround them with belongings seen in museums at Pompeii and Naples, to hear them speak the words of Martial, Juvenal,

JUPITER JABS *a bolt of lightning through the Naples night toward Vesuvius. Brooding sky evokes the "horrible black cloud torn by sudden bursts of fire in snakelike flashes" that Pliny the Younger saw on an August day,* A.D. *79. The eruption killed his uncle, Pliny the Elder—fleet commander and naturalist, drawn to the scene as much by scientific curiosity as by duty. It entombed Pompeii, six miles south of Vesuvius.*

A wind-whipped hail of lapilli, pellets of pumice, scourged fleeing Pompeians (below); some shielded heads with roof tiles or pillows. Ash mired many, deadly vapors felled others. Three days later the pall lifted, but the port and its environs, plus 16,000 dead, lay under 20 feet of volcanic debris.

"Even for gods this was going too far," complained the poet Martial of the holocaust that made a time capsule of the tragic town.

NAPLES AT NIGHT BY JAMES P. BLAIR,
POMPEII PAINTING BY PETER V. BIANCHI,
BOTH NATIONAL GEOGRAPHIC STAFF

WHERE NATURE *rampaged, scholars now reconstruct, striving to portray Pompeii at her moment of doom. Prof. Amedeo Maiuri (left) led them for 37 years; in World War II he stuck to his site until bullets sang, then fled wounded on a bike.*

Discovered in 1748, the forgotten city was mined for treasures. Excavators now leave things in place. Blooms gladden House of the Vettii (right); root holes showed where to plant. Ancient lead pipes again feed founts in the peristyle garden and the pool in the atrium, or central hall. Rebuilt roof shields murals.

Horace, Petronius, and other Roman writers who so delighted in conversation!

"He's already started wading into Greek and he's keen on his Latin," I fancy I overhear a guest say as he reclines on his couch at dinner. "The older boy, now, he's a bit slow. If he doesn't stick it out in school, I'm going to have him taught a trade. Barbering or auctioneering.... But every day I keep pounding the same thing into his head: 'Son, get all the learning you can. It's money in the bank.'"

"Parents no longer bring up their children to behave and be honest," grumbles a companion. In these affluent days of empire, he says, youngsters "get to be fresh, with no respect for themselves or anybody else."

Out on the stone-paved street the last knots of tourists head for the gate as shadows lengthen. In the sudden hush Pompeii magically comes to life. I hop onto the narrow sidewalk to let an imaginary chariot rattle past. I smell fresh-baked bread at an open shop and pity the slave who turns its stone mill, grinding grain. I nod to the cobbler, the potter, the felt maker, the gem cutter bent over his little piles of agate, jasper, carnelian, and lapis lazuli. I stroll past a modest *hospitium,* or hospice, with only a single *triclinium,* or three-couch dining room. Its sign is the figure of an elephant, for its founder served with Caesar in Africa.

Houses turn their backs on the streets, but the people's voice — *vox populi* — cries out on the walls. Red-lettered political posters proclaim: "Numerius Barcha, a fine man; I appeal to you to elect him...." And "Numerius Veius Barcha, may you rot!" Scribbles trace love's uneasy course: "Here Romula and Staphylus met" — and, alas, "Here Staphylus met Quieta" — and, inevitably, "Do you think I'd mind if you dropped dead tomorrow?"

Beside the Forum I pass one of the elegant baths with radiant heating. Marble, murals, and sculpture adorn it. Some 1,300 lamps illuminate it. Here Pompeians steam, swim, and chat into the night, men and women in separate sections.

In the covered market, men do most of the shopping. Several women parade past,

16

wearing elaborate coiffures and cloaks of Indian cotton or Chinese silk. Gold and pearls weight their ears; the jewelry copies Greek, Syrian, and Egyptian designs. Slaves shade their mistresses with parasols. "She buys all the creams the slender Indians send us," complains a husband. At bedtime he chides her: "You lie stored away in a hundred little jars . . . your face does not sleep with you!"

A patrician sniffs at the street scene. His white wool toga falls in exquisite folds —obviously he owns a fine *vestiplicus,* or valet. He points out a plump Pompeian in silk tunic, inelegantly loose at the waist. "Came up from nowhere," he comments. "Used to tote wood on his back." This fashionable resort where the great Cicero once had a villa surges with the new-rich. "Ambition pulls everyone forward, chained to the wheels of her gleaming chariot," he continues; "nobodies, some-bodies, everybody." Merchants, artisans, manufacturers of *garum,* a pungent fish sauce much esteemed, are turning mansions into homes with shops. A cloth mer-chant has inscribed in his vestibule *Salve Lucrum*—"Hurrah for Profit!" No wonder respectable people are moving out of Pompeii to suburban villas!

Gladiators lure them back to the amphitheater. Big enough to seat the city's 20,000 people, it has seen fired-up fans commit mayhem. Once, when Pompeians massacred neighboring Nucerines there, Nero closed it for a decade.

Raised voices arguing about gladiators draw me to the *thermopolium*, a tavern that sells mulled wine. Asellina owns it—patrons have scrawled her name on a wall along with those of Smyrna and Maria Aegle, her obliging wenches. Now a "regular" rages about some broken-down fighters: "Puff at them and they'd fall down dead. Why, I've seen better men tossed to the wild animals." His comrade speaks of a big show coming up. "Not the same old fighters either; they've got a fresh shipment in and there's not a slave in the batch. There'll be cold steel for the crowd, no quarter, and the amphitheater will look like a slaughterhouse."

Not for me, even though a poster promises scented water will be sprayed on the crowd. Instead, I'll visit the small, roofed Odeon for a concert, or a big open theater near it. It's free, as are the games, and the spectators bring food and drink and cushions for the long siege on stone seats. Women dress for maximum effect and gleam with jewels. "They come to see and be seen," the cynics say. The program? Slapstick farce adored by the people—the misadventures of Maccus, glutton turned banker; of Pappus, dotard running

LEE E. BATTAGLIA

POMPEII LIVES *today because it died so swiftly, preserved in mid-stride under a shroud of ash. Nuts, bread, figs, intact eggs seem to await a diner—perhaps the merchant whose scale is balanced with a bronze Mercury, god of trade (and thieves!). Ghost of plaster memorializes a merchant's dying struggles; engulfing mud hardened into a mold, which scholars filled. Famed murals (opposite) in Villa of the Mysteries show forbidden Bacchic rites. An initiate awaits a whiplash that ensures fertility as a Bacchante whirls to castanets.*

19

WALTER MEAYERS EDWARDS, NATIONAL GEOGRAPHIC STAFF. BOTTOM: ADAM WOOLFITT. UPPER RIGHT: ENGRAVING BY PIETER SCHENCK, LATE 17TH CENTURY; MANSELL COLLECTION, LONDON.

for office and after girls. In the interludes, on come dancers, acrobats, clowns, bawdy comics—and, for a grand finale, a parade of nude showgirls!

SUCH WAS LIFE IN POMPEII, arrested by the eruption of Vesuvius on August 24, A.D. 79. For more than 16 centuries the city and its neighbor, Herculaneum, slept in tombs of hardened ash and mud. Then in the eighteenth century scraping shovels revealed them. Studying their statues, Johann Joachim Winckelmann, pioneer art historian and archeologist, proclaimed the rediscovery of the ancient world, faultless in its beauty, transcendent in its art.

The coaches of the Grand Tour rattled up, and a procession of notables came to marvel at these subterranean cities spared the ravages of time. Pompeii and Herculaneum captivated the tastemakers of an age. Borne by poets, painters, and collectors, news of the wonders swept a modern world once again falling in love with

20

CRUMBLING CROWN *of golden Rome, the Colosseum rears its ramparts through an aureole of auto lights. It kindles awe today as it did when Grand Tourists came to survey its silent shell (above) and Shelley wandered its "ruined stairs and immeasurable galleries." Statues that once filled upper arches stand on a coin of Emperor Titus (below, right). He opened the Flavian Amphitheater, named for his clan,* A.D. *80, passing out slaves as door prizes to lucky ticket holders. Baptized in blood, it rang for four centuries to the roar of beasts, the screams of dying men, the clang of the* gladius, *the short sword that named gladiators.*

An even grander marvel preceded it: Domus Aurea, Nero's Golden House. On 200 acres cleared by the great fire some said he set, the paunchy playboy (pictured on his coin below) sang and sported amid gold- and jewel-bedecked rooms, a mile-long triple colonnade, banquet halls with ceilings that revolved or showered revelers with blossoms and perfume. His fanciful frescoes, later found buried as if in grottoes, inspired our word "grotesque." In the entry stood a gilded-bronze colossus of Nero as sun god, taller than the Statue of Liberty. "At last," sighed Nero, "I can live like a human being." Successors razed the palace, drained its lake for the arena, moved aside the colossus. It toppled 1,200 years ago, yet its name stands in the Colosseum.

COINS OF NERO, A.D. 64-66, AND TITUS, A.D. 80; BRITISH MUSEUM

DOME OF THE PANTHEON,
*model for a thousand capitols
and shrines around the world, soars
toward its unglazed eye in the sky.
Emperor Hadrian designed antiquity's
most daring and majestic vault about* A.D. *120,
using arched brick ribs to reinforce concrete,
a material the world all but forgot for 1,400 years.
The dome forms a perfect hemisphere. If it were a
sphere, it would touch the floor, for the dome's height
equals its diameter — 142 feet. Five rows of coffers adorn
and lighten it. Engineers today use them for the same purpose.
Through the 29-foot open window to heaven beat the bright rays
of Sol and the rains of Jupiter Pluvius, drained by a sloping pavement.
Warm light from this sole source once bathed a rotunda sheathed in marble,
bronze, and gleaming gold, and rich in statuary honoring seven planetary deities.
Now amid impressive simplicity it touches tombs of Raphael and two Italian kings,
and altars of a more enduring faith. Since* A.D. *609, Christians have worshiped here under
Hadrian's harmonious dome and "the eye of God" in Rome's best-preserved ancient building.*

the ancient one. Arbiters of fashion went Pompeii-mad. From palaces of Catherine the Great's Russia to pseudo-Greek mansions of Mississippi Valley planters, neo-classicism reigned. Pompeian arabesques decorated English drawing rooms; Pompeian cupids adorned French boudoirs. Marie Antoinette led women out of virtue's rampart, the hoop, into the soft, clinging gowns of the new "Grecian mode." Josiah Wedgwood founded a Staffordshire pottery town to meet the demand for urns decorated with classical garlands and "Herculaneum figures." In rapt obedience to Winckelmann's edict — "imitation of the Ancients is the shortest way to perfection in the fine arts" — artists chiseled and daubed to supply ardent collectors with what passed for Greco-Roman style.

Archeology became the rage. Nelson's mistress, Lady Hamilton, and her husband, British ambassador at Naples, considerately timed "finds" of reburied objects with the arrival of distinguished guests. And what the Grand Tourist couldn't turn up with a spade, he bought at inflated prices, often from swindlers. Art dealers fattened on foreign purses in this age of easy authentication, when English lords sent home statuary by the shipload. "If the Colosseum were portable," Romans quipped, "the English would carry it away."

The Romans themselves had almost carried it away. For centuries they used it as a quarry. They also razed temples, blew up one shrine to get stone for stables, operated lime kilns in the Forum. Christian zealots hammered heads off pagan statues. Fortunately Rome was not unbuilt in a day, and some statues survived to adorn Renaissance palaces. In 1506 young Michelangelo rushed to a vineyard to see the sculpture, unearthed in Nero's Golden House, of the Trojan priest Laocoön and his sons being strangled by Athena's serpents. Its dynamic movement had compelling effect on Renaissance art, steering it toward the exuberant Baroque.

"ROME IS THE GREAT OBJECT of our pilgrimage," wrote Edward Gibbon. He conceived the idea of *The Decline and Fall of the Roman Empire* "in the gloom of evening, as I sat musing on the Capitol, while the barefooted friars were chanting their litanies in the temple of Jupiter...." Goethe, Keats, Shelley, Byron, Washington Irving, Henry James — all came, saw, and were conquered. Rome became essential to a gentleman's education. "I entered Rome with full classical enthusiasm," Boswell wrote Rousseau. "I remembered the rakish deeds of Horace and other amorous Roman poets...." Love was part of that education. And if fortunes were lost pursuing it in the palatial parlors of courtesans, or at the gaming tables, that was hardly surprising. Our word "money" was coined here — in the temple of Juno Moneta, ancient Rome's mint.

Concepts of the Roman Republic were the currency of 18th-century political thought. Repelled alike by the absolutism of kings and the despotism of the mob, the French jurist Montesquieu studied ancient institutions. And where he wrote that there can be no exercise of sovereignty but by the will of the people, our Declaration of Independence states that governments derive "their just Powers

VENUS DE MILO, *island of serenity amid a swirl of admirers, stands alone in ageless allure. Gone are the arms that perhaps held a polished shield to reflect the ideal beauty of the love goddess who rose from the sea. Yet she mirrors in marble the quest for perfection that ennobled ancient Greece.*

"THE YEAR'S YIELD *burgeons . . . in nodding heads of grain . . . the generous olive yields its juice . . . and high upon the sunlit rocks the vintage ripens mellow."* In lines as rich as the farmlands he extolled, the poet Virgil sang of the staple crops of the ancient world. *Our cereal invokes Ceres, Roman grain goddess; most of our wines flow from the grape species Odysseus knew.* In lands once Rome's, Turks winnow wheat (above) and a Spanish woman tips a water jar. Italians tread grapes and winnow olives (opposite) in Virgil's *"earthly paradise, mighty mother of crops and mother of men!"*

from the Consent of the Governed." He warned that "power should be a check to power," that legislative, executive, and judicial functions should be separate. The founders of our nation spelled it out in the Constitution.

This was the theory of the Roman Republic—*S.P.Q.R.*, "the Senate *and* People of Rome," governing through elected magistrates, each group checking and balancing the others. Romans split the executive; they had two consuls. Like our Founding Fathers, they trusted no one man with unlimited power (except in crisis). Rome's Senate took its name from the Latin for "old men." This council of elders stood as a father to the people, so senators were patricians, from *pater*, or father. Champion of the plebeians, the commoners, was the tribune (originally the leader of a tribe—a voting district). His cry, *"Veto—I forbid!"* could block a bill.

Cicero's cadences ring in our oratory. Burke, Pitt, Patrick Henry modeled their speeches on his, and later statesmen unconsciously borrowed his style. When

Lincoln said "of the people, by the people, for the people"; when Churchill said "Victory at all costs, Victory in spite of all terror, Victory however long and hard the road may be"; when John F. Kennedy said "where the strong are just and the weak secure and the peace preserved," all were using the triple link and the repeated hammerblow—Greek devices which Cicero perfected.

As our nation underwent its birth pangs and citizens filled journals with letters signed "Brutus" and "Civis," it was only natural that our borrowed institutions found homes in classical buildings called capitols from Rome's Capitoline. Jefferson designed the first—Virginia's "Republican-style" Capitol in Richmond, inspired by a Roman temple he had seen at Nîmes while U. S. minister to France. And our money seemed safer in banks built like solid Greek temples. Benjamin Latrobe designed these, envisioning that "the days of Greece may be revived in the woods of America, and Philadelphia become the Athens of the western world." He

SACRED DELPHI, *revered by its pilgrims as the womb of Greece, nurtured religion, statecraft, and the arts. Zeus loosed two eagles, one from where the sun rose, the other where it set; and where they met, here in a realm "tortured by the rages of the Earthshaker," a stone marked the omphalos, the very navel of the earth. Here Apollo spoke through his Oracle to man; and here throbbed the political intelligence center of the ancient world. Above the templed sanctuary thrusts Mount Parnassus, haunt of the Muses.*

HELEN AND FRANK SCHREIDER, NATIONAL GEOGRAPHIC STAFF

Americanized his columns for the U. S. Capitol with tobacco and Indian-corn motifs.

As Greek columns and Roman domes marched westward, and early steam engines chuffed in little Doric temples, ancient names spread over the new land: Rome, Athens, Carthage, Corinth, Sparta, Syracuse, Utica, Troy...Augusta, Hannibal, Cicero. Cincinnati was named for the society formed by officers retiring after the Revolutionary War. They honored the patriot Cincinnatus who led Rome to victory over her foes, then laid down his sword and returned to his plow. Inevitably Washington would be portrayed in sculpture as *Pater Patriae*—a bare-chested Jupiter in classic robe, arm raised in a Ciceronian gesture. Enthusiasm for antiquity even led a painter to enlist Rome's goddess of love and god of medicine in a salute to progress—a painting titled "Venus Vaccinated by Aesculapius."

F ROM A CRAG in the shadow of Mount Parnassus, I looked out upon a scene that symbolized all Greece. Stark walls of rock soared from a valley where darkly gleaming olive groves curved down through the lowlands to the shining Gulf of Corinth. I felt apart from the world, exalted, blessed with eagle vision.

"ATHENS, SO THEY SAY, EXCELS in piety.... Yet, when it comes to me, where is her refuge?" Lament of homeless Oedipus rings down the ages as Athenians breathe life into Sophocles' Oedipus at Colonus. Sequel to his towering Oedipus Rex, it restores to glory the king who gouged out his eyes after realizing that unwittingly he had slain his father and married his mother. "Now let the weeping cease," it ends. "Let no one mourn again."

Gone from plays are choruses that chanted such lines, and the masks they wore for comedy or tragedy (right). But Greek tragedy speaks to us yet, grips us with scenes of noble striving against omnipotent fate. We glimpse hope in the abyss of despair, man triumphant even in death.

No wonder, for I was at Delphi, where the gods have watched the saga of Greece unfold since the Mycenaean earth goddess, Gaea, reigned here in the Bronze Age.

Invading Dorians pushed the goddess aside. Her son and protector, Python the serpent, was slain by a newcomer, Apollo. He stayed at Delphi and counseled mortals.

For more than a thousand years, pilgrims trudged up Delphi's Sacred Way to consult his Oracle. As the Greeks tamed the land and cultivated their minds, so did their gods mellow. Warlike Apollo became a patron of arts, maker of laws, healer of the sick. His father, thundering Zeus of the roving eye, evolved into a benevolent patriarch. Poseidon, Earth-shaker who rent the Delphic landscape, had long since picked up a trident and taken to the sea, a realm the Greeks would make their own.

Delphi saw warrior-aristocrats with precious bronze weapons give way to trade-rich tyrants whose militia were armed with cheaper iron—and later, that civil weapon so costly to tyrants: the vote. The shrine welcomed elected leaders from a lodestar city named Athens and kings from a realm turned fortress, Sparta. Rivals in rare peace and frequent war, they both raised monuments here. Athens commemorated her defeat of the Persians; Sparta, her destruction of the Athenian fleet. Earlier, Delphi had inspired the first confederation in a land that knew no nationhood, when 12 city-states banded to protect the Oracle.

Along the Sacred Way small "treasuries" rose to house offerings to Apollo. Gold tripods, sculptures, bronzes came from all over the world the Greeks had colonized: city-states in Sicily, North Africa, the Black Sea.

I paused before the reconstructed Treasury of the Athenians. From this I could envision the scattered ruins restored to beauty, and the Sacred Way ringing with footsteps and voices as figures paraded to Apollo's Shrine out from misty valleys of legend and bright plateaus of glory. Here trod

Oedipus, King of Thebes, to learn of his dreadful fate. Pythagoras the philosopher came, and trained a Pythia, the priestess voice of Apollo. Herodotus the historian came: "My business is to record what people say, but I am by no means bound to believe it." Plutarch the biographer served here as a priest. What a lofty place for him to look out over the landscape of men and discern those towering among them! One who came would be called Alexander the Great.

Roman emperors came—conquerors, yet conquered by the soul of Greece. Then about A.D. 390 the Christian emperor Theodosius closed the pagan shrine. Pagan? Of course. But as I stood within the ruined Temple of Apollo, I thought of what the Greeks had done. They brought their gods down to earth—and raised the human mind into the realm of the immortal.

Apollo, some say, took annual leave from his shrine, allowing Dionysus, god of wine, who had a cave on Parnassus, to reign for three months of revelry, a riotous respite from lucid sanity. The Greeks had two souls in their breasts, one striving for clarity, temperance, moderation, the other impelling them toward orgy and

MILI. TRAGIC MASK (UPPER), 5TH CENTURY B.C. BRONZE FROM PIRAEUS; NATIONAL MUSEUM, ATHENS. COMIC MASK, HELLENISTIC TERRACOTTA FROM MELOS; BRITISH MUSEUM

rapture; love of order coupled with violence; the serenity of civilization and the cry of the cave. We find that opposition between Apollonian and Dionysian traits in drama, which the Greeks invented. Such conflict gives it enduring power.

In theaters like the one that fans out above Apollo's temple at Delphi the Greeks watched man confront himself and his fate. They experienced a catharsis, a purging of pity and terror through witnessing a noble character brought low through some flaw or blindspot—often *hybris,* overweening pride. And when the three great tragedians, Aeschylus, Sophocles, and Euripides, spoke in Greece's golden century, they spoke to us across 24 centuries. From Seneca to Shakespeare, from Racine to Goethe, to Schiller, to O'Neill, playwrights echoed their voices—just as majestic

FIFTH-CENTURY FOOTRACE IN ARMOR AT OLYMPIA; PAINTING FOR NATIONAL GEOGRAPHIC BY TOM LOVELL. BELOW: RUNNERS PASS OLYMPIC TORCH, SYMBOLIC FLAME FROM GREECE, AT 1956 OLYMPICS IN AUSTRALIA; GEORGE LEAVENS FOR "SPORTS ILLUSTRATED"

LONG RUN *of the Olympic Games—they began in 776 B.C. and lasted 12 centuries—fostered Greek athletic ideals. From a sprint in a local one-day festival at Olympia, the Olympics grew to a Panhellenic week of events bringing rival cities' champions under a truce to compete for garlands and glory in honor of Zeus.*

Outlawed as pagan in A.D. 394 by Christian emperor Theodosius, the Games began anew in Athens in 1896. Every fourth year the torch of sportsmanship draws amateurs of many nations, who compete in "the cause of peace."

chords of Homer and Virgil resound in epics of Dante and Milton. Eugene O'Neill transfers the family curse and inbred hatreds of the house of Agamemnon to an America darkened by the tragic shadow of civil war.

Each age has taken from those ancient writings what it would. From a Greek myth the Roman poet Ovid shaped his tale of Pygmalion, the sculptor who fell in love with his creation and persuaded Aphrodite to bring the statue to life as Galatea. From Ovid the tale passed to W. S. Gilbert of Gilbert and Sullivan fame, who created *Pygmalion and Galatea*. George Bernard Shaw, with wit and irony, modernized the myth as *Pygmalion*. This became Lerner and Loewe's *My Fair Lady*.

Some plays need never change. The antiwar message in Aristophanes' *Lysistrata* is as trenchant today as it was in 411 B.C., when Athenians first saw it. A short time before, they had sent more than 30,000 men to their deaths in a senseless war on Syracuse.

In Sophocles' *Oedipus Rex*, Freud perceived dark passions: a son's desire for his mother and hatred of his father. This Oedipus complex—a boy's unconscious desire to supplant his father—is the core of Freudian psychology. Greek drama ever sought the central issues of life and probed beneath them. The plays spring from myths that, Gilbert Highet writes, "go far beneath the sunlit levels of reason, into the rayless ocean of the subconscious, a realm peopled by thousands of mysterious beings who, although they inhabit our minds, are strange to us, and when they appear prove to be temptingly beautiful and often disturbing and sometimes messengers of terror and madness and death."

MUSIC, like myth, could both charm and disturb, soothe and intoxicate. With Apollo's divine instrument, the lyre, Orpheus nearly spirited his beloved Eurydice out of Hades. Spartans drilled and warred to the Dionysian shrilling of double flutes—not our dulcet flute but twin oboes that skirled like Scottish bagpipes.

Music could heal, turn an Olympian ear to your cause, pacify civil disorders, subvert a state. The numerical relations of its harmonic intervals explained to ancients the relative positions of the planets; thus did Pythagoras, while giving us earthlings our science of acoustics, hark to the heavenly music of the spheres.

When the Muses brought *mousike* (which included poetry) down to earth from Parnassus, the Greeks joined this ancestor of our "liberal arts" with *gymnastike*, art of

TO ENLIVEN LIMBO, *Etruscans dance on a tomb wall in Tarquinia. Music and dance moved both men and gods. Rome saw its first stage show, Livy tells us, in 364 B.C. when "performers from Etruria danced . . . not ungracefully' to placate deities in time of plague.*

Terpsichore, Muse of choral song and dance, inspired the sinuous, subtle half-steps of Greek festival dancers. Greeks hymned Apollo and Asclepius; dithyrambs (choral chants) to Dionysus led to drama. Dialogue was soon wed to dance and song; the marriage lives in musicals and opera today.

Singers plucked the cithara (below), one string at a time, for Greek music was melody without harmony. Pipers puffed the aulos, or double flute, and Panpipes of the shepherd's god.

Roman architect-engineer Vitruvius urged music for soldiers so they could "tune catapults by striking the tension skeins."

"No sober person dances," asserted Cicero. Few Romans did, but many loved pantomime. "Man," said a fan, "'tis as if your hands were tongues!"

the body, to form the basis of education. But they watched it carefully: Asian melodies in the lascivious Phrygian and mournful Lydian modes undermined the character. Lawmakers agreed that the Dorian mode, austere and manly as the northern invaders, was best for building spirited soldiers in Sparta, responsible citizens in Athens. At the great Panhellenic festivals, Greeks honored Muse as well as muscle. Delphi's Pythian Games, resounding in the stadium high above the theater, began as a musical contest. Then athletes came to compete, and Pindar rhapsodized on victories of "glorious-limbed youth." Juvenal, a Roman, caught the essence of the Greek idea: "A sound mind in a sound body."

From the stadium's enduring stones my thoughts drifted to fragile treasures of papyrus and parchment containing fragments of Greek writings. What miracles saved them! Manuscripts from Alexandria's Library, preserved in Egypt's desert air, have shown up in mummy cases. Aristotle's books and notes, stored in a cellar by a pupil's heirs, were rescued in Asia Minor by the Roman general Sulla. Later the books were lost. All we have of Aristotle came from the surviving notes.

Of some 150 Greek tragedians, we have works by only 3. Of 82 plays written by Aeschylus, we have 7; of Sophocles' 123, 7 also; of Euripides' 92, we have 19. We know of about 170 writers of comedies; all we have are 11 plays by Aristophanes, 6 nearly complete by Menander. But we do possess both epics of Homer, all of Plato, all of the histories of Herodotus and Thucydides.

We seek not only what the ancients wrote but how they lived. Probing, sifting, interpreting, archeologists find in great city or humble artifact pieces of our

JONATHAN S. BLAIR

MEMORIES IN MARBLE *glow in a Turkish sunset at Aphrodisias,*
Greco-Roman city whose tumbled treasures speak to scholars. "Choice
sculptures roll out of the sides of ditches," reports Dr. Kenan T. Erim,
leader of excavations aided by National Geographic research grants.
Crews date potsherds, clean coins, restore art of this Carian center.

Roman ghosts haunt thermal baths, a mighty stadium, a buried theater,
and the Temple of Aphrodite (above), which Christians turned into a
basilica. Head of a deity, paint still clinging to eyes and hair (below),
bears witness to the skill of sculptors whose art graced the Roman world.
Salesmen of the city hawked sarcophagi with unfinished figures;
features of occupants could be added post mortem.

On the acropolis (right) workers dig down through time to clear
Bronze Age walls 4,500 years old. "We have only skimmed the surface,"
said Dr. Erim. What may yet lie buried speeds the spades of archeology.

story. They glean from a fragment of pottery knowledge
about those who made it, traded it, used it, broke it, and
didn't bother to sweep up the pieces. Some families were
"disgustingly clean," grumbled Carl Blegen, an excavator of
Troy. "Any archeologist prefers dirty housekeepers."

Today's archeologist digs for roots beneath roots: Etruscan entwined with Roman; Minoan and Mycenaean with
Greek. He goes aloft to hunt traces of ruins that earthbound
eyes would never see. He analyzes forgotten languages with
computers. He peers into sealed tombs with periscopes,
hovers in a two-man submarine over the spilled cargo of a
Roman wreck. We may read of a new discovery tomorrow,
for the search for our golden heritage is page-one news.

We can search too. Look at the Parthenon, pure and serene, familiar, open to view. No secrets here. Look again.
See it the way Athenians saw it: frieze and pediment ablaze
with gaudy red, blue, and yellow paint. How the ancients

would mock our reverence for white marble statues! The almost unendurable tension of their drama should tip us off that these were no serene white-marble types. Centuries have scrubbed off the color they delighted in — just as our awe has whitewashed so much that is fascinating in their age. If the Greeks argued philosophies in the agora, they also roared at bawdy comedies in the theater. If they preached the Golden Mean, they also practiced brazen excess. Pygmalion-like, Athens fell in love with the democracy she created and it sprang to life. Jealously, she would not share it with those who came under her sway. A thousand squabbling city-states resisted unity until conquerors forced it on them.

We revere Homer no less if we peel away layers of folk memory from the hard kernel of historic fact. And we revere the Greeks no less if we call them human. They built their Parthenon with misapplied funds. Slavery tarnished their Golden Age. They curbed overpopulation by infanticide, and one island's social-security program consisted of dispensing hemlock to persons over 60.

Greece was a poor country lacking in most resources but the resourcefulness of man. Athens' culture did not leap full-armed from the head of Zeus as her patron Athena did. Greeks borrowed what they needed, across island stepping-stones

CHARLES R. NICKLIN, JR. BELOW: FLIP SCHULKE, BLACK STAR. OPPOSITE: JOHN G. CASSILS

that linked them with Asia and Egypt: the alphabet spared them from memorizing thousands of characters as the Chinese do; concepts of architecture and statuary enabled them to immortalize their vision of the good and the beautiful. Stones alone do not make a Venus de Milo or a Parthenon; words do not inevitably carry the wisdom of Plato, the insights of Sophocles, the music of Sappho and Pindar. What the Greeks did with their borrowings excites wonder.

They shaped simple letters into an instrument capable of encompassing thoughts of grandeur and subtle shadings. But on their finely tuned ears other languages grated like *bar-bar-bar*, and in their hybris they scorned non-Greek speakers as barbarians. Even in Greek, free speech sometimes grated. Aristotle exiled himself lest "the Athenians should sin a second time against philosophy." The first time was against Socrates, who never took a penny for his thoughts, never published a word of them—and lives on because his executioners could not snuff them out.

"Life unexamined is not worth living," he said. Greeks examined life by participating; anyone who did not was an *idiotes*. Instead of being a rebel, the artist worked with polis as patron to adorn his city, where each citizen knew every other by sight. Intellectuals fought political battles—and the polis' wars. Aeschylus fought at Marathon, trod a deck

at Salamis, and sheathed his sword to write *The Persians*, our oldest historical play.

Their gods, as quarrelsomely human as the Greeks themselves, gave them neither creed nor commandment. Divine indifference bred Skeptics, Cynics, Stoics, Epicureans: a philosophical pantheon of probing, questioning men. They hailed man, in Socrates' words, as "that being who, when asked a rational question, can give a rational answer." They enhanced intellect with logic as clear as the Mediterranean sunlight, gave it such tools as the syllogism and the theorem. Their inventions were mainly abstract. They left to the Romans the invention of concrete.

Bringing Greek thought down to earth, the Romans shaped an empire. Along the great straight roads that led from Rome marched the Christian heirs of Athens and Rome. Greek was the tongue of their Testament, Roman the organization of their Church. When Jesus confronted Pilate with "I have come . . . to bear witness to the truth," Pilate asked, as Socrates would have asked, "What is truth?"

The Christian answer filtered for centuries through Greek-trained minds in a Roman-ruled world. And from *fides*, faith, and *foedus*, league, came federal ideas in a later age when questions about life, liberty, and the pursuit of happiness churned in minds debating the merits of the Greeks' face-to-face democracy and the practicality of the Romans' republic. I like to think a Greek would feel at home in our House and a Roman in our Senate. Surely they would find much that was familiar as they watched us, fallible as we are, wrestle with problems of reconciling freedom with order that magnify as you move from polis to metropolis to megalopolis to continent-girdling superpower.

They are with us still, the Greeks and Romans, even as, thrust by Saturns, nestled in Apollos, we take to the stars an odyssey of man that began on the shores of a wine-dark sea.

JEWEL OF A GOLDEN AGE, *sunlit crown of the Acropolis,*
the matchless Parthenon lures questing pilgrims, as it once did
devotees of Athena. Amid the treasures of Athens and Rome
we drink at wellsprings of art and eloquence,
of law, liberty, and government which yet refresh our souls.

WILLIAM EPPRIDGE

By Emily Vermeule

The World of Odysseus

*T*O MOST PEOPLE who delight in the past,
"the world of Odysseus" means the bright
world of sea adventure and palace intrigue
made immortal in Homer's *Odyssey*. Homer created
a timeless journey of love and loss, danger and
self-discovery. He drew from verses of earlier poets
and dim memories of an earlier time, spiced with
the fresh color of his own world, the eighth century B.C.
Yet Odysseus, so far as he was real at all, lived in the
Late Bronze Age of the 13th century B.C. Between his world
and Homer's came the Dark Ages—grim centuries
when Greeks suffered hungry times, livestock grew scarce,
art declined, and knowledge of writing faded. We still cannot
explain these disastrous centuries. Perhaps some climatic change
shifted rain-laden trade winds, parching once-fertile regions.
Tradition points to an invasion by Dorians from northwestern Greece.
But the widespread dislocations forced many peoples to migrate—
east, west, and south. The Dorians may have taken advantage
of the situation; it is unlikely that they caused it.
After Greece emerged from its misery, about 900 B.C., men looked
on the massive stone citadels of their Bronze Age forebears
and created legends of giants who might have lifted such

"Cyclopean" stones into place. Their poets peopled palaces with heroes who fought in bronze armor and sailed to impossibly distant places. Surely they must have been demigods, so great their strength, so wise their counsel, so terrible their weapons, so close their ties to the gods. Surely the hive-shaped royal tombs held treasuries of gold. How else could the ancients have afforded their luxuries?

One of the great Bronze Age fortress-palaces stood at Mycenae, its yellow-gray walls guarding a pass between Argos and Corinth in the northeastern Peloponnesus. Mycenae gives its name to the era Odysseus would have known. Its glories grew in the telling of tales by firelight during Greece's Dark Ages, when all were poor and fearful. Yet the Mycenaean Age, like the Elizabethan, was in truth one of those rare times when men tried new things, did them well, and lived in splendor and excitement. In recent decades archeologists have been digging up and putting in a sensible pattern the true "world of Odysseus." If the picture looks different from Homer's, that is the difference between poetry and truth recovered from the dirt.

In 1876, when earth and brush had filled Mycenae's gates and houses almost to the top, Heinrich Schliemann found the Royal Shaft Graves just inside the Lion Gate,

BENEATH HOMER'S "HOLY SOUNION, *the cape of Athens," crowned by a temple, mariners prayed to*

where headless lions stand guard. Here in six deep shafts sunk under a stone-ringed
terrace lay treasures of gold still unmatched, for here the princes of Mycenae
had been buried with their wives and children in the 16th and 15th centuries B.C.
Men and animals had walked above those gold-clad bones for more than a hundred
generations without disturbing the richness below.

Gold literally covered the 19 bodies. Even a baby wore a complete suit of gold foil.
Other skeletons in the rectangular chambers were showered with gold rosettes and
disks, diadems and belts, masks and heavy pins. The list goes on: ropes of amber
from Baltic lands, ostrich eggs from Nubia, a silver stag from Asia Minor. Great
swords buried with the princes suggest careers not wholly spent in peaceful trade.
War and looting and a command of chariot fighting must have added to their riches.

Of all Schliemann saw, the gold mask of a bearded warrior impressed him most:
"I have gazed on the face of Agamemnon!" We know now that more than 300 years
separate the gold mask and Homer's legendary king of Mycenae. The shaft-grave princes,
whose names remain a mystery, lived at the beginning of true Mycenaean civilization.
The Trojan War, in which Agamemnon led the Greek forces, heralded the end of the era.

Poseidon for safe passage on his storm-swept sea—highway of destiny for rocky, island-fringed Greece.

FLAMES IN THE CENTRAL HEARTH *of a Mycenaean king's megaron dance to the tale of a bard. Strumming his lyre, he composes as he chants—for hours, even continuing his epic night after night. Lusty nobles reveled in "the famous actions of men," Homer tells us. His* Iliad *and* Odyssey *contain kernels of Bronze Age fact and clearly picture a warrior society's bold ideal: The hero, strong and valiant, rules by might and gains glory garnering spoils stained with the gore of men he has slain.*

It has taken years to correct Schliemann's image of the Mycenaean Age, and of the older civilizations of Crete and Asia Minor which so much influenced it. Archeologists Chrestos Tsountas and Sir Arthur Evans, Alan J. B. Wace and Carl W. Blegen, and cryptographer Michael Ventris helped piece together the picture we now have of the first Greek-speaking civilization, which reached its peak in the 14th and 13th centuries B.C.

Warrior nobles built fortresses to command nearby harbors, olive groves, and vineyards, and turned their citadels into oases of luxury. The Greeks delighted in Cretan art; it became stylish with every mainland brigand who aspired to elegance. Cretan fashions were shown from court to court. Craftsmen offered bargains in jewelry, ivory trinkets, frescoes, and bronze tools. Under the Mycenaean code nobles themselves never made anything. Of all Homer's heroes, only Odysseus could plow, shear a sheep, or slaughter a pig. This, perhaps, made him seem less than heroic to his peers at Troy. But he came from the small, rocky island of Ithaca, and he had to learn farming as well as fighting.

Richer kings needed only to hunt, fight, and govern. Any hero could fix weapons or soothe a horse in a tangle of overturned chariots. But he had no interest in making beautiful objects. If goblets looked the same at Tiryns and Pylos, it mattered little. Nobles simply wanted the best material, the most conspicuous style.

To PICTURE LIFE among the Mycenaeans, let us follow a ship captain on his travels in the fall of 1230 B.C. Aktor of Troezen, trader and part-time pirate, carried fine pottery and trinkets from the Peloponnesus to the Cyclades. At times he sailed to Cyprus or the polyglot colonies on Asia Minor's south coast to buy caravan goods: ivory, woven cloaks, ingots of copper, cakes of

tin, figurines of divinities, jewels of lapis lazuli. This afternoon, Aktor ascended
the long road from the harbor at Nauplion to seek the High King's help in the
palace at Mycenae. Officials had impounded his cargo of painted wine bowls and
goblets from Corinth, all packed in straw for a trip to Cyprus. Rich Cypriotes
kept dying—from overeating, Aktor always thought—and were buried in state
with dozens of vases, ropes of beads, and piles of cloth crammed into their tombs.

But now Aktor's dreams of profit were blocked by the greedy men of Nauplion.
They had been in bad repute with Greeks ever since one of their kings had ravished
a Cretan princess destined for Mycenae and sent her on her way diminished
in dowry and desirability. Yet the High King could control them. His dynasty
was related to nearly every important family in Greece; when blood ties failed
to enforce his policies, his trained army succeeded.

Tired, dusty, scratched by thorns, Aktor sighted Mycenae in late afternoon.
It rose in circles on a hill, blending curiously with the landscape, commanding

47

AGAMEMNON'S CITADEL OF MYCENAE,
"where the sons of the gods were born,"
shoulders its Cyclopean stonework above the plain of Argos.
Bronze Age Greeks—Homer's "Argives"—buried royalty with
weapons and treasure in shafts within the curved wall.

FARRELL GREHAN

the whole magnificent view to Tiryns, Argos, and the waves. A flock of black goats, homeward bound in the twilight, scrambled uphill beside Aktor. Two climbed into an oak tree to eat the tenderer bark—one reason the forest was dying. In a field of barley a plowman unhitched from his clumsy wooden plow a team of oxen—the prized red-and-white breed whose hides made tough shields. Other small fields were yellow with wheat, green with vines, red with raw earth. On a rock outcrop a glowing dot marked where Mycenae's famed beacon signal system started, fires flaming with messages to observers on mountaintops throughout the kingdom.

As he rested under a fig tree Aktor watched a work party opening a passage to an old rock-cut tomb. Soon a group of mourners came into view carrying a white-shrouded corpse on a bier. In the tomb, where the bones of old skeletons had been brushed neatly into a corner, they set their burden down. Others laid vases or bouquets of field flowers beside it. From a mixing bowl of wine, the mourners

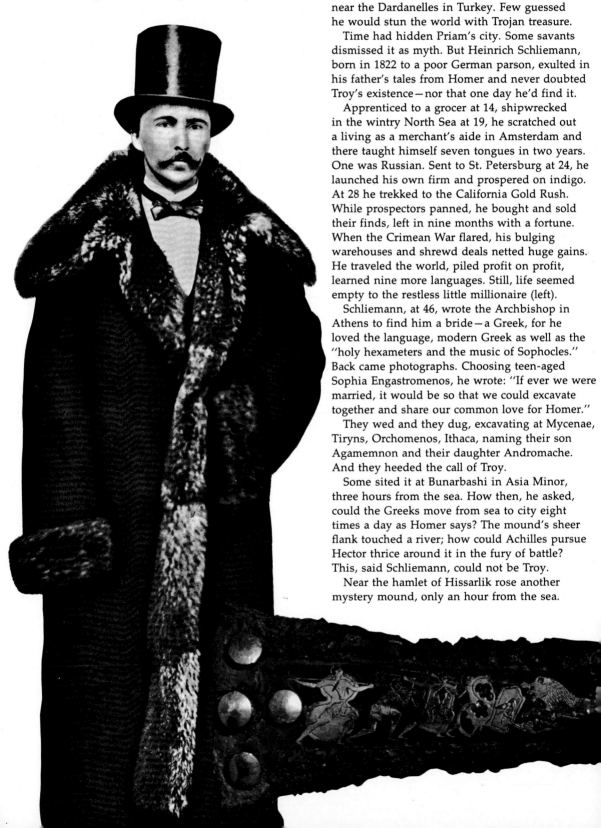

While scholars scoffed, Schliemann followed Homer to the gold of Troy and Mycenae

"HAVE I to take a tent and iron bedstead and pillow with me...? Do I require pistols, dagger and rifle?... What sort of hat is best...?" Problems plagued the middle-aged merchant as he girded for his dig at a mound scorned by experts, near the Dardanelles in Turkey. Few guessed he would stun the world with Trojan treasure.

Time had hidden Priam's city. Some savants dismissed it as myth. But Heinrich Schliemann, born in 1822 to a poor German parson, exulted in his father's tales from Homer and never doubted Troy's existence—nor that one day he'd find it.

Apprenticed to a grocer at 14, shipwrecked in the wintry North Sea at 19, he scratched out a living as a merchant's aide in Amsterdam and there taught himself seven tongues in two years. One was Russian. Sent to St. Petersburg at 24, he launched his own firm and prospered on indigo. At 28 he trekked to the California Gold Rush. While prospectors panned, he bought and sold their finds, left in nine months with a fortune. When the Crimean War flared, his bulging warehouses and shrewd deals netted huge gains. He traveled the world, piled profit on profit, learned nine more languages. Still, life seemed empty to the restless little millionaire (left).

Schliemann, at 46, wrote the Archbishop in Athens to find him a bride—a Greek, for he loved the language, modern Greek as well as the "holy hexameters and the music of Sophocles." Back came photographs. Choosing teen-aged Sophia Engastromenos, he wrote: "If ever we were married, it would be so that we could excavate together and share our common love for Homer."

They wed and they dug, excavating at Mycenae, Tiryns, Orchomenos, Ithaca, naming their son Agamemnon and their daughter Andromache. And they heeded the call of Troy.

Some sited it at Bunarbashi in Asia Minor, three hours from the sea. How then, he asked, could the Greeks move from sea to city eight times a day as Homer says? The mound's sheer flank touched a river; how could Achilles pursue Hector thrice around it in the fury of battle? This, said Schliemann, could not be Troy.

Near the hamlet of Hissarlik rose another mystery mound, only an hour from the sea.

He paced around it with a watch, found it
right for Hector's flight, and in the first
hour of digging struck ancient walls.

His workers bared several cities, each atop
ruins of its predecessor. Schliemann counted
seven as he impetuously trenched straight
through the mound. "As it was my object
to excavate Troy . . . I was forced to demolish
many interesting ruins," he said. Ironically,
he dug right past the level archeology now
labels Homeric Troy (page 73) and designated
the far older "Burnt City," second from the
virgin soil, as the one sacked by the Greeks.

A stone building came to light. "Priam's
Palace!" trumpeted Schliemann. Watchmen
of the local pasha greedily eyed each spadeful.
But, wearied after three seasons' toil in the icy
north winds, blinding dust, and stifling heat,
Schliemann decided to call it quits.

On May 31, 1873, shortly before the dig
was to end, he watched a pickax hole a wall—
and glimpsed gold. Sophia, at his side, saw
it too, but no one else did. With the cunning
of Odysseus, he told her to call a holiday
to mark his birthday—still six months off!
Homeward trooped the delighted workers,
and soon the Schliemanns' locked cabin blazed
with gold as Heinrich fingered goblets and
Sophia modeled bracelets, necklaces, rings,
and gleaming diadems—8,700 pieces!

Now famous, Schliemann posed seated beside
the Lion Gate (above) at Homer's Mycenae,
"rich in gold." Others had dug outside the
gate; he dug behind it, heeding Pausanias'
2d-century *Description of Greece*. He found
gold-clad skeletons in treasure-rich shafts—
a hoard that gave the name Mycenaean to an
age. He saw hunters with Homeric shields
brave lions on a bronze dagger. He named a
vessel "Nestor's cup" after the golden goblet
of the *Iliad*'s king of Pylos. He thought the
bracelet and eagle necklace worthy of Helen.

Archeologists now date these priceless relics
three centuries before the Trojan War. But in
the flush of finding the golden mask on page 42,
Schliemann telegraphed the king of Greece:
"I have gazed on the face of Agamemnon!"

FINDS FROM MYCENAE, 16TH CENTURY B.C.; NATIONAL MUSEUM, ATHENS.
OPPOSITE: SCHLIEMANN IN ST. PETERSBURG, 1860; DR. ERNST MEYER.
LION GATE, 1876; GERMAN ARCHEOLOGICAL INSTITUTE, ATHENS

51

SACRED TREE *of Athena,*
who brought forth the first
with a touch of her lance,
the olive thrives in the poor,
dry soil of Greece.

Ancient Greeks paid taxes in
olive oil to their kings, offered
it in rituals to their gods.
They cooked with it, burned it
in clay lamps, used it as
butter on bread, as soap when
scraping themselves clean.
Women anointed their bodies
briskly against the cold of
unheated quarters. An oil and
honey dip kept cloth supple.

Panorama of the industry,
taken from 6th century B.C.
vase paintings, shows men
shaking down ripe fruit.
Workers at right use a beam
weighted with a net of stones
to press oil from a woven
container. Customer at left,
haggling, sniffs a sample.

"Unguent boilers" mixed in
rose, sage, and coriander to
produce perfumed oil—a major
export and royal monopoly of
Bronze Age realms, which were
led by warriors, run by clerks.
At Nestor's Pylos, 40 scribes
kept a clay census of men,
beasts, even vintage of wines.

filled thin-stemmed clay goblets and wished their relative bearable fortune on the dangerous trip to the land of the dead. Filing out, they waited until men filled the doorway with rocks, then smashed their cups against the stones. The labor gang filled in the passageway to thwart thieves.

The family had provided wine and a roasted ox haunch for the workers; children gave each man a green branch to carry. As the evening breeze wafted a thrush song and shuttled olive branches about, the mourners keened their ceremonial cries and struck their cheeks, one woman until the blood came.

Aktor now joined a throng crowding the shadowed chute leading to the Lion Gate, for at nightfall the double oak doors with bronze studs would be closed and barred. Somehow the staring stone lions seemed more frightening than the soldier with his spotted hound who stood behind the gate to screen entrants.

Suddenly a loud rattle announced a late chariot driven by one of the king's couriers. Painted wheels and spotted oxhide body swung past Aktor to a space inside the gate where men steadied the team. The charioteer, swaying after miles of jouncing on footrests a few inches above ground, noted Aktor, travel-stained like himself,

and called out the usual friendly greeting: "Where are you from, stranger?
Do you need food and drink, or will you come with me to the palace?"

Gladly accepting company, Aktor followed his guide above the terraced circle
where the old kings lay buried. Before them roofs and columned courts spread
toward the fierce thick walls. The path turned in angles and branched off into
alleys, rising steadily to the foot of a broad stair which led to the palace forecourt.
In the afterglow of sunset Aktor looked across a deep ravine to a scene of
breathtaking loveliness: the great green plain of Argos spreading mistily to the sea.

In a square apartment off the forecourt Aktor took a bowl and sponge from
a barefoot servant girl to freshen himself, but refused her offer to look after
his pouch—he carried a few trinkets in it for palace gifts. At the inner
porch a guard removed Aktor's dagger and hung it beside a rack of spears.
The challenge over, Aktor passed into the megaron, the great hall.

Torches were being hung on the walls and dim light filtered down from upstairs
windows. No fire glowed in the hearth at this time of year, but its flame pattern
in black and red had been freshly retouched, and green boughs lay across it.

53

Six nobles in embroidered blue tunics stood by the wooden throne. And there, with his feet on a stool inlaid with ebony and ivory, sat the High King of Mycenae.

Before him stood the charioteer, Aktor's guide, delivering his message in an undertone. The king dispatched one of the nobles. Aktor heard something about reinforcing a hill garrison on the northern coast. Though the king seemed a little fat, with stubby hands and crooked nose, a look of quick temper, perhaps, and a bit of greed, Mycenae's ruler was obviously a tough and able administrator.

In the background a singer in a long robe faintly tuned his heavy lyre. Aktor had never seen such a large and lovely lyre, with its five long strings and ivory finials shaped like sphinx heads. He hoped he would be invited to listen.

But his business was quickly done. The king solved Aktor's problem by dictating an order giving him free passage through all ports in the realm. A scribe with inkpot and reed pen marked it down on a strip of leather, rolled the strip, and tied it. Aktor recalled that at home in Troezen they had had a scribe long ago, but he had died. Now business was by word of mouth, leading to endless quarrels.

Aktor knew that palace records were kept on clay tablets packed in wicker baskets in a guarded room. Sometimes they circulated to farm overseers and harbor masters, and to priests at country shrines. He wondered whether he could learn to make these complicated little marks . . . but he was not of the guild, and anyway the sedentary life of a scribe had little appeal for him. His eyes were too attuned to far horizons to cope with a clay tablet held six inches away.

Even in this great hall Aktor felt confined, eager to be back on ship. He gave the king a small blue faïence monkey he had picked up in Egypt and a tooled scabbard for a dagger, and bowed himself away. A last glance at the scenes of chariots and soldiers around the walls, at the bard, still dreaming a song, and he left for a congenial inn where barley beer and wild stories would refresh him before sleep.

SEAMEN LIKE AKTOR out on the Aegean often would shelter at night among the islands that form a rough wheel around Delos—a circle that gives them their name, Cyclades. To baffle pirates, the small, wiry men of the Cyclades hid their villages in the folds of steep hills and built heavy rubble walls. At most, raiders might catch some sheep, or women washing clothes. Island women were prized as slaves or concubines, but they were not easily caught. Villagers themselves preyed on ships beached for the night, slipping down familiar paths. One can imagine the sudden havoc, bodies thrown into the sea, loot divided by torchlight.

One day near the year 1500 B.C., a tremendous, almost unimaginable explosion shook the Mediterranean world. Boulders the size of houses shot far into the air.

WHERE HORSES STRAIN *to the plow, mules and oxen labored in Homeric days. The chariot steed, "delight of proud luxury," never set hoof to humble tasks. Odysseus could manage a farm household, or* oikos *(whence our word "economy"); he scorned the "lawless outrageous Cyclopes who . . . neither plow with their hands nor plant anything." But his world owed more to flocks than fields. Sheep and goats (lower), at home in rough terrain, yielded milk, cheese, and meat; wool for clothes; skins for rugs and bottles. The* Iliad's *heroes dined on meat and flat barley bread.*

Showers of lava, cooled to pumice, rained down on land and sea. The sea bed shuddered and the shock ran along the fault which cleaves the underwater crust between Turkey and Sicily. Clouds of ash drifted through the sky 500 miles from the blast, and sulphuric mists polluted the air. The volcanic island of Thera was erupting.

Only 70 miles north of Crete, Thera closes the circle of the Cyclades at the south. It is still an active volcano. Today it resembles an oval doughnut, its huge hole formed when the interior of the mountain hurled itself skyward and the shell collapsed into the sea.

Prehistoric life on Thera was revealed a century ago when engineers, seeking hydraulic cement to build the Suez Canal, began quarrying pumice and ash. The eruption had heaped 30 to 120 feet of this debris over the Bronze Age surface of the island. Digging into it, workmen came upon house walls. Scientists probed two sites and found frescoes, pottery, farm tools, and chunks of wood and obsidian. Then, in 1967, the Archeological Society of Athens, in an exploration directed by Prof. Spyridon Marinatos of the University of Athens, began to uncover one of the old sites.

It lay in a gully where the village of Akrotiri dominates Thera's south coast. Here winter floods and erosion had cut ravines, exposing two- and three-story houses the ancient townspeople had hurriedly left when the huge volcano erupted. Excavation revealed room after room nearly intact. Sealed under a

BLASTS *even more cataclysmic than the 1883 eruption of Krakatoa shook the Aegean about 1500 B.C. when an explosion rent Thera. Tidal waves 160 feet high roared on Crete, only 70 miles away. Some scholars think Minoan civilization died under the ashfall. Did such a disaster give rise to Plato's legend of lost Atlantis?*

Cliff-top town, reached by 587 steps, whitens the lip of Thera's drowned crater, too deep for ships to anchor in. In 1967 scientists four in the ashes three-story houses: a city 3,500 years old. Jars studied by the author and Prof. Spyridon Marinatos, the expedition leader (right), stored wine and olive oil.

Mycenae •

• Athens

THERA

• Knossos

CRETE

THERA

PAINTING BY NED M. SEIDLER
GEOGRAPHIC ART DIVISION

56

protective cover of pumice and ash, ceiling beams and wooden beds were preserved. So were storage chests, pottery painted with plant and animal designs, pieces of looms—even bits of straw and some snails, items seldom encountered after the passage of 3,500 years. Impressively beautiful scenes in brilliant colors leaped from the plastered walls of many houses, an extraordinary panorama of country landscapes and religious life. In this provincial but artistic town, gifted painters had rendered antelopes and mating swallows, Africans wearing gold-hoop earrings, priestesses bearing cups for a sacrament, girls—with thorn-scratched legs—picking flowers.

Gradually the shape of the town has become clear. Streets of stamped earth ran from the shore up to squares and odd-shaped plazas on which fronted tall, yellow houses of notable townsmen. Over the narrow doors, tall windows threw light into reception rooms and bedrooms, rooms often painted with scenes depicting the owner's life. One residence may have been built by a sea captain; its upstairs walls display an unforgettable frieze showing a great fleet calling on seashore towns. Ships and seamen are painted with loving and knowledgeable talent. Sailors and rowers bend to their tasks, helmeted soldiers recline under deck awnings, dolphins frolic. In the distance one sees a flowing river, animals hunting, goatherds gossiping, women looking down from the roofs of pink and yellow buildings, young men marching, defeated enemies falling. No finer look into the long-ago world of Odysseus has come down to us.

Professor Marinatos died in 1975 in a fall from a third-floor wall on which he was working. But Greek archeologists carry on, freeing the town from its volcanic burden, fixing roofs over the houses, replacing furniture and pottery, repairing stairs. Thus we learn how the people of Thera lived before the fumes and showering pumice drove them away—how they escaped with small valuables but left ordinary things behind. And ancient Akrotiri, like a little Pompeii, emerges as an indelible glimpse into the Bronze Age.

Islands like Thera reflect the influence of ancient Cretan culture, but they cast only a soft shadow of the brilliance of Crete itself. Any sailor, from the Stone Age onward, must have caught his breath at his first sight of it. Icebound mountains form the island's spine; rich valleys, rivers, outcrops of white gypsum, coves and harbors

BULL LEAPERS *thrilled Cretans at King Minos' palace at Knossos. Frescoes show youths vaulting, heels over head, from horns to back to ground. A missed hold, like this, invited a gory death. Legend says the mighty sea king sacrificed Greek youths and maidens to a monster, half man, half bull, kept here in a labyrinth. Athenian prince Theseus killed it and escaped by following a thread given him by Ariadne, the king's daughter. Slaying the Minotaur (Bull of Minos), perhaps a priest-king in ritual mask, may reflect Mycenaean conquest of Crete.*

PAINTING FOR NATIONAL GEOGRAPHIC BY H. M. HERGET

59

punctuate a rugged shoreline. Perhaps to the early settlers from wild mountain-girt harbors of southwest Asia Minor it seemed like home. To Egyptian travelers it must have looked exotic; to Greek mainlanders, lusher than their own rough land.

*T*HE CULTURE we call Minoan, after the legendary King Minos of Crete, unfolded in three stages. Early Minoans, who lived from about 2500 to 2000 B.C., dwelt in valleys slightly withdrawn from the sea. In stone tombs they placed their dead with fine raiment and delicate gold jewelry. Clearly Crete was in touch with rich regions like Egypt and the Levant. Shortly after 2000 B.C., in a spurt of energy and grandeur, Cretans began building large palaces around central courts.

LABYRINTHINE RUINS *at Knossos recall the power of the Minoan empire 3,500 years ago. Processions*

Knossos, Phaistos, and Mallia took on forms we see now, however battered they appear. In this Middle Minoan Age luxuries grew more expensively delightful, government more sophisticated, with records kept in the scratchy script we call Linear A. Visiting Greeks saw the elaborate palace architecture, the brilliant frescoes, the writing techniques, and opened their minds to a new way of life.

Toward 1600 B.C. some natural disaster, probably an earthquake, badly hurt the island. The Cretans rebuilt as the Late Minoan Age got under way, but around 1500 B.C. another catastrophe severely damaged the palaces. Present knowledge points to Thera's eruption as the destroying force. Only Knossos seems to have recovered, slowly. Perhaps its weakened state allowed mainland Greeks to take over

climbed broad stairs to the audience chamber amid the multi-level complex of apartments, storerooms, courts.

GILBERT M. GROSVENOR, NATIONAL GEOGRAPHIC STAFF

Sir Arthur Evans came to Crete
in search of signets—and discovered
the Minoan civilization

62

CURIOUS SYMBOLS on tiny seals in Athens' shops caught the nearsighted eye of Arthur Evans, rich, dynamic, Keeper of Oxford's Ashmolean Museum. Prehistoric writing? He raced to the dealers' source, Crete, where his second day's digging hit on a Bronze Age palace.

Having bought the Knossos site in 1899, Sir Arthur (above) spent a fortune and half his life resurrecting the civilization he named Minoan. From his Villa Ariadne he ruled like King Minos, jealous of sharing priceless written records, indefatigable in his reconstructions, fierce in the fights that swirled round him ("I can see him snuffing up the tainted breeze and pawing like a warhorse," a relative wrote of the former Balkans war correspondent).

The Minoan art he revealed to the world breathes zest for life. Mother goddess in flounced skirt (right) grasps snakes, skin-shedding symbols of renewal. She and figurine at far left bespeak the bold, dark-eyed Cretan women, who drove chariots and married as equals. Knossos' luxurious, bright-frescoed palace—maze of downward-tapering columns (left), light wells, and dogleg halls where the Minotaur seems to lurk—gets its name Labyrinth from the labrys, or double ax (upper left), mark of Minoan power. Octopuses writhing on vases evoke the encircling sea, road to empire, defensive moat of unfortified Knossos. Sarcophagus from Hágia Triáda's royal villa shows that Cretans even crossed the Styx in style: Priestess with attendants pours a last libation.

In the 16th century B.C., Knossos hummed with 80,000 people, sophisticated hub of Europe's first sea power. Natural disasters and conquest by Mycenaeans marked the end of her golden age.

gradually from Minoan princes. New weapons, horses, chariots, military paintings, use of an altered script—Linear B—for writing Greek, all attest to the presence of Mycenaean power in Crete at this time. At the beginning of the 14th century Knossos fell again and finally, damaged by savage fire, collapsed. From then on Crete was a minor power, with Greeks in the ascendancy until the Trojan War.

A GREEK who visited the northern coast of Crete would have come by the dockworks near modern Herakleion. Here wealthy ship captains controlled the shoreward end of the road which ran through low hills to the palace at Knossos. The traveler could rest and wash at a pretty inn whose wall paintings— a frieze of partridges and hoopoes among sprays of greenery—evoked the island's rich gardens and wild game.

The palace itself, called the Labyrinth after the holy symbol of the *labrys*, or double ax, spread across a rise beyond a small river. Towering above the houses of noblemen, the massive complex gleamed in pale stone set off by red columns with black, yellow, and white accents. Colonnades etched it with shadows, balconies caught the sun. Gardens surrounded the whole with splashing fountains and carefully tended beds of crocuses, irises, roses, and lilies.

Like most Mediterranean palace centers, Knossos lavished luxury on its ruler. Brilliant show was the right hand of diplomacy; an impressive setting convinced neighbors of a king's power. Visitors might wonder at the absence of fortifications. But with merchantmen and warships trading and patrolling, an enemy would have found it hard to mount a surprise naval attack. And neither spies nor thieves could freely enter the palace; its ground floor had no windows.

By the time a visitor had threaded narrow corridors to the heart of the palace, walking past shadowy walls where life-size painted figures seemed to move with him, he would feel lost in a maze. Each segment had its logical order, but connections between them seemed haphazard: recesses, stairways, dark passages, light wells, doors opening into hidden places. Partitions muffled the sounds of life— soft voices, bare feet padding across plaster floors, the chuckle of running water. Glimmering pools offered relief in hot weather. Off private chambers were sunken bathrooms, some with flush toilets. Drains running under the floors mingled their murmur with the chatter of green monkeys, the song of caged birds, the slithering of house snakes, the distant bellowing of the sacred bulls. It must have been a relief to reach the sunlit central court. Here there could be no secrets or monsters, only ordinary people passing by or leaning over balconies, and the excitement of the royal bull games.

Perhaps 5,000 people would watch one of these graceful exhibitions, the most spectacular entertainment in Minoan court life. Young men and girls, trained in a precise series of motions, exhausted the bull. Apparently they worked in trios,

HOSPITABLE, *handsome, and fertile, as Odysseus called it, Crete was once the hub of the Mediterranean. Snow-crowned Mount Ida, Zeus' birthplace in later tradition, looked on cypress forests that yielded timber, chief Minoan export. Today flocks nibble on barren slopes.*

FARRELL GREHAN

65

Michael Ventris and "Linear B" gave tongue to Odysseus' world

THE MYSTERY of Minoan writing highlighted a 1936 London lecture by Sir Arthur Evans, then 84. In 1900 at Knossos he had dug up clay tablets he still could not decipher. Most were in a script he labeled "Linear B" to distinguish it from an earlier, somewhat different "Linear A." Michael Ventris, 14, listened spellbound. An avid linguist, the schoolboy vowed to solve the riddle.

Evans had published only 120 of his 3,000 tablets. "King Nestor's Palace" at Pylos, discovered in 1939, yielded 600 more. But World War II blocked work. What language underlay such records? Hittite? Etruscan? Certainly not Greek, decreed Evans.

In 1951, publication of the Pylos Linear B tablets spurred Ventris, now a London architect. He noted 88 signs—too many for an alphabet, too few for a system of ideographs such as Egyptian hieroglyphs. This system must build words on in-di-vi-du-al syllables. He sought patterns, grouped and regrouped signs with similar vowels on a grid, tested sounds on syllables linked with recurring pictorial symbols. During a 1952 BBC talk on Evans' tablets Ventris startled listeners: Linear B was archaic Greek!

American archeologist Carl Blegen, excavator of Pylos, sent confirmation: On a newfound tablet (above) Ventris' key unlocked the word *ti-ri-po*, from the Greek for three-legged pot, or tripod. A picture of a three-handled pot was coupled with *ti-ri-o-we*; a handleless pot with *a-no-we*— the negative prefix *an* plus *o-we*, "ear."

Greek first followed Semitic style, right to left; then it read back and forth—boustrophedon, "as the ox plows," like Crete's Code of Gortyn (below), proclaiming 500 B.C. law. In 403 Athens adopted the left-to-right Ionic script of classical Greek. Romans 300 years earlier took the Chalcidian script Etruscans got from Greeks in Italy. Christianity carried the Latin alphabet worldwide.

Phoenicians used 22 letters (opposite), classical Greeks 24, Romans 23. Chalcidian had *vav* and *koph*; they passed into Latin as F and Q. Romans invented G to give a harder sound to their hard C. *Zeta*, 6th Greek letter, became Roman Z, following Y, a *vav*-like form of *upsilon*. Medieval J, U, and W complete the 26-letter alphabet used in this book.

About 12 percent of our words stem from Greek; note subtle shifts in meaning (opposite, lower).

TI-RI-PO tripod | TI-RI-O-WE 3-handled pot | A-NO-WE handleless pot

Though skeptics remained, many scholars hailed the amateur cryptographer as another Schliemann. His book on the decipherment still on press, Ventris, 34, was killed in an auto accident. But he had proved that the Greek language had a 3,300-year history, rivaled only by Chinese; opened unique records of Mycenaean life; exploded Evans' stranglehold view that the mainland was merely a backwater of Minoan Crete. Mycenaeans even ruled Knossos, converting its Linear A into B in adapting the script to their Greek tongue.

Mycenaean writing perished with its civilization c. 1200 B.C. After four dark centuries, Greeks took a Phoenician form of the world's oldest alphabet. Semitic signs *aleph* (ox) and *beth* (house), once pictographs, lost descriptive meanings in the Greeks' *alpha* and *beta*. Instead of writing only with consonants (like lwyr for "lawyer"), Greeks coined vowels: *alpha, epsilon, iota, omicron, upsilon.*

PHOENICIAN Letter Name		GREEK Letter Name		ROMAN	
ALEPH	𐤀	ALPHA	A	A	
BETH		BETA	B	B	
GIMEL		GAMMA	Γ	C	
DALETH		DELTA	Δ	D	
HE		EPSILON	E	E	
VAV				F	
				G	
HETH		ETA	H	H	
TETH	⊕	THETA	θ		
YOD		IOTA	I	I	
KAPH		KAPPA	K	K	
LAMED		LAMBDA	Λ	L	
MEM		MU	M	M	
NUN		NU	N	N	
SAMEK		XI	Ξ		
AYIN	O	OMICRON	O	O	
PE		PI	Π	P	
SADE					
KOPH				Q	
RESH		RHO	P	R	
SHIN	W	SIGMA	Σ	S	
TAW	T	TAU	T	T	
		UPSILON	Y	V	
		PHI	Φ		
		CHI	X	X	
		PSI	Ψ		
				Y	
ZAYIN	I	ZETA	Z	Z	
		OMEGA	Ω		

GREEK WORD	ANCIENT MEANING	ENGLISH DERIVATIVE
ΑΓΩΝΙΑ agonia	contest, struggle	agony
ΑΠΟΛΟΓΙΑ pologia	defense	apology
ΑΡΑΚΤΗΡ harakter	mark, emblem, signet	character
ΚΡΙΤΙΚΟΣ ritikos	able to discern	critical
ΔΕΣΠΟΤΗΣ espotes	master	despot
ΔΥΝΑΜΙΚΟΣ ynamikos	powerful	dynamic
ΚΚΕΝΤΡΟΣ kkentros	off-center	eccentric
ΚΚΛΗΣΙΑ kklesia	assembly of citizens	ecclesiastic
ΣΧΟΛΗ chole	leisure, discussion	school

each person trying to keep his teammates from being gored or trampled. One would approach the bull's head, slip his arms over the horns, kick his feet with the bull's toss and somersault onto the bull's back, then leap off behind his tail. Life depended on perfect timing and control.

The legend of Prince Theseus of Athens, who faced a man-eating bull in the Labyrinth, suggests that foreigners were trained as victims in the bull games. But Minoan art shows bold young Cretans freely taking part.

In rocky sanctuaries, in caves, on peaks, or in palace shrines the Minoans worshiped the Great Goddess who controlled their lives. Wind and wave obeyed her; angered, she could disrupt the cycle of seasons. She gave men grain and children. Despite her many forms—her emblem might be the double ax, a serpent, a dove, or the horns of consecration that recalled the island's great bulls— the Great Goddess was a single power.

Mycenaean religion differed. Each mainland center had its Potnia, or Mistress Lady, in addition to specialized gods—Poseidon for the sea and swift horses, Zeus for the sky and thunder and lightning, Athena for handicrafts, Artemis for childbirth, Demeter for the fruits of the land. The Linear B tablets of Pylos give us the names of many powers who did not survive the Dark Ages, but Poseidon and various Potnias did and are clearly the strongest in the crowd.

WHEN MYCENAEANS went to war, the gods attended them and watched the outcome. The few records of Bronze Age Greece we have fail to document the battles they fought. Homer remains our most vivid reporter of the warfare at Troy, but his exciting pictures do not quite fit the discoveries of archeologists in the mound at Hissarlik, site of the beleaguered city.

For nine years, Homer tells us in the *Iliad*, Agamemnon ravaged the region around Troy but could not take the city itself. In the tenth year Apollo, protector of Troy, sowed discord among the Greeks by making Agamemnon give up

67

a concubine. The Greek chieftain replaced her with a favorite of Achilles, his most powerful warrior. In a mighty rage, "darkly brilliant" Achilles dropped out of the war, warning Agamemnon that "you will eat out the heart within you in sorrow." When battle resumed, Achilles was sorely missed. "Immortal Panic" gripped the Greeks; Agamemnon now offered to give back the girl, untouched, along with gold, horses, more women, and seven strong citadels. Though old Nestor, "the lucid speaker of Pylos," believed none could scorn these gifts, wrathful Achilles held out. The fighting intensified. Led by their great champion, "manslaughtering Hector," son of King Priam, the Trojans drove back the Greeks, disabling Agamemnon, Odysseus, and most of the other heroes.

When his dearest friend Patroclus fell, Achilles rejoined the fray. Just the sight of him and the sound of his mighty war cry checked the Trojans. After a bloody battle the Trojans fled behind their city's walls, Hector remaining outside to meet Achilles in single combat. But "the shivers took hold" of Priam's son; he broke and ran. Three times around Troy's walls Achilles chased the Trojan prince. Then Athena, partisan of the Greeks, tricked Hector into standing firm, and Achilles finished him off. The *Iliad* ends with the burial of Hector. In the *Odyssey* we hear of the death of Achilles, of Odysseus' cunning use of the wooden horse, and of the fall of Troy.

Prof. Carl Blegen of the University of Cincinnati Expedition probed the ruins of Troy's layered cities with surgical accuracy in the 1930's and judged that Troy VII A (page 73) must have been the one Homer's heroes besieged. This was a weakened citadel whose people had mended the earthquake-battered walls of Troy VI. Around the time of the Trojan War, it burned fiercely. Many coastal cities of Asia Minor, Syria, and Palestine suffered the same fate in this era of sacking, burning, and forced migrations which saw the collapse of the old Mediterranean powers.

This burning of Troy VII A and Homer's tale of that burning by the victorious Greeks seemed to promise insight into the Trojan War. But the two stories scarcely touch. Professor Blegen found only the wreckage of a crowded stronghold, one skeleton of dubious date on the hillside below it, parts of three skulls, some bones in a doorway, one arrowhead. Yet combining Homer with what we know of Mycenaean military lore gives us an idea of what the Trojan War must have been like.

IN HIS JOYOUS RETURN *to Athens,*
Theseus (below) forgot to hoist
a white sail to signal success.
His despairing father, Athens'
King Aegeus, flung himself into
the sea thenceforth named Aegean.

The reality behind the legend
of Theseus and the Minotaur?
Tribute, certainly, for Minoan sea
power ruled the Aegean; but Athens
more likely paid Knossos in grain
and oil than in youths and maidens
for a man-eating monster.
Minoans traded with those too
strong to be raided, like Mycenae,
and preferred tribute to the torch.

Then, in the 1400's, the tables
turned. Mycenaeans took over
Crete. Now their colonists, traders,
and raiders churned the Aegean.
Families, sometimes several towns,
might join in a coastal foray.
Once, Homer says, all the kings
gathered at Aulis for a mass attack
on Troy in revenge for the
abduction of Sparta's Queen
Helen, "shining among women,"
by Paris, son of Troy's King Priam.
Menelaus, the husband, got his
brother Agamemnon to lead the
vendetta. Personal ties drew
forces from fragmented Hellas
that "launch'd a thousand ships."

Modern Helen (right) measures
bullion from the sea—an "oxhide"
of Cyprus copper equal in value to
a cow. The galley it rode sank off
Cos at the time of the Trojan War.

CRUSTED COPPER INGOT, 32 CENTURIES OLD, FROM BRONZE AGE SHIPWRECK; PETER THROCKMORTON.
LEFT: DETAIL OF FRANÇOIS VASE, ATHENIAN, 6TH CENTURY B.C., IN ARCHEOLOGICAL MUSEUM, FLORENCE; SCALA

PAINTING BY LISA BIGANZOLI
GEOGRAPHIC ART DIVISION

69

Greeks and Trojans had similar racial backgrounds and had been trading with each other since at least 1800 B.C. Astride land and water routes at the crossroads of Asia and Europe, Troy dominated a fertile plain where rivers ran from Mount Ida to the sea. Here the Mycenaeans could find woolen cloth, silver, and the famed Trojan horses, "born of the north wind." Rivalry between Troy and the newer Mycenaean colonies in Asia Minor might have strained relations. Some quick grievance—the abduction of Helen from Sparta by Hector's brother Paris—could have sparked a blaze of anger which helped ruin both civilizations.

*H*OMER SHOWS US Greek longships drawn up on the beach several miles from the Trojan stronghold; men building timber-and-thatch houses against the winter and for storing loot from raids on neighboring settlements. He treats chariots as taxis to carry the heroes to their dueling grounds before Troy. But we know that Mycenaean nobles fought from chariots and wore special panoply for chariot warfare—a cuirass, or breastplate; a helmet with cheek pieces and plume. Two charioteers manned the light, unstable vehicle. The warrior carried a pair of long spears with hardwood shafts and bronze heads to inflict damage from a distance while the driver maneuvered, warding off trouble with whip, knife, and warning yells. Chariots attacked individually. Pole, yoke, and traces often parted or tangled a team, and one of the two men might have to spring down and quiet the horses.

We can picture the whole Homeric armory: ash spear, polished goat-horn bow, battle club of olivewood studded with bronze spikes, hunting javelins, slings. A duel between foot soldiers opens with spears flying, striking the ground or thudding into a leather shield. Then swords come into play, no longer the two-handed slasher, but a more manageable cut-and-thruster entrusted only to nobles. Homer delights in describing livers and eyeballs quivering on spear points, arrows slicing past corselets at neck or belt, dismembered corpses rolling like logs through the press of combat, men hamstrung or left helpless with cut ankle tendons. (Long after Homer the legend arose that Achilles died of a wound in the heel, the spot where his mother held him when she dipped him in the River Styx to make him invulnerable.)

Anger sometimes caused a warrior to humiliate a fallen foe, to jab his body and kick it. Proper burial of friends was an emotional necessity, or their ghosts might become reproachful and troublesome. Concepts of justice played no part in shaping a soldier. The grief of captives did not stir him. Slaughtering children, dragging women from their houses, and firing palaces was part of the day's work. The Homeric hero judged skill and honor by loot. After ten years of ravaging

WOODEN HORSE, *Odysseus' stratagem, disgorges Greek warriors inside sleeping Troy. Spear in its side was thrown by the priest Laocoön to warn his fellow Trojans by its hollow thud to beware of Greeks "even when they are bearing gifts." Athena cut him short (Virgil relates in the* Aeneid*), sending two huge sea snakes streaking ashore, "tongues flickering like flame . . . mouths hissing." Seizing his two sons, sinking fangs in "piteous flesh," they crushed Laocoön in scaly coils as he cried to heaven. Trojans breached their walls to drag the horse inside, then celebrated the Greek withdrawal. Dire prophecies of their princess Cassandra went unheeded—and their city was destroyed.*

the plain of Troy, bold men had amassed treasures of bronze cauldrons, red iron, fast horses, skilled and pretty captive women. Achilles, who sacked 23 cities, grew bored by promises of ransom from prisoners of war and killed them.

The story of the Trojan Horse remains one of the most famous in Greek mythology. The invaders burn their houses by the shore and sail off. Only Odysseus and the elite among warriors remain with the wooden horse, " sitting within and bearing death and doom for the Trojans." We may never know what Mycenaean invention gave rise to the legend of the Trojan Horse. A great siege engine, perhaps.

But Troy fell. Trojans who escaped moved westward, like Aeneas, whose story became Virgil's *Aeneid,* or south to Africa where their chariots astonished the Libyans. Some Greeks settled in Asia Minor. Some were blown off course to Egypt and western islands. Many who reached home without shipwreck or suffering found strife waiting them. Wives had not stayed faithful for all those years. Rivals occupied thrones. People grumbled at poverty, aggression, and greed. Tales of returning heroes—of Odysseus—fit well enough the archeology of the Mediterranean in the 13th century B.C.

Most Greek towns were looted and destroyed. In place of the imposing Mycenaean palaces rose flimsy and squalid buildings. The Dark Ages descended. Only poets guarded the knowledge of the lost, sunlit Bronze Age and its heroes, resourceful and determined in their battles and in their homeward striving.

Spades of science unearthed not one, but nine Troys

Stronghold of kings, shelter for surrounding populace, "well-walled" Troy guarded the plain by the Hellespont where heroes fought for Helen. Archeologist Carl W. Blegen sifted the sherds of three millenniums to establish a chronology for nine settlements built one atop the other (right). He identified Homer's Troy as VII A— a thousand years later than Schliemann's city.

ATTIC CUP PAINTING FROM VULCI, 6TH CENTURY B.C.; BRITISH MUSEUM

MERLE SEVERY AND (RIGHT) JOHN W. LOTHERS, NATIONAL GEOGRAPHIC STAFF

TROY IX c. 300 B.C.-A.D. 400

Hellenistic Ilion and Roman Ilium. Temple of Athena, theater. Fell into oblivion.

TROY VIII 700-300 B.C.

Greek colonists reoccupy the mound. Xerxes invading Greece, Alexander invading Persia offer sacrifices here.

TROY VII 1300-1100 B.C.

Late Bronze Age citadel: Homeric Troy, though less grand than described in the *Iliad*. People crowd into "sheepish cubicles" along fortress wall, repaired from Troy VI (opposite). Jars set in floors perhaps held siege rations. Public well in plaza. Troy VII A was sacked and burned c. 1260, says Blegen (traditional date: 1184). Rebuilt, invaded c. 1190 by Thracians who made knobbed pottery. This citadel, Troy VII B, destroyed by fire at dawn of Iron Age. Site uninhabited 400 years.

TROY VI 1800-1300 B.C.

In Middle Bronze Age a new people, probably same stock as Hellenes then invading Greece, bring horses, build site's strongest citadel; towered wall of dressed stone 15 feet thick. Large stone houses on terraces. Gray Minyan ware resembles Mycenaean. Cemetery reveals cremations. Earthquake shatters citadel.

TROY V 1900-1800 B.C.

Houses roomier, neater, with corner seats and benches of clay. Pottery brighter colored, more symmetrical. Town demolished.

TROY IV 2050-1900 B.C.

Rebuilt citadel grows to four acres; houses revert to mud brick. Domed ovens, often outside. Destroyed by unknown cause.

TROY III 2200-2050 B.C.

Stone-walled apartment dwellings. Venison main meat. Horn diadems. Houses razed.

TROY II 2500-2200 B.C.

"Burnt City" with extended, towered walls and royal treasure mistaken by Schliemann for Homeric Troy (page 51). King's megaron (great hall with portico and central hearth) like those at Mycenae and Pylos. Potter's wheel produces flaring bowls and goblets found from Bulgaria to Syria. Large number of terracotta whorls heralds rise in wool textile output. Trade, perhaps tolls yield gold, silver, bronze.

TROY I 3000-2500 B.C.

Rubblework wall protects region's ruler at dawn of Bronze Age. Mud-brick houses, probably windowless, framed in wood with flat clay-and-reed roofs. Pottery hand-shaped. Settlement razed by fire.

In the Wake of Odysseus

Sail with Ernle Bradford to Cyclops' cave and Calypso's isle,
tracing Homer's hero across the "wine-dark sea" on a

Voyage in Search
of Fabled Lands

W HEN HOMER'S HERO, ODYSSEUS, strayed into the western Mediterranean, his voyage had all the excitement of today's space travel. In that misty age following the Trojan War, he knew less of the world into which the winds tossed him than the captain of a spacecraft knows of the moon. Though Minoans and Mycenaeans had traded in Italy and Sicily as early as 1600 B.C., memory of these voyages had dimmed by Homer's day, and he launches his hero into the unknown. Conqueror of men and monsters, master and lover of goddesses, much-enduring wanderer over the "fish-infested" sea, Odysseus symbolizes man's questing spirit.

I have always felt that Homer's geographical descriptions, his treatment of wind and weather, indicated an original source based on fact. And since World War II, when I spent three years cruising the Mediterranean with the

Gentle breeze wafts the author to Ithaca, "a rugged place, but a good nurse of men"; Winfield Parks, National Geographic photographer

"So he crept into the wide-wayed city," scouting Troy's defenses (below)
before hiding in his wooden horse that conquered the city.
Similar wiles served Odysseus well while wandering homeward.
Scholars since antiquity have sought to chart his course.
Exploring from seaward, the author plotted these landfalls (opposite),
based on ship speeds under sail and oars. The hero's side trip to Hades,
"at the limit . . . of the deep-running Ocean" beyond the Pillars
of Hercules, may be an interpolation in Homer's epic reflecting
a hazy memory of Minoan seafaring into the Atlantic.

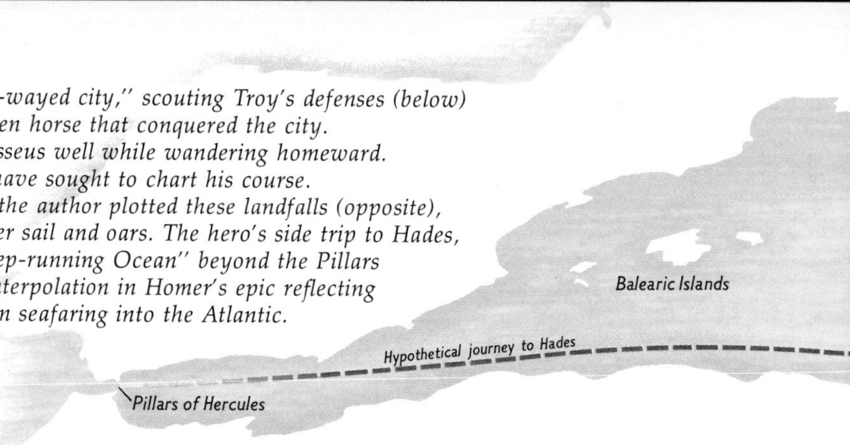

Balearic Islands

Hypothetical journey to Hades

Pillars of Hercules

ROMAN STATUE, 1ST CENTURY, MRS. ISABELLA STEWART GARDNER MUSEUM, BOSTON; ERICH LESSING, MAGNUM

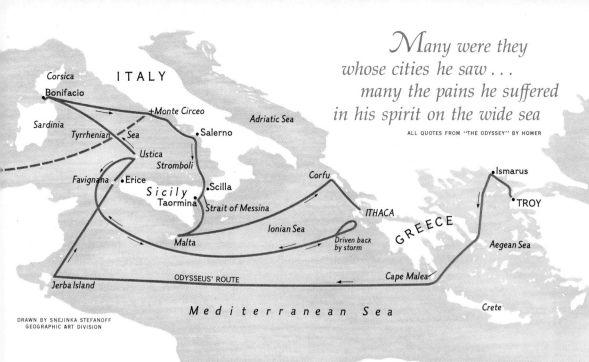

*Many were they
whose cities he saw . . .
many the pains he suffered
in his spirit on the wide sea*

ALL QUOTES FROM "THE ODYSSEY" BY HOMER

Royal Navy, I have followed the wake of Odysseus. I have skippered a small sloop, a staysail ketch, and a 20-ton cutter. I have crewed with friends aboard their yachts. I have taken caïques and fishing boats to remote islands. I sailed with the Admiralty's pilotage instructions for the Mediterranean in one hand, Homer's epic in the other. The conviction of the *Odyssey*'s geographical authenticity grew. Time and again I felt that certain anchorages, cliffs, and turbulent straits were familiar. It seemed as though I were gazing at the world through someone else's eyes.

KING OF ITHACA, an island off western Greece, Odysseus had joined the expedition that sailed under Agamemnon to wreak vengeance on Troy for the rape of Helen. He first tried to avoid taking part by feigning madness, for an oracle had warned that if he left home, he would not see his wife Penelope nor his son Telemachus for 20 years.

Homer's hero is depicted as reddish-haired, with a jutting beard, short legs, and broad shoulders. I believe he walked with a slight limp from the boar wound in his thigh. As Ovid later wrote—using the Latin name that is now more familiar—"Ulysses was not beautiful, but he was eloquent." He was, in fact, a man of many wiles, boastful, but loyal to his friends and courageous in adversity. The goddess Athena admired his "many-colored mind ever framing some new craftiness."

Odysseus spent ten years in the siege of Troy. Finally his cunning stratagem, the Trojan Horse, won victory for the Greeks. While Priam's citadel still smoked above its plain, Odysseus' men hauled in the sleeping stones (pierced mooring rocks so named because mariners generally beached their craft at night) and headed homeward. He would hug the shoreline, for he had no maps, no compass, and little knowledge of weather or currents. He rode a primitive, pitch-covered "black ship"

77

They wanted to stay . . .
feeding on lotus, and
forget the way home

Jerba, island oasis off Tunisia,
weaves the spell of Homer's
land of the "Lotus-Eaters."
It needs no "flowering food"
to drug visitors. Ivory beaches
and swaying palms bid them stay
forever. Village women (right)
wear the **petasus**, conical hat
of Hermes, patron of travelers
and bringer of dreams.

Steadfast, the author (opposite)
continues his odyssey northward.

with no deck, with a simple square sail when the wind was favorable and the arms of his oarsmen when the wind was adverse. Some 40 freemen took turns at the 20 oars—10 to a side—while Odysseus and other nobles gave orders and steered.

Heading northwest with his squadron of 12 ships, Odysseus made a landfall at Ismarus in Thrace, near modern Alexandroupolis. Here his raiding mariners brought aboard many jars of "honey-sweet red wine." Then a savage storm from the north swept the ships southward down the Aegean, past islands of the Cyclades—Delos, Seriphos, Siphnos, Melos, Thera. From the deck of a small boat I too have seen these isles, often trailing banners of cloud before that same wind.

Odysseus made for the channel between Cape Malea, at the southeastern tip of Greece, and the island of Cythera. He planned to skirt the Peloponnesus as he worked north to Ithaca. But the wind rose again and the swell plucked the vessels away from land. Hard though the men strained at their oars, they could not double the cape. The wind sent them scudding southwestward, hurling them across whitecapped waters, starting Odysseus on his long adventure. It would be another ten years before he set foot on Ithaca again.

"NINE DAYS then I was swept along by the force of the hostile winds . . . but on the tenth day we landed in the country of the Lotus-Eaters. . . ." Strabo, the Greek geographer of the first century, and other authorities identified this place with the isle of Jerba off Tunisia. I agree. Under good sailing conditions Odysseus' ships could make about three knots; under oars, two. Driven by a strong northeasterly wind, the squadron would have sailed 648 nautical miles. Jerba lies about 620 miles from Cape Malea.

The inhabitants offered the weary Greeks "honey-sweet fruit of lotus." Those

WINFIELD PARKS AND (OPPOSITE) JOHN J. PUTMAN, BOTH NATIONAL GEOGRAPHIC STAFF

He cried aloud to the other Cyclopes,
who live around him in their own caves
along the windy pinnacles

who ate it wanted to desert for a life of happy indolence
The lotus may have been the sloe-like fruit of the *cordia
myxa*, which still grows in grape-like clusters on this coast
In any event, the sailors' feelings here were hardly surprising. They had made a safe landfall and found plenty to eat
If male Lotus-Eaters greeted them, surely there must have
been women too.

I was torpedoed off this coast during the war and spen
nearly a week here. But for the Naval Discipline Act, I doub
if I would have left to hazard the sea once more. There are
worse things than resting in the shade when the sun is high
swimming in the cool of the evening, and feeling a deep
trance-laden peace. I think one must look beyond the lotus
for the seaman's reluctance to leave.

Determined to return home, Odysseus dragged his men
aboard and led his ships away from that drowsy African
shore. He had no idea how far west of his destination he
had been carried. So he headed northward, on a course tha
put him aground on a "wooded island" that held "wild
goats beyond number."

By my reckoning this was the island of Favignana of
western Sicily. In classical times it bore the name Aegusa
Goat Island—hardly a coincidence. Fog shrouded the beach

Like mist, the Cyclops legend
wreathes Sicily's lofty Erice.
Here Odysseus plied Polyphemus
with syrupy, unwatered wine,
blinded the drunken giant (below),
and fled his cave clinging
to the fleece of a ram (right).

when Odysseus' ships ran up on it. Fog rarely forms in this part of the world—except off this corner of Sicily. When I came here in a staysail ketch I also hit fog. Hearing the murmur of rollers, we dropped anchor in a rush; seconds later the mist parted and there was the island, a hundred yards dead ahead. From here Odysseus could hear the bleat of sheep in the land of the Cyclopes across the strait. And from here I heard the sound of traffic along Sicily's coast road.

Leaving all but his own crew to feast on Favignana's wild goats, Odysseus struck out for the mainland, his vessel tracking the still water with her oar thresh. He probably used Mount Eryx (Erice), towering 2,400 feet above the coastal plain, as his landmark, just as sailors have used it ever since. Landing somewhere near modern Trapani, he led his raiding party up the hillside and into the cave where the Cyclops Polyphemus kept his sheep.

Polyphemus, the one-eyed giant—here's a sailor's yarn! Men who escape danger often exaggerate when later telling the tale. And Odysseus knew no tradition of the "stiff upper lip." The "giant" who trapped him was probably an oversize Sicilian shepherd who objected to foreigners stealing his sheep! Homer tells how Polyphemus rolled a huge boulder, "a piece of sky-towering cliff," across the cave mouth.

ALONG THE STEEP STREETS *of Erice walk silent black-mantled women. The stark and solitary citadel was named for Eryx, son of Aphrodite and an Argonaut she rescued from the sea. Ruins of her temple, clinging to a dizzying spur, recall her ancient cult. Here, locals say, girls paid homage to the love goddess by sacrificing their virginity to homecoming mariners.*

In spring, spawning tuna blunder into traps off nearby Favignana. Befuddled giants wander sheeplike through a labyrinth of nets into the "chamber of death." Here fishermen hoist the net and reap a thrashing harvest. Odysseus' men preferred red meat. On Favignana they found "the game we longed for"—goat.

WINFIELD PARKS AND (LEFT) LUIS MARDEN, BOTH NATIONAL GEOGRAPHIC STAFF

Seizing two Greeks, he "slapped them, like . . . puppies, against the ground. . . . Then he cut them up limb by limb and got supper ready, and like a lion, reared in the hills, without leaving anything, ate them. . . ."

Crafty Odysseus plied Polyphemus with that strong wine from Ismarus, and when the giant had fallen into a drunken sleep, he blinded him with a sharpened staff heated in the fire: ". . . and the blood boiled around the hot point, so that the blast and scorch of the burning ball singed all his eyebrows and eyelids, and the fire made the roots of his eye crackle. . . . He gave a giant horrible cry and the rocks rattled to the sound. . . ."

Neighboring Cyclopes thronged about the closed cave, asking who was doing Polyphemus harm. "No-man!" he shouted, for Odysseus slyly had told him his name was Noman. And hearing that no man had hurt their friend, the Cyclopes went away.

In the morning the agonized giant pushed the great

*Giants . . . along the
cliffs pelted my men with
man-sized boulders, and
a horrid racket went up*

Eerie haze drapes Bonifacio harbor,
pincered between walls of limestone
at Corsica's southern tip.
Here the cannibalistic Laestrygonians
smashed Odysseus' fleet and speared men
for the pot. Only his black ship escaped.
   Giant prehistoric burial stones knob
the French island, birthplace of Napoleon.
Fjords knife into its coast; jagged peaks
and gorges scar its wild heart. Shepherds
still chant harsh, wailing airs, calling
to mind the ballate, ancient lament of
keening women. Murder occasioned the
singing of the voceri to incite a vendetta.
Families often consumed one another
in these blood feuds. Outlawed killers
formed a banditry—"lords of the maquis"—
unchecked until the 1930's. "Maquis"
(bushland) earned fame when French
guerrillas took the name in World War II.

stone aside to let his flock out to pasture, but passed his hands over each beast to make sure no Greek escaped. Odysseus, wily as always, had his men cling to the wool on the bellies of the sheep to avoid detection. He was last to leave, choosing the finest ram. Polyphemus felt the thick fleece: " 'My dear old ram, why are you thus leaving the cave last of the sheep? Never in the old days were you left behind by the flock, but long-striding, far ahead of the rest would pasture on the tender bloom of the grass. . . . Perhaps you are grieving for your master's eye. . . .' "

Safely aboard ship, Odysseus hurled taunts. " 'Cyclops, if any mortal man ever asks you . . . tell him that you were blinded by Odysseus, sacker of cities.' " In fury the giant flung boulders toward the mocking voice. Sicilians point them out now — great spears of rock, still a hazard to mariners.

Northeast the Greeks sailed, to where Aeolus lived "on a floating island, the whole enclosed by a rampart of bronze. . . ." Tradition — and many scholars — link this home of the wind god with the Aeolian Islands northwest of Messina, but I favor the island of Ustica, 60 miles from Favignana. When I first saw it, a heat haze hid its base, so it "floated." Homer mentions no other islands near it, and Ustica is the only solitary island in this part of the Mediterranean. The *Mediterranean Pilot* warns of its "steep and inaccessible" shoreline. This must be what Homer meant by his "rampart of bronze." Sailors today speak of an "iron-bound coast."

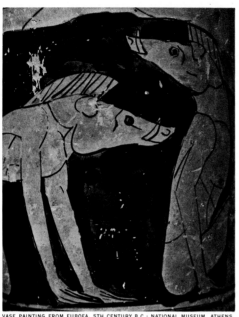

VASE PAINTING FROM EUBOEA, 5TH CENTURY B.C.; NATIONAL MUSEUM, ATHENS

WINFIELD PARKS, NATIONAL GEOGRAPHIC PHOTOGRAPHER

*Hawk's-eye view from a temple ruin sweeps Italy's coast from Terracina
to distant Cape Circeo, jutting like an island. There Circe ("she-hawk" in Greek)
turned Odysseus' men into swine. Modern Circe (opposite) casts a subtler spell.*

Aeolus gave Odysseus a favorable wind to speed him back to Greece. He packed the other winds in a bag and told Odysseus not to open it until he was home. But with Greece in sight at last, Odysseus allowed himself a proper sleep. Some crewmen, thinking the bag contained treasure, opened it. A gale blew up and drove them from their homeland. Now they knew the ordeal of Tantalus, whom the gods punished by keeping food and water just out of reach—"tantalizing" him.

The Greeks fetched Ustica again, but Aeolus spurned them. So they rowed off into the unknown sea. For six days and nights they bent to their oars, then came to a "glorious harbor, which a sky-towering cliff encloses on either side, with ... two projecting promontories facing each other...." At the head of the harbor the sailors were out of sight and sound of the sea.

Such places are rare in the Mediterranean. Since ancient times men have sited this port in eastern Sicily or western Italy. But I sailed back and forth along these coasts and could find no natural harbor to fit the description. I finally came upon it, as I suspect Odysseus did, entirely by accident.

Sailing up the strait between Corsica and Sardinia one summer day, I decided to put into Bonifacio for the night. The *Mediterranean Pilot* should have given me a clue: "Port de Bonifacio consists of a cove from three-quarters of a cable to one cable wide, formed by the peninsula on which the town is built.... The entrance is difficult to distinguish from a distance." As we closed the coast, it was a long time before we could make out that break in the cliffs.

Tacking constantly, we worked our way in—and suddenly it dawned on me. Cliffs stood high on either hand. Through the heart of them ran a knife thrust of the sea. Here was the harbor I had vainly sought! Here an arm of the sea winds inland for nearly a mile to a secure anchorage. Bonifacio lies about 240 miles northwest of Ustica—on the radius of a ship making less than two knots for six days. Odysseus, of course, should have headed eastward around Sicily, but by now he may well have lost all sense of direction.

Rowing their ships into the harbor, the Greeks were trapped by the savage Laestrygonians, who hurled boulders on them and sank them. Only Odysseus and his crew escaped. Ever wary, he had waited outside.

Now the frightened survivors steered east and found the unknown mainland of Italy barring the way to Greece. According to my calculations, they sighted it where Monte Circeo, Circe's Mountain, looms out of the sea. I came here once after 57 hours of hard sailing against a northerly, and I remember with what relief we hailed the first sight of the Pontine Islands, south of the mountain. Our bodies were bruised, our hair stiff with salt, our eyes red from lack of sleep. We anchored at Terracina just below the mountain, and we knew how Odysseus and his men must have felt when they limped into this haven.

Odysseus probably intended to lay up for the winter. It was fall when I first came here, and the smoke stood up still and blue from San Felice Circeo. Perhaps near here Odysseus' men saw the smoke rising from the palace of Circe.

The "dread goddess" invited the mariners to a feast and bewitched them with a potion. Smiting them with her wand, she penned them in pigsties, "and they took on the look of pigs, with the heads and voices and bristles of pigs, but the minds within them stayed as they had been before."

Provided with a countermagic by the god Hermes, Odysseus forced the goddess to restore his shipmates. Impressed, Circe not only obeyed but became his mistress. Her maids served him wine and bathed him, "mixing hot and cold just as I wanted, and pouring it over shoulders and head, to take the heart-wasting weariness from my limbs." Amid such luxury Odysseus lingered nearly a year.

Could it be chance, I wondered, that until a few years ago all roads leading toward Circe's Mountain displayed the sign, "Motorists, Beware of Boars"? A few miles away lies the pre-classical temple to Feronia, goddess of the beasts. And who else, I thought, was Circe, who changed men into beasts? Wandering about the mountain one day, I saw a dark-haired young woman make her way to a stream. She carried a wicker basket. Would this modern Circe fill it with the same herbs

The swift ship as it drew nearer was seen by the Sirens, and they directed their sweet song toward us

Lashed to the mast, Odysseus suffers the Sirens' lure to disaster. But his companions, ears sealed with wax, "dashed their oars in the gray sea" and pulled safely by. Eye on prow, believed to help a ship see its way safely, looks out for danger on Sicilian fishing craft today. Bradford (below, at right) explores Li Galli rocks, which may have been the Sirens' lair. Nearby Capri, cliffs crowned with villas ancient and modern, lures throngs with pleasure's "honey-sweet voice."

WINFIELD PARKS, NATIONAL GEOGRAPHIC PHOTOGRAPHER
RIGHT: VASE PAINTING FROM VULCI, 5TH CENTURY B.C.; BRITISH MUSEUM

from which her ancestress had made her potion? Far more prosaic, I discovered. It held the family wash, which she rinsed and hung over spiky bushes of yellow broom.

Later, as I sat over coffee in the market square of San Felice Circeo, the *padrone* offered to show me the site of "Circe's cave" if I came back after his siesta. But I had seen plenty of caves on the mountain, and I had pictured the goddess in a palace, as Homer said. The cicadas shouted on the shimmering slopes as I returned to my boat. A pair of hawks lifted over the ridge. The afternoon was drug-laden with peace and an ancient stillness.

CIRCE WARNED ODYSSEUS of the Sirens, "enchanters of all mankind," on whose shores lay "boneheaps of men now rotted away." She cautioned him to plug the ears of his crew with beeswax so they could not hear the Sirens' song, for those who listened never returned home. If Odysseus wished to hear it, he must get his men to bind him to the mast and pay no heed to his pleas to be set free.

Strabo identified the Sirens' rocks with the Li Galli islets just east of Capri at the

entrance to the Gulf of Salerno. In this region I have come nearer shipwreck than anywhere else — shipwreck of energy, of ambition, of all desire to struggle for survival. I sailed here in a small boat after the war and fell under the Siren spell. Something called out: "Abandon activity; stay forever!" During calm September days when mists varnished the peaks of Anacapri and the scent of melons from a fruit boat hung on the sirocco-laden air, I nearly did abandon my voyage to Greece,

The next thing we saw was smoke and a heavy surf, and we heard it thundering

"Lighthouse of the Mediterranean,"
Stromboli has spit lava by day,
fire by night since history began.
The more violent eruptions of the
3,038-foot cone turn sea to steam
with molten rock—the "storms
of ravening fire" Odysseus braved.

Hephaestus, Greek god of fire,
worked a forge on the nearby isle
of Vulcano. From Vulcan, his Roman
counterpart, we get "volcano."

my voyage to anywhere. Once a man finds the quiet center of the spinning world, there seems little point in moving. But my bankers were cool to any suggestion of extending an overdraft. My yacht insurance would soon expire. I had a story to write.

I have been back since, but it has never been quite the same. Something fades as we grow older, and we hear the Siren voices less clearly.

ODYSSEUS HEARD THEM clearly enough. But his sailors, their ears plugged, smote the water and ignored his pleas to turn him loose. Not until well away did they set Odysseus free. Then their strong shoulders drove the boat to the next hazard, the wandering rocks.

Of these, too, Circe had forewarned the hero: "No ship of men that came here ever has fled through, but the waves of the sea and storms of ravening fire carry away together the ship's timbers and the men's bodies."

Does any spot in the Mediterranean fill this description? And if so, would it lie on Odysseus' course?

The answer is yes: The volcanic islands of Stromboli and Strombolicchio lie 112 miles south of the Li Galli rocks. I have sailed by Stromboli at night when rivers of lava hissed into the sea and spears of lightning crackled above the mountain. What would I have thought of such phenomena 3,000 years ago, when men had the fears and imagination children have today? I would have equated a frowning peak with, perhaps, a dangerous giant, a tranquil cove with a beautiful nymph—and a volcano with an angry god.

Despite his crew's terror, Odysseus guided his ship through the dangerous waters and headed for the Strait of Messina, inhabited by two fearsome monsters, Scylla and Charybdis. The first was a man-eating female with 12 feet and "six necks upon her, grown to great length, and upon each neck there is a horrible head . . . full of black death." The second was a giant whirlpool. Circe described how it "sucks down the black water," and told Odysseus to drive his vessel past quickly and cut close to Scylla, "since it is far better to mourn six friends lost out of your ship than the whole company."

Charybdis still lies over toward the Sicilian side of the strait and, though tamed since Homeric times, still appears on modern charts. Countercurrents churn the whole area with turbulent water. I once came through at dawn, with the wind astern and the tide running against us. Suddenly the boat would not answer her

WINFIELD PARKS, NATIONAL GEOGRAPHIC PHOTOGRAPHER
OPPOSITE: BRONZE MIRROR HANDLE FROM TARENTUM,
4TH CENTURY B.C., THE LOUVRE, PARIS; ERICH LESSING, MAGNUM

*Running south through the Strait
of Messina, graveyard of mariners
down the centuries, small craft still
hew to Odysseus' course. They hug
Italy's toe, haunt of the fabled sea
monster Scylla (opposite). Thus they
clear the maelstrom Charybdis. Here
tides of the Tyrrhenian and Ionian
Seas clash, forming whirlpools that
can suck a skiff down into the abyss.
The channel's powerful currents
swiftly reverse every six hours.*

helm. Wheel hard to port, we were being inexorably dragged to starboard. All around us the water seethed. It had a curious oily look. Then up from the sea bed boiled a patch of deep, cold water. We switched on our engine to pull clear of the maelstrom, but not until we added full power did the rudder respond. Changes in the sea floor even in the last 150 years have weakened these whirlpools. How fearsome they must have been to the Greeks in their open boat, under oars!

If Charybdis is fact, what about Scylla? Well, it's just possible that huge squid might have inhabited these rocks 3,000 years ago. Today squid and octopus fishing plays a large part in the local economy.

Between the village of Scilla, as Italians spell it today, and the coast of Sicily, less than four miles away, lies the finest swordfishing ground in the Mediterranean. I have sailed with the swordfish boats here and shall always remember that moment of fabulous excitement when the harpoon strikes home and a great swordfish jumps, shining, from the sea.

At the end of one hot day I watched a swordfish boat come into Ganzirri, almost opposite the whirlpool of Charybdis. Among waiting children stood a little girl with an armful of lilies and gladioli. When the huge fish were brought ashore, she placed a flower in the jaws of each. I asked a bystander why. "The fish are beautiful," he said, "and so are the flowers. . . ." He spread his hands in a fanlike gesture, as if this explained everything.

Approaching the terrors of the strait, Odysseus followed Circe's instructions to the letter. He hugged the Italian shore by Scylla's rock, while across the way Charybdis "sucked down the sea's salt water . . . and the rock around it groaned terribly, and the ground showed at the sea's bottom, black with sand; and green fear seized upon my companions."

While they gazed at this awesome sight, Scylla stretched her long necks and snatched six of the crew. Now proud Odysseus knew pity as "they cried out to me and called me by name, the last time they ever did it. . . . they gasped and struggled as they were hoisted up the cliff. Right in her doorway she ate them up. They were screaming and reaching out their hands to me in this horrid encounter. That was the most pitiful scene that these eyes have looked on in my sufferings as I explored the routes over the water."

From the Sirens, Odysseus had heard the enchanting song which told him that all things have happened

*She fishes, peering
all over the cliffside,
looking for dolphins or
... some sea monster*

*Where monster Scylla fished for men
swordfishermen now stalk their
monstrous prey. The geographer
Strabo told how fish spotters
on bluffs directed men in skiffs.
Today's lookouts guide harpooners
from tall masts of feluccas (above).*

*Success crowns one fisher (right)
at Ganzirri, across the strait from
Scilla (opposite). There a castle
caps the famous "Rock of Scylla."*

before, that all will occur again, and that the course of true wisdom is to take our ease in the shade. From Scylla, symbol of all the sinister aspects of the sea—storm, rock, whirlpool, waterspout, and sea monster combined—he heard the cry of elemental forces that crush men.

Mourning his loss, Odysseus headed for the domain of the sun god Helios. Circe had cautioned the Greeks not to touch the "handsome, wide-browed oxen" that grazed there, lest disaster befall. In the evening Odysseus reached a "hollow harbor, close to sweet water...."

By my calculation the Ithacans must have spent nine days at sea and were probably low on water. They clamored to go ashore for the night, instead of sailing past as their captain wanted to do. Reluctantly, Odysseus agreed to put in, warning his men again not to harm any of the sacred cattle.

This natural harbor with fresh water at hand must have been the Sicilian port of Taormina. It lies 30 miles south of the strait, just about the distance one would

expect the vessel to have reached with the oarsmen pulling their hardest. There are no other anchorages for many miles. Taormina sits high on a hill overlooking the harbor. Two small rivers, the Alcantara and Minissale, flow into the sea nearby — fresh water for the taking. Long after Homer's time Greeks believed that the sun god's cattle roamed the plains between here and Mount Etna. Their old name for the area, Tauromenion, stems from their word for bull, *tauros*. Some object that Homer called the sun god's island *Thrinakia*, a name never applied to Sicily. I am not disturbed. With the change of three letters — the kind of slip writers make every day — we have *Trinacria*, Three-cornered Island, a common name for Sicily in ancient times, and a fitting one.

I was disappointed to see few cattle at Taormina; the industrious Sicilian farmer has found better use for the land. Vines, olives, date palms, and mulberry trees now spread their green over the dark soil. One name, Val del Bove, Valley of the Ox, preserves the memory of what was once cattle land.

A long spell of bad weather detained Odysseus here. First, an offshore gale blew itself out, then "the South Wind blew for a whole month long. . . ." They had what we call sirocco weather — the wind sweeping across the Mediterranean from North Africa in winter, picking up humidity as it moves north. Those who have never experienced it can have no idea of its effect on body, nerves, and temper. I have heard that there was a time in Sicily when any sirocco that blew for more than ten days got the blame for crimes of passion committed during the spell of weather. And the Greeks endured a whole month of sirocco!   (Continued on page 102)

*Handsome . . . horn-curved
      oxen were pasturing . . .
   not far from the
         dark-prowed ship*

Sacred cattle of the sun god Helios tempted Odysseus' crew, stranded and starving. Despite dire warnings, the men butchered enough beef for a six-day feast — and doomed themselves to Olympian wrath.

The author equates the "island of Helios" with Sicily, largest in the Mediterranean, colonized by Phoenicians, Carthaginians, and Greeks. Sheep and goats graze hills above the sea, where fishing boats spread lateen sails and a patriarch, dreaming in the sun (opposite), evokes Tennyson's Ulysses:
*"Old age hath yet his honour and his toil . . .
Some work of noble note may yet be done,
Not unbecoming men that strove with Gods."*

VASE PAINTING FROM CERVETERI, 6TH CENTURY B.C.;
THE LOUVRE. OPPOSITE: FISHING VILLAGE OF MONDELLO;
LUIS MARDEN, NATIONAL GEOGRAPHIC STAFF

"HELIOS WHO BRINGS JOY to mortals" still beams on Taormina, famed resort squeezed on terraces high above Sicily's sandy shore. Behind soars 10,958-foot Mount Etna, loftiest active volcano in Europe. Refugees from the nearby Greek colony of Naxos, sacked by Syracuse in 403 B.C., found haven here, as Odysseus did. At Taormina's Greek theater, rebuilt by Romans, visitors view ancient drama in a setting described by Goethe as "the most colossal work of nature and art."

PAUL A. ZAHL, NATIONAL GEOGRAPHIC STAFF

Terracotta from Cumae smiles in memory that here Greeks bore gifts of art and alphabet to Etruscans, then to Romans, when Euboeans set roots in Italian soil c. 750 B.C. Thrice Cumae stemmed an Etruscan march southward; in 474 she and Syracuse broke Etruscan sea power. Relief rests in National Museum in Naples—Neapolis, "New City" founded from Cumae c. 600. Galleys below, with landing ladders lashed, sail on 6th-century Athenian cup in the Louvre.

Naples
Neapolis

Cumae
Kyme

Paestu
Poseido

Velia
Elea

Bold mariners sailing in the wake of Odysseus carried the flame of Hellas west to Magna Graecia

Lion-hearted Syracuse crushed Carthaginians at Himera, 480 B.C., the year Athens beat Persians at Salamis. National Archeological Museum in Syracuse holds this spout from Himera's temple of victory.

Himera •

• Segesta

"Most beautiful city of mortals," the poet Pindar said of Agrigentum, whose temples, like Paestum's on the mainland, are Doric glories. Founded by Gela in 580, it rivaled Syracuse. Its tyrant Phalaris roasted opponents in a brazen bull.

S I C I L Y

Selinus
•

Agrigentum
Acragas

• Gela

Graceful 5th-century flutist in Rome's Terme Museum typifies art of Locri, founded by Dorians c. 700 B.C. Art from Selinus is as impressive as the earthquake-tumbled ruins of its 10 temples.

Metapontum •

• Tarentum
  Taras

Heraclea •

Trade-rich, luxury-
loving Sybaris,
where late sleepers
banned roosters,
coined this silver bull
and our word "sybarite."
Croton razed it in 510 B.C.

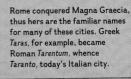

Rome conquered Magna Graecia,
thus hers are the familiar names
for many of these cities. Greek
Taras, for example, became
Roman *Tarentum*, whence
Taranto, today's Italian city.

0   50
STATUTE MILES

• Sybaris

• Thurii

Bronze sphinx in city's
National Museum kept
guard at Rhegium,
founded in the
8th century B.C.

Croton •

• Hipponium

Strait of
Messina

Locri •

• Rhegium

Taormina

• Naxos

"EUREKA!" cried Archimedes of
Syracuse, deducing in his bath
the principle of buoyant force.
Here he applies it to test Hieron's
crown in the 3d century B.C.
He found the gold adulterated.

yracuse
•

"STRANGERS, who are you?" Cyclops asks Odysseus and his companions. "From where do you come sailing over the watery ways? Is it on some business, or are you recklessly roving as pirates do...?"

A good question. Leaving Troy, Odysseus' crew had fallen on Ismarus, slain its men, seized its women in a tradition that scarcely distinguished raid from trade.

Earlier, Mycenaeans had taken over Crete's trading outposts from Syria to Sicily. But the Dorian invasions disrupted that trade, drove settlers to Aegean isles and Asia Minor. Land hunger spawned Hellenic settlements "like frogs around a pond." Greeks colonized the Black Sea region, founding Byzantium 1,000 years before Constantine renamed the city for himself. Merchants from Miletus secured a port at Naucratis in the Nile Delta; Thera farmers founded Cyrene in Libya.

The main thrust was westward, starting near Naples about 750 B.C. Famine-ridden Chalcis of Euboea sent a tenth of her number to found Rhegium. To Tarentum came Sparta's exiled "sons of virgins," sired while her warriors were away fighting a 20-year war. Naxos, Sicily's first colony, was planted in 735 B.C. The following year Corinth settled Syracuse, future kingpin of the west. Colonists brought sacred fire and soil as symbolic links with mother cities but cut political apron strings. Corfu, strategic way station, even fought its parent, Corinth.

Latins in Italy called the newcomers *Graeci* after an obscure tribe of colonists, hence the name "Greeks." *Magna Graecia*, Great Greece, came to rival the homeland in philosophy and science. Pythagoras, who said "all things are numbers," founded a mystic society at Croton. Elea boasted the Eleatic philosophers: Xenophanes, who rejected the Homeric pantheon in favor of one god; Zeno, famed for paradoxes; Parmenides, who claimed the world was round. Empedocles of Agrigentum postulated a universe of four elements: earth, air, water, and fire, joined by Love, severed by Strife. Herodotus completed his *History* at Thurii; Archimedes lived in Syracuse; Aeschylus died in Gela when, Pliny says, an eagle dropped a turtle on his bald head, mistaking it for a rock.

Phocaeans from Asia Minor colonized today's French Riviera and Spain's Costa Brava, and ventured beyond the Pillars of Hercules to Tartessus, near Cadiz. When Persia sacked Phocaea, they moved *en masse* to Corsica. Navigator Pytheas of Marseilles, a Phocaean colony, sailed round Britain in the 4th century B.C., then on to "Thule" (perhaps Iceland or Norway) near a "congealed sea." Greek wanderlust had reached even the Arctic ice pack.

Food began to give out. Exhausted trying to keep order, Odysseus went to pray for help and succumbed to a natural Mediterranean urge—understandable when the sirocco has reduced a man to a limp bundle of exacerbated nerves. He fell asleep.

He awoke to find his men had been listening to the rebellious Eurylochus, one of the nobles. Eurylochus had grumbled that "hunger is the sorriest way to die" and that he "would far rather gulp the waves and lose my life in them once for all, than be pinched to death on this desolate island." So the crew had killed and eaten some of the cattle.

How sad the Greeks did not know that the little rock-fringed cove of Taormina holds some of the sweetest lobsters in Sicily! Mooring here once on my way south to Syracuse, I bought five sea-green beauties for the equivalent of an English pound. In the big hotels they would have cost a pound apiece. The lobsters were still damp from the sea, trailing a little weed between their spiny legs and blowing sad bubbles from their whiskered mouths. The Sicilians, amazed to find that I sailed alone with my wife, were deeply touched by her plight: "A woman working like a sailor!" We popped the lobsters into a bucket of salt water on the roaring galley stove. One needs little more in this world than a fair wind, the sun going down behind Etna, the sound of the sea, hot lobster, good rough bread, and the red wine of Taormina. . . .

But Odysseus' crew ate beef. Frightened to stay any longer in the sun god's land, he decided to put to sea and try to reach Greece before the crime was discovered. Unfortunately the news had already reached the gods on Olympus. No sooner had the ship set out than exactly what Circe had prophesied took place. The vessel was overwhelmed by a storm. "My men were thrown in the water, and bobbing like sea crows they were washed away on the running waves all around the black ship, and the god took away their homecoming."

Some scholars have maintained that the shipwreck scene—the speed with which the ship is overcome—proves that Homer didn't know what he was talking about. But thunderstorms come up quickly in this part of the Mediterranean. A sudden squall snapped the forestays. The backstay was made of leather, extra strong to withstand the strain of a squaresail filled to a following breeze. Now, without the counteraction of the forestays, the backstay caused the mast to collapse onto the stern, crushing the helmsman's skull. The ship broke up in pounding seas. Odysseus lashed mast and keel together to form a raft. He was the sole survivor.

"FROM THERE I WAS CARRIED along nine days, and on the tenth night the gods brought me to the island Ogygia, home of Calypso with the lovely hair. . . ." For seven years Odysseus was to be detained by this goddess on her mysterious island, described by Homer as "the navel of the sea." We know from the poem that the hero drifted southward on his raft along the coast, away from the Strait of Messina. Some 50 miles to the south of Sicily lies the Maltese archipelago. No other islands are in this area—no land at all until one comes to the North African coast.

All day long her sails were filled as she went through the water, and the sun set, and all the journeying-ways were darkened

BRADFORD, ABOARD A STAYSAIL KETCH, CONTINUES HIS QUEST; WINFIELD PARKS, NATIONAL GEOGRAPHIC PHOTOGRAPHER

It seems likely, then, that Calypso dwelt on Malta or its sister island Gozo. The description "navel of the sea" fits them perfectly. They are dead in the center of the Mediterranean trade routes, almost equidistant from Gibraltar and Cyprus and half way between Italy and North Africa.

Ortygia, the small Sicilian island on which the city of Syracuse was built, has been claimed as the island home of Calypso. But it lies so near the mainland that it has been connected, at least since classical times, by a mole or by a bridge. Odysseus, a good swimmer, could easily have swum across. Yet he remained marooned on Calypso's island for seven years, looking out across "this endless salt water," unable to escape until the nymph showed him how. I feel that Ortygia is unacceptable.

The Phoenicians, who used Malta's Grand Harbor, called the island Maleth, "the hiding place." In Greek, Calypso means hidden or hider. Calypso, moreover, lived in a cave as a kind of mother goddess. Malta's ancient inhabitants worshiped a mother goddess whose temples, made of stones carved by sharpened flints, resembled caves.

Calypso conceived a passion for Odysseus and offered to make him a god. But he longed for home. "By nights he would lie beside her . . . against his will, by one who was willing, but all the days he would sit upon the rocks . . . as weeping tears he looked out over the barren water."

Calypso's cave or rock temple could well have been on Malta's south coast, where caves honeycomb cliffs that stoop to the sea. I visited the cliff temples of Mnajdra and Hagar Qim, looked past their limestone blocks, across the fields of oats, wheat, and barley golden in the May sun, and could well picture the ambrosial den of Calypso: "There was a great fire blazing on the hearth, and the smell of cedar split in billets, and sweetwood burning, spread all over the island. She was singing inside the cave with a sweet voice as she went up and down the loom and wove with a golden shuttle."

WHEN CALYPSO finally relinquished her reluctant lover, she showed him where to get the materials for a raft. She also told him to set course for Greece by "keeping the Bear on his left hand." A glance at the map shows that if a man sailed from Malta with Ursa Major (the Great Bear), the most prominent constellation in northern skies, on his left, he would head eastward—toward Greece and the Ionian Islands where Odysseus lived.

Homer describes Odysseus' raft in detail. It had a mast, a steering oar, and built-up sides of plaited osier twigs to

Calypso, shining among divinities, kept me with her in her hollow caverns

Jumbled megaliths of Hagar Qim whisper of ancient temple rites when men of Malta worshiped their mother goddess. Somewhere here in the labyrinths of legend "divine Calypso" welcomed Odysseus when he drifted ashore amid debris of his last ship, lightning-struck by Zeus. Captive of love in her cavern, Homer's hapless hero let seven years slip by.

Honeycombed with caves, Malta sheltered Stone Age men and refugees from World War II bombs. Today visitors come to explore eerie reaches of the Blue Grotto (opposite) below Hagar Qim.

protect him from spray. He carried water, wine, grain, and plenty of "appetizing meats." If he left Malta in summer, with westerly winds, he could well have crossed the Ionian Sea. The voyage took 17 days. Since Corfu, his landfall, lies 330 miles from Malta, he would have averaged less than a knot—likely enough for his craft.

As he neared Corfu, the sea god Poseidon, rankling at the fate of his son Polyphemus, raised a great storm: "... and the North Wind born in the bright air rolled up a heavy sea." The most dangerous wind in these waters is the *bora,* the north wind that hurtles down from the Adriatic and splinters the Ionian into jagged seas. A mountainous wave tore the steering oar from Odysseus' hands, sent mast and sail overboard, and washed the hero into the sea. He climbed back aboard the raft and crouched amidships, at Poseidon's mercy.

I fell afoul of the same kind of weather while crossing the Ionian to Corfu with two friends. The wind was too strong for canvas. We sprang a leak. Our pumps jammed. All that terrible night we toiled to free the pumps and hold the yacht head-to-wind under engine. We were luckier than Odysseus, for ours was a 20-ton vessel instead of a raft. I remember how beautiful Corfu looked at dawn, under banks of cloud, lit by a glowering sun.

So it must have looked to Odysseus, flung from the last plank of his raft and swimming for shore. But the land was steep-to; the swell thundered on it and exploded in spray. He grasped a rock, but undertow plucked him off, tearing skin from "his bold hands." Clear of the sizzle and boom of surf, he swam along the coast and finally felt the coolness of fresh water flowing out to sea. Wherever a river enters the sea there is a clean inlet and the

*The Earthshaker, Poseidon . . .
stirred up an unspeakable sea . . .
and drove me to your shore*

Wrecked by the wrathful sea god, Odysseus swam to the isle of the Phaeacians: Corfu. By a river (right) he met Nausicaa "of the white arms." She had come to do the family linen— role of princess as well as peasant in Homeric days.

waves round about are flattened. So the wanderer swam landward into the mouth of a sweet, fresh stream. He was safe at last.

The island of Corfu fits the phrase: "like a shield lying on the misty face of the water." Seen from a small boat, Corfu does resemble a Greek shield, with Mount Pantocrator forming the central boss. And only Corfu has a spot that meets Homer's description of Odysseus' landing place. At Ermones Bay on the island's west coast a stream cascades down to a sandy beach. Here Odysseus went ashore and, moving inland, lay down to rest. Less than a quarter of a mile from the beach I found a shoulder of high land, shaded by olive trees, where I believe the hero fell exhausted when Athena "shed a sleep on his eyes. . . ."

He awoke to the sound of young women laughing. Shielding himself with an olive branch, for he had lost all his clothes, he looked down and saw Nausicaa, daughter of the king of the Phaeacians, playing ball with the handmaidens who

had helped her with the washing. Her attendants were terrified by this naked wild man, but she took pity on him and led him home. Over a banquet at the palace of King Alcinous, Odysseus revealed his identity and told the story of his wanderings.

Alcinous and his family, ancestors of today's hospitable Corfiotes, sent the hero on his last lap home, laden with gifts, in one of their large, 52-oared galleys. A passenger for once, Odysseus fell asleep as Corfu receded astern and the galley drove south toward Ithaca.

By dawn next day the Phaeacians were within sight of Odysseus' kingdom. They entered a cove where two headlands "jut out, to close in the harbor and shelter it." They lifted their guest ashore "and set him down on the sand . . . still bound fast in sleep." They set his possessions beside him, "next to the trunk of the olive."

I have sailed here and looked at "the harbors where all could anchor, the rocks going straight up, and the trees tall growing." I have seen the jutting headlands

What are the people whose land I have come to . . . are they . . . hospitable to strangers and with minds that are godly?

Odysseus would find the staunch folk of stone-walled Leucas as friendly as their olive groves are fruitful, as pious as their donkeys are patient. Land is their pride; in his day it spelled power, measured by how many retainers it could feed. His storeroom stood at the heart of his great house.

Schooled at mother's side to spin and sew, to grind grain, bake bread, and make cheese, a girl wed at 16. Suitors offered "gifts of wooing." Homer tells of "cattle-bringing" maidens; wealth lay in cattle in those coinless days. Without a return gift —the dowry—no marriage took place.

Boys learned to handle bow and javelin, to hunt, fish, and swim. They harked to the warrior's code in the tales of bards, saw their fathers share each meal with protecting gods. Ritual was simple, worship joyous; from burnt offerings at palace hearth or shrine, priests carved a generous slab of meat for themselves.

Some scholars identify Leucas as Odysseus' long-sought isle. But most say neighboring Ithaca was where he "kissed the grain-giving ground."

WINFIELD PARKS, NATIONAL GEOGRAPHIC PHOTOGRAPHER

WINFIELD PARKS, NATIONAL GEOGRAPHIC PHOTOGRAPHER. OPPOSITE: TERRACOTTA FROM MELOS, 5TH CENTURY B.C.; THE LOUVRE

which shield the entrance to Vathi, modern port and capital of the island. The winding hill-paths and the sandy beach with its olive trees are recognizable today.

In that cove—on my port hand—Odysseus awoke in the twentieth year since he had left his home. As my boat slid into Port Vathi to drop anchor, I pictured him standing on that small beach with his jutting beard, his torn hands, his boar-wounded thigh, and his indomitable heart.

For ten years he had known "battle, murder, and sudden death" at Troy, and for ten more years he had known every aspect of the Mediterranean—the summer mornings that bloomed on its unruffled surface, the knifing winds of winter that scored it, the sirocco draping the mountains with cloud and beading his forehead with sweat, staining his squaresail with its damp breath.

I walked toward the Raven's Rock, where Odysseus met his faithful friend, the swineherd Eumaeus, and learned of the suitors who infested his palace, seeking Penelope's hand. These he would slay to regain his wife and throne. Near the

110

*O respected wife of Odysseus . . . no longer
waste . . . in lamentation for your husband*

beetling rock I met a modern Eumaeus with his wife. Theirs was a lonely life in their cottage, but they seemed content. As I talked to them, a jet airliner passed high overhead, spinning its contrails across the soft Ionian sky.

"Those people will be in Athens soon," said the shepherd. I stirred at the thought of the city of Athena, the goddess who had never forsaken Odysseus, whose favor had saved him from Poseidon's wrath. The shepherd continued. "What do I want with that city? Odysseus went everywhere in the world, but he came back to Ithaca, not Athens."

He looked at me intently. "You are a stranger, but surely you know that this is the island of Odysseus?"

My own quest had brought me so close to Odysseus that I almost cried out to the man: "Don't you recognize me?"

Her 20-year vigil nears its end, faithful Penelope learns from an old beggar—Odysseus in disguise. First he must fight his way back to power in his own palace, where nobles consume his wealth while wooing his queen. (She had insisted they wait until she finished the cloth on her loom; by night she undid what she had woven by day.)

Shadowing his hero home (opposite), the author ends his odyssey at Ithaca. Here Odysseus, aided by Athena, slew the suitors and—unlike doomed heroes of the Iliad—found a happy ending.

111

By Paul MacKendrick

The World of Pericles

THE MORNING SUN warmed the citizens gathered just
outside Athens on a bright winter day 431 years before
the birth of Christ. In rapt silence they listened to an orator—
a bearded, high-browed man who wore an air of aloof authority.
Pericles, son of Xanthippus, perennially elected leader
of the city, was delivering a funeral oration over the first
young Athenian warriors to be slain in the war with Sparta.
He sang the praises of the city for which they had died:
"Athens alone, of the states we know, comes to her testing time
in a greatness that surpasses what was imagined of her. . . .
Future ages will wonder at us, as the present age does now."
His audience stirred with pride, for the words distilled
that sense of discovery that was as much a part of the Athenians
as the sea-scented air they breathed. They were creating a kind
of society the world had never before seen, where, as Pericles said,
"Power rests with the majority instead of a few."
The phrases fell like newly minted coins, gleaming with
freshness. For this aristocrat was talking about *democracy*—
a Greek word for an Athenian invention: rule by the people.
The concept had developed over the long centuries since
the Dark Ages. Spared from the destruction which had claimed
every other Mycenaean fortress town, Athens grew to dominate
its peninsula of Attica, a rocky triangle half the size of Delaware.
Its form of government changed in ways that the Greek tongue

"Olympian" Pericles led Athens during her Golden Age. Roman copy in British Museum of 5th-century B.C. *bust; Adam Woolfitt*   113

aptly defined: Monarchy (single rule) gave way to oligarchy (rule by the few). In the seventh century B.C. the legislator Draco gave Athens laws so strict they were said to be writ in blood. A generation later Solon as archon, or chief magistrate, repealed these measures. His cousin Pisistratus seized power and became the city's tyrant (lord). Athens flourished, sparkling with new buildings, with poets and artists. But the citizens soon tired of one-man rule and created an assembly to govern themselves—a town meeting type of democracy. Years later they would grow to despise the word tyranny and give it a hateful meaning.

War with Persia pushed Athens into greatness. Victories at Marathon and Salamis established the city-state as leader of a confederation which Pericles turned into an empire. Never again would a metropolis of only 150,000 citizens achieve such greatness in statesmanship, philosophy, and the arts as Periclean Athens.

Totalitarian, plodding Sparta came to fear these restless Athenians, whose traders and merchants swamped competition from outside the Athenian empire. In 431, Sparta's forces set out to free Greece from what they alleged to be the "tyrant city." So now the new dead lay in their cypress coffins. As Pericles finished his address the citizens turned quietly to pay reverence, then passed through the Dipylon Gate and re-entered the bustling life of their city.

I HAVE STOOD in the Ceramicus, "fairest suburb" of the city, where Pericles spoke. I have worked with archeologists who excavated the Agora, the marketplace where Pericles strolled, and I have held in my hand an ostracon—an inscribed potsherd—bearing Pericles' name. I have deciphered inscriptions of laws written in Pericles' time. I have sat in the reconstructed Odeon of Herodes Atticus and watched performers

ACROPOLIS, *"High City"* of ancient kings, rises 260 feet above Athens. Its temples flamed *when Persians stormed the citadel in 480* B.C. *Rebuilding, Pericles added the gleaming Parthenon.*
PHILLIP HARRINGTON

reproducing the solemnity of Aeschylus, the mellowness of Sophocles, the iconoclasm of Euripides—playwrights who stimulated Pericles and his people. This personal acquaintance with the Golden Age of Pericles prods my imagination as I picture the life of a young Athenian in those exciting days.

Let us call him Megacles. We follow him as he strolls thoughtfully through Athens with Pericles' funeral address ringing in his ears. Though he is preoccupied, he cannot resist the lively Agora where, the Persians claim, "Greeks meet to cheat one another." He walks the Panathenaic Way, lined with plane and poplar trees. Beyond the Agora, houses nestle at the foot of the Acropolis, the rocky, windswept hill crowned with temples around which the city crowds.

On Megacles' left, voices rise in one of the stoas, the Painted Porch. A famous Sophist has arrived—one of those traveling teachers whose theories of the way to material success so excite the young men of Athens. His name is Protagoras, and eager students surround him as he expounds a revolutionary doctrine: "Man is the measure of all things." Man, not the gods; the relative, not the absolute. No wonder the conservatives fume. Pericles himself supports the new doctrine and even is friendly with the philosopher Anaxagoras, who upset the older generation by claiming the sun is not a god but a red-hot stone no larger than the Peloponnesus!

A former pupil now confronts Protagoras. "We agreed I didn't have to pay you," the lad says, "until I won my first case. Now, suppose you sue me for non-payment of fees. If I win, I don't have to pay you according to the judgment; if I lose, I won't have to

EVZONES *of the Palace Guard hold ranks but crack smiles as a 6-year-old takes command. Mountaineer kilts recall short-skirted tunics that bare-thighed Periclean warriors wore under armor (page 32).*

PHILLIP HARRINGTON

117

pay you according to our agreement!" Megacles smiles, for the argument reflects almost exactly the subtle, tricky style of reasoning ("sophistry") the Sophists teach.

Crossing the Agora, Megacles pauses outside the law courts, where citizens have gathered around the allotment machines, a pair of slotted pillars each with a funnel and tube. A sampling of those who want to serve as jurors have had their tickets inserted in the slots. Now an official feeds black balls and white balls into the funnel. If a black one drops from the tube first, all those with names in the first row will be dismissed. If a white ball appears, the men in the first row will serve. At least this, the world's first blackballing, has the virtue of being random rather than spiteful and it makes jury tampering difficult. The lucky ones will receive a jury fee of two obols, enough to support a man for a day.

Inside the court a speaker is just finishing. His time is measured by a *klepsydra* (water stealer), a pair of clay pots set so that water flows from one to the other, taking about six minutes. Each juror has two wheel-shaped bronze ballots. A solid hub means "not guilty"; hollow means "guilty." Concealing the hub, he deposits the ballot he wants to count in an urn, the other in a discard bin. No one knows how he votes.

"BANISH PERICLES!" an Athenian urges a fellow citizen inscribing his ostracon in the walled-off Agora. "Pericles [son] of Xanthippus" reads a potsherd ballot (below, right), recalling that Athenians vented ire on too-powerful leaders by trying to ostracize them. Voters entered at ten gates, one for each political unit, (Antiochis at far left). Conical roof beyond marks the Tholos, where the city council's committee of the day lived. Temple of Hephaestus rises behind.

Toplike disks (below) served as jurors' ballots. Hollow-hubbed disks condemned the philosopher Socrates (lower), Plato's "bravest, wisest, most just man," for impiety and for corrupting youth. Fearless in the pursuit of truth, ever questioning, a gadfly provoking men into thought, Socrates deemed the unexamined life not worth living.

An Athenian court has no judge or public prosecutor, no professional lawyers. An official administers rules of procedure, citizens conduct their own cases. The litigant may hire a ghostwriter; still, he memorizes and delivers the argument. Appeals to passion abound; also gross irrelevancies and hearsay evidence. But Athenians love this free-for-all justice. An abiding faith in the amateur lies at the core of their democracy.

Departing, Megacles notices workmen fencing off part of the Agora, leaving only ten entrances, one for each voting district. A vote on ostracism is about to take place.

Mindful of the tyrants of old, Athenians have instituted ostracism so they can act against any popular figure who, they fear may try to dominate the government. On a bit of broken pottery, or ostracon, a citizen can scratch the name of the man he thinks most dangerous to Athens. If 6,000 voters living in the city vote against a man, he will be banished for ten years—without dishonor and without loss of citizenship or property rights.

Personal or political enemies of men in power sometimes try to rig the vote. A hawker with a basketful of sherds offers one to Megacles. He refuses, but notices it is already inscribed—it bears the name of Pericles! Enmity is one price Pericles must pay for keeping Athens a democracy. Fortunately for the citizens, they will never quite succeed in ostracizing him.

Shops crowd one side of the Agora: the barbers, where men talk politics; the perfumers, where they compare essences; the flower shops, where they bargain for roses and irises. At the green-cheese shop, Megacles recognizes a group from Athens' loyal Boeotian ally, Plataea. They rendezvous here when they are in town. At the bookseller's, Anaxagoras' latest pamphlet is going fast, even at a whole drachma (two days' pay for a laborer) for the scroll. Innumerable booths offer wide varieties of fruits, vegetables, and delicacies. Sausage sellers and fishmongers balance trays, crying their wares.

BIRTHPLACE OF DEMOCRACY, the Agora dozes at the foot of the Acropolis. Athenians thronged here to discuss, harangue, litigate, philosophize. Boys frolic before the reconstructed Stoa of Attalus II, 2d-century king of Pergamum who built this arcade of shops and courts in gratitude for his Athens education. Spirited talk in nearby flea market (left) reminds us that the word agoreuo, "I make a speech," stems from same root as agora, marketplace.

MICHAEL KUH. RIGHT: PHILLIP HARRINGTON

Megacles passes them all by, for he has no slave with him to carry his purchases.

He leaves the Agora, bound for the town meeting on the rocky hill of the Pnyx. The proceedings had begun at dawn with a proclamation by a herald. Then Scythian police in their trousers (a symbol of barbarism!) herded a quorum of citizens to the Pnyx with a red-dyed rope. Those who escaped the rope, but picked up red stains, face a fine for non-attendance. Prayer and the sacrifice of a pig opened the meeting.

Approaching, Megacles hears shouts, whistles, and stamping—a demagogue has roused sentiment against Pericles' leadership. Athenians are exercising their freedom, but Megacles turns angrily away. He is related to Pericles and approves of his policy: "in theory a democracy; in practice, rule by the first citizen."

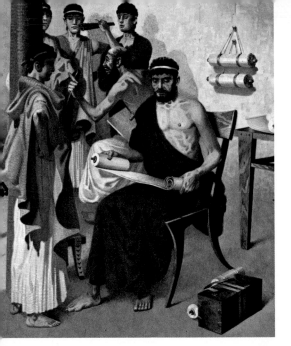

To calm his anger, Megacles makes for the gymnasium, one of his favorite haunts. In its frescoed portico he undresses, anoints his body with oil, then takes a few sprints on the track, long enough for a 200-yard dash. He hopes to win the race at next year's Panathenaic festival.

At the palaestra wrestlers grunt and twist in spirited workouts. Some wrestle upright, two out of three throws to win, others prone, straining to pin an opponent. Megacles works out on punching bags in the boxing room, but he does not go in for the sport, because the nails or lead bosses in the leather straps over the knuckles could disfigure him.

Joining some friends on the javelin and discus range, he marvels at the speed of the elderwood

STRIPPED FOR ACTION, *youths work out in a gymnasium—from* gymnos, *"naked." Athenians scorn a man who can't swim and wrestle, and decry the potbelly. Smeared with olive oil, they box, hurl discus and javelin, lift weights and leap with them, sprint a* stade, *200-yard dash that gave us "stadium." With a strigil one youth scrapes off oil his bath won't remove.*

Seeking the Periclean ideal—"wisdom without loss of manly vigor"—Athenians exercised minds and bodies in three famed gymnasiums: the Academy, where Plato expounded his philosophy of the ideal republic; the Lyceum, where Aristotle strolled the walks (peripatoi), *teaching disciples called Peripatetics; the Cynosarges ("agile dog"), where Cynics growled at riches and preached self-denial. A Cynic, Zeno, teaching at the Painted Stoa, or porch, founded Stoic philosophy.*

A boy went to private school (above) escorted by an old slave —a pedagogue. He learned music, numbers, how to read papyrus scrolls and write with stylus on waxed tablets. At 18 he entered civic and military training.

PAINTINGS FOR NATIONAL GEOGRAPHIC BY H. M. HERGET

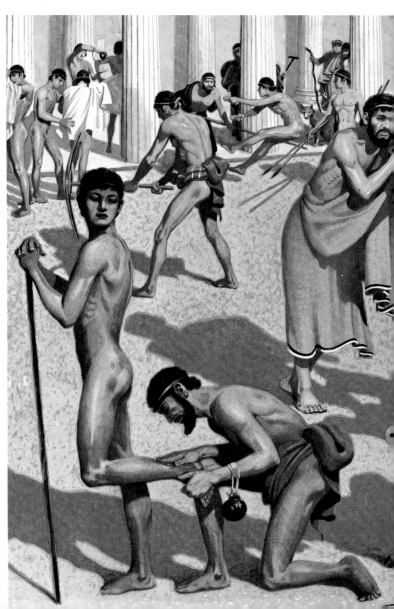

javelin. A thong wound around it gives it a spin so that it pitches on its point. He admires, too, the graceful sweep of the discus thrower. To Megacles—and many another Athenian—it's the look of the thing that counts, not just training until you are muscle-bound like a dull professional. He does not envy athletes like Bybon, who once threw a 316-pound stone over his head with one hand!

He wanders over to the stable to see his horse. He has ridden this fine Corinthian thoroughbred on patrol along the frontier of Attica with other young aristocrats. But he will not ride now, for he is anxious to clean up. With a strigil, or scraper (his is bronze), he rids himself of oil and sweat. Then, bathed and dressed, he sets out to join his friends in what he loves best at the gymnasium—conversation.

Sophists like Protagoras scoff at "overemphasis" on athletics, quoting Euripides:

> *Now of ten thousand curses that plague Hellas*
> *There's none so pestilent as this breed of athletes . . .*
> *For what stout wrestler, or what nimble runner*
> *Or discus-thrower, or brave jawbone-breaker*
> *Profits his country, gone a-gathering garlands?*

BEST PRESERVED THEATER *in the ancient world spreads its giant fan of stone at Epidaurus, across the Saronic Gulf from Athens. Perfect acoustics bring every whisper of Euripides' Ion to the 14,000 seats of this theatron, or seeing place, built 2,300 years ago. The orchestra, or dancing place where the chorus sang in early plays, evolved from a threshing floor marked out by circling cattle; altar at center made a performance a sacred rite to Dionysus. The skene, or stage, which began as a booth or tent where actors dressed, became the scene for the drama, or action. A cranelike machine enabled a god to make a sudden dramatic appearance — deus ex machina.*

It's a knotty problem for a young Athenian, the relative claims of brains and brawn. Megacles would like to take it up with Socrates. By great luck there is the philosopher, pacing the portico and talking animatedly. Megacles recognizes the waddling gait, the snub nose, the wall eyes, the potbelly. Socrates has a slave boy with him, and by his famous method of priming with questions, he has just gotten the lad, who has never studied geometry, to the final proof that in a right-angled triangle the square of the hypotenuse equals the sum of the squares of the other two sides.

Socrates' brilliance, which infuriates many, fascinates Megacles. To him, Socrates, ugly as he is to look at, seems beautiful within. After hearing him, Megacles has few doubts about the relative importance of brain and brawn.

All in all it has been a good day in the gymnasium—rigorous exercise for both body and mind. Tomorrow Megacles can give the brain another workout, for there will be plays in the theater of Dionysus at the foot of the south slope of the Acropolis.

*T*HE LENAEA, winter festival of Dionysus, god of fertility, wine, and song, generally offers comedies, which do not draw so wide an audience as the Great Dionysia in March. This time, however, the archons are reviving a ten-year-old tragedy, Sophocles' *Antigone,* to compete with the other plays. The prize: a wreath of ivy. Sophocles, now 65, has long been a favorite with Athenian playgoers. Like his friend Pericles, Sophocles served as a general, elected to that rank perhaps as a reward for the political wisdom of this very play. It should prove most appropriate for wartime, thinks Megacles.

He has never seen the play, but he knows the story of Antigone, who buried her disgraced brother in defiance of a tyrant's decree, thus fulfilling what Greeks considered a sacred obligation. Sophocles must have given the old tale some religious meaning, for this is a religious occasion. The priest of Dionysus and his wife will enjoy the best seats in the open-air theater—"front row center." Megacles and his friends will sit on wooden seats built on the side of the hill. Even the poor can attend, thanks to a state subsidy established by Pericles.

Tragedy originated as a song and dance marking the return of spring, the budding of the vine leaves sacred to Dionysus. "Tragedy" stems from "goat song"; perhaps the word entered the theater because the ritual dancing accompanied the sacrifice of a goat, or because performers once competed for the prize of a goat. A century ago the poet Thespis arrived in Athens with a chorus and an actor—called the hypocrite (answerer)—who gave set speeches. Since then Aeschylus, Sophocles, Euripides, and the skilled "thespians" who perform their works have developed tragedy into a sophisticated art. Messengers report actions in speeches that stir the imagination more than would a portrayal of the actions. The chorus, drawn from Megacles' fellow citizens, reacts to the plot and brings relief from the growing tension. Actors and

ARISTOPHANES' LINES, *after 2,300 years, sparkle under the stars in the Odeon of Herodes Atticus below the Acropolis. In his comedy* Plutus, *Chremylus explains to Blepsidemus his plan to lead the blind god Wealth to Asclepius' shrine. Sight restored, Wealth (Plutus) will reward honest men (like these two) instead of villains.*

THEATER BUILT IN 2D CENTURY A.D.; MICHAEL KUH

chorus wear masks to magnify their voices and increase the solemnity of the scenes. Costumes seem larger than life; ten-inch elevator shoes raise gods above mortals.

Megacles feels conflict develop as Antigone faces her alternatives: obey the edict of the tyrant Creon, or follow her own conviction that she must bury her brother in accordance with the will of the gods. She chooses the latter course, putting gods above tyrant, but the guard catches her. Creon apparently has won. Then she commits suicide. The tyrant's life becomes a living death: His wife and son also take their own lives. Antigone's defiant conscience wins after all.

Megacles leaves the theater humbled at seeing man's painful way in this pitiless universe, exalted by the moral strength of the heroine, proud to be an Athenian brought up to defy tyranny, determined to follow his individual conscience.

Tonight, Megacles has invited friends in for a symposium, literally a "drinking together." A hired caterer frees the host to enjoy the occasion fully. Guests number from three to nine: "neither fewer than the Graces, nor more than the Muses." As they arrive they remove their sandals and a slave washes their feet. When they take their places at the couches, other slaves bring basins for washing their hands, and portable tables for the meal. Meat arrives, ready cut for eating with the fingers. Diners wipe their lips and mop up their plates with bread, which they throw under the tables to dogs.

At first Megacles' friends drink wine sparingly, diluting it with water, for only barbarians would take this syrupy wine unmixed. After the main course a flute player sounds a note, and someone begins one of the old songs about a battle fought long ago when the world was young.

Slaves bring on dessert—dried fruit, nuts, whatever else may best induce thirst. The diners anoint hair and beards with myrrh and put wreaths on their heads or around their necks. Now from a large mixing bowl the celebrants dip more wine with shallow cups. One of these cups, dating from around Pericles' time, shows a flute girl holding the head of a young man who has drunk too much. A considerate host like Megacles would have supplied a basin for one so stricken—and a chamber pot as well.

The toasts now fly—to Zeus, to the heroes, from host to guest, from person to person around the couches. A toss of dice selects a toastmaster, who sets a new proportion of water to wine, decides when to call for larger cups, fines the obstreperous, proposes topics for discussion.

Plato describes a symposium attended by his teacher Socrates and by Aristophanes, the master of Greek Comedy. The toastmaster proposed the topic "Love." Aristophanes, recovering from a fit of hiccups, tells how men were once spherical, with four of everything they now have two of, and two of everything they now have one of. Then Zeus split men in two, and ever since they have been looking for their other halves. This is love!

Socrates, more serious, expounds the theory that has since been known as "Platonic love": We must progress

REFRESHING INTERLUDE *brings on flute girl and courtesan at a symposium, or drinking party. Sumptuous meal over, the wine is dipped from a* krater, *the large mixing bowl on the floor. Entertainers, riddles, impromptu verse divert garlanded guests— males only. If the mood takes a philosophical turn, they may discourse deep into the night.*

from love of a beautiful body to love of beautiful thoughts, laws, institutions, until we gain a mystic vision of the good, the true, and the beautiful.

Megacles' symposium, though witty enough, is more typical. Repartee is quick, debate eager, examples apt. Guests quote Homer and the lyric poets. They sing to the lyre, perhaps one of the hits from Euripides' new play, *Medea*:

> *Fortunate forever the sons of Athens,*
> *Sons of the blessed gods, enjoying*
> *A land holy, unravaged by war,*
> *Feasting on famous wisdom, and always*
> *Walking buoyantly through shining air.*

When originality flags, some guest asks a riddle. This bores Megacles and he signals for the flute and lyre players, jugglers, contortionists. In the *Symposium* of the historian Xenophon, a boy and a girl mime the loves of Dionysus and Ariadne.

130

The girl does a sword dance and throws a dozen hoops in the air. Socrates, a guest here too, praises the girl's talent as an example of women's ability to learn. Well, someone asks, why doesn't Socrates teach good temper to his shrewish wife Xanthippe? "My great aim in life," he replies, "is to get on well with people and I chose Xanthippe because I knew if I could get on with her I could with anyone."

"T HE WARES of the whole world find their way to us," claimed Pericles in his funeral oration. They found their way to Athens' port of Piraeus four miles away. Let us stroll there with Megacles between the Long Walls. They stand 200 yards apart, finished by Pericles to make Athens a snug fortress where most of the population of Attica could live on seaborne provisions. The streets of Piraeus, cleaner than those of Athens, lie in regular lines with spacious squares. In the naval harbor triremes are fitting out to drive the Spartans from the sea. Smells of tar, pitch, and oakum fill the air. From forts at the harbor mouth, chains can stretch across to close the port.

PHILLIP HARRINGTON AND (OPPOSITE) FARRELL GREHAN

FISHING VESSELS *nod at yachts in Tourkolimano, one of three ancient harbors comprising the port of Piraeus. Themistocles (page 157), early fifth-century advocate of Athenian sea power, built up Athens' port with ship sheds and colonnaded warehouses for produce from merchantmen that crowded the main harbor. At anchorage of Zea, an arsenal served ram-prowed warships. For 400 years Piraeus, its grid of streets laid out in Europe's first city planning, ranked as the leading Mediterranean port.*

Shipyards (right), trade, and industry spur a new rise to fame.

Stevedores unload grain ships at the deepwater commercial harbor. Waterfront wineshops do a brisk business. Hook-nosed merchants in embroidered robes consult their supercargos, just arrived with trinkets from Phoenicia. A galley from Cyprus unloads copper ingots. Ships are in from Naxos, Cos, and Lemnos in the Aegean; from Ephesus, Halicarnassus, and Byzantium; from Amphipolis in Macedonia and Abdera in Thrace. Megacles recognizes the famed Herodotus, ever ready to hear a good story, talking to bearded seamen with rings in their ears just back from beyond the Pillars of Hercules. Herodotus has produced an account of the Persian Wars, which he calls an inquiry—a *historia*. Athens marvels at it.

Today in modern Athens, when I walk from the American School to the Agora, the last stage of my journey takes me through the street of the hardware shops—

called Hephaestus Street after the god of blacksmiths. The smith-god's temple, the Hephaesteum, stands almost perfectly preserved, 200 yards away. Since Pericles' time and before, this has been a quarter for blacksmiths. Many relics of their craft have been unearthed here.

Other trades had their own locations. We hear of the street of the sculptors and the street of the boxmakers. Periclean Athens was a city of small shopkeepers; the largest known establishment, a shield-maker's, employed 120 slaves. On the streets drovers with sheep and goats impeded farmers with pack asses and solid-wheeled mule

TO MARKET *flock the Athenians, sampling, haggling, jostling, joshing. Stoa of the Herms rises beyond stalls where hucksters bawl the virtues of fish and fabrics, cheese and wine, statues and slave girls. Acrobats twirl, beggars moan their woes, fences offer stolen goods. In the Agora you could buy anything under the sun, quipped a poet: "turnips, pears, apples, witnesses, roses, medlars, porridge, honeycombs, chickpeas, lawsuits . . . water clocks, laws, indictments."*

carts laden with wood or vegetables. At the miller's, horses, mules, oxen, or slaves turned the millstone. Market inspectors checked size and weight of bakers' loaves, then peddlers hawked them noisily, treading streets made muddy and filthy by the refuse housewives threw from their front doors.

Athenians wore a white wool chiton, or tunic, woven by their women and cleaned by fullers. Their chief cleaning agent was urine. The tanneries stood outside town. Pericles' successor, Cleon, was a tanner, and his reputation was as odoriferous as his trade.

Jewelers worked the silver from the Laurium mines near the tip of Attica into trinkets, vases, and mirrors. Coinage was a state monopoly. At a corner of the Agora excavators found the mint with its furnaces and water basins, and the bronze disks, or flans, from which coins were struck. Athenian silver coins, Athena on one side, her owl on the other, were standard in the eastern Mediterranean for 200 years after Pericles.

Slaves on their bellies dug for the silver in yard-high tunnels; they worked shifts of about two hours. Archeologists have found rings for chaining the slaves to the tunnel walls. The mines had streets, crossroads, squares, wells, and workshops. Miners pulverized, washed, filtered, and superheated the ore—and produced silver more nearly pure than today's sterling.

FIRED BY A LOVE OF BEAUTY *even in everyday things, Greeks made the humble pot into a work of art, portraying a parade of crafts.*

A smith (far left) hammers a slab of red-hot iron into shape; like many artisans, he works to order on material furnished by the waiting customers. An artist with a paintpot beside him decorates a bowl. A butcher carves a quarter of beef for the well-to-do; meat is a luxury. A sandalmaker stands a client on his worktable and cuts leather to a perfect fit.

Unearthing a shoemaker's shop in the Agora, archeologists found iron hobnails, bone eyelets, and a pottery cup inscribed "Simon." Plutarch and Diogenes Laërtius, biographers in Roman times, tell how in the easy democracy of Athens, Socrates and Pericles often met at Simon the Shoemaker's.

Potters, providing jars for export of wine and olive oil, led Athens' industry. Their district, Ceramicus, got its name from ceramics. In the sixth century vase painters favored black figures on red; in the fifth, red figures on a black background.

Today, on Hephaestus Street, the ancient street of the smiths, a coppersmith (below) plies his trade.

Pottery was Athens' chief export. Vase paintings show potters at work: a slave stokes the kiln, a boy turns the wheel, older men throw the clay, a young man paints a finished vase, his paintpot on a stool beside him. Potters understood reduction—reducing the air in the kiln and so turning the clay black; and also oxidizing—introducing air to keep the clay red. Their handsome wares were in demand all around the Mediterranean.

Athenian artisans were freeborn citizens, resident aliens, or slaves. The aliens, or metics, paid taxes, could run businesses, and enjoyed the protection of the courts, but could not marry a citizen or vote. Slaves accounted for one-third of the total population of Attica in 431 B.C., but you could not tell a slave from a freeman if you met him on an Athenian street. They worked side by side on the Parthenon and earned the same wage. Slaves could buy their freedom, and if a slave girl had a child by her master, as she often did, the child was born free. Slavery helped make possible the Periclean culture, but it was not the most important factor in the Athenian economy, nor did it exempt freemen from hard work.

An extraordinary simplicity marked the life of the ordinary people of those days, both slave and free. As the British scholar H. D. F. Kitto put it, "The Greek got up as soon as it was light, shook out the blanket in which he had slept, draped it elegantly around himself . . . and . . . was ready to face the world in five minutes."

MEGACLES' HOME, along with thousands of others, crowds inside the five-mile circumference of the city's walls. Most are modest—painted mud-brick walls set on stone foundations, with flat roofs where people sit in the cool of the evening. Burglars—called "wall-diggers" in Greek—can easily burrow through these walls. But then they are virtually fireproof, so Athens needs no fire department.

Neither do the houses need central heat in this climate. Residents dull the winter chill with portable braziers; smoke escapes through roof holes. At night torches and oil lamps supply light, but Athenians do little work by artificial light. Most go to bed at dark and rise with the dawn.

A visitor to Megacles' house quickly realizes he has entered a wealthy home, for just inside the front door a porter with a chained dog greets him. Only a few upstairs windows look out on the street side. The life of the house faces inward, toward the courtyard with its altar and its menagerie of pets wandering freely about— the frisky dog with his tail arched in a plume over his back, the geese and quail. A caged cock reflects the current fad of cockfighting.

A mosaic floor and frescoed walls adorn Megacles' best room, the scene of his symposium, which also opens onto the court. Some of his rich neighbors collect books; Euripides has one of the first libraries. A few connoisseurs boast picture galleries. Yet the master bedroom, typically, seems a mere cell. Megacles wants a guest suite, but well-off as he is, he cannot afford it. He puts up overnight guests in the portico overlooking his courtyard.

The simple furniture exhibits proud craftsmanship—chairs with beautifully carved backs; couches with lathe-turned legs; carved chests, tables, three-legged stools. Woven rugs and curtains add color to the decor. The house lacks a private well and private bath. Female slaves fetch water—and have a good gossip—at the public fountain; men and women resort to the public baths at separate hours.

For Megacles and his friends, their living rooms extend to the Agora and the streets of Athens; this is a man's world. Women confine themselves to the home. They occupy separate quarters and bear in mind the words Pericles addressed to them in his funeral oration: "Great is your good name when you give men the least occasion to talk about you, whether for praise or for blame."

The bad temper of Socrates' wife Xanthippe was notorious; most Athenian wives were not shrews. Neither were they bluestockings like Pericles' mistress Aspasia, who wrote poetry and conversed with philosophers. Xenophon, offering a guide to proper relations between man and wife, wrote of a husband setting about to make his 15-year-old bride "docile, and domesticated." She must be a good manager, must choose the least gluttonous and bibulous of her female slaves as housekeeper, must draw up a budget and take care not to spend in a month what should last a year. She must see that the grain is stored in a dry place and the wine in a cool one.

"A WOMAN should be good for everything at home, but abroad good for nothing."
Thus the playwright Euripides summarized Periclean policy toward the secluded sex.
With distaffs and spindle whorls, women spun wool and flax in their own quarters,
then wove bedding and clothing on handlooms. Grain was bruised with mortar and pestle.

5TH-CENTURY STELE, CERAMICUS MUSEUM, ATHENS. CUP DETAILS, BELOW: ASHMOLEAN MUSEUM; OPPOSITE: MUSEUM OF FINE ARTS, BOSTON; (LOWER) ROYAL MUSEUM OF ART AND HISTORY, BRUSSELS

She must care for the slaves when they are ill. "I don't mind," the poor girl comments, "as long as they are grateful."

To Xenophon, a former soldier, the ideal household meant a place for everything and everything in its place. Clothes, shoes, armor, linen, sacrificial equipment—all must be neatly stored.

One time the young wife, who could hardly be accused of leading a gay life, appears before her husband powdered and rouged. He is shocked. "Cosmetics may fool strangers," he sniffs, "but I'm bound to catch you unpainted, when you're just out of bed, or the bath, or have been sweating, or in tears." (With *that* husband it would have been tears.) And he adds: "It's not beauty, but the practical virtues that make for happiness." Fortunately, not all husbands were that stuffy.

While girls might marry in their teens, young men like Megacles often waited until they were 30. A couple might not set eyes on each other until their wedding, for parents arranged marriages.

The bride solemnly dedicated her girdle, toys, or a lock of hair to Artemis, goddess of virginity. On her wedding day she took a ritual bath and put on bright clothes and a veil. Celebrants sacrificed an animal at her home, removing the victim's gall lest bitterness mar the marriage. The wedding feast over, the happy couple retreated to their new home—perhaps escorted there by the best man. Guests swarmed around the door, singing bawdy songs. Next day the new wife, unveiled, received gift-bearing friends.

Upon the birth of a baby son, the father hung an olive branch over the door; for a daughter, he displayed tufts of wool. (Some parents might "expose" a baby girl —leave her in a basket at a temple in hope that someone would adopt her.) Five days after birth, a nurse or female relative took the infant and ran around the central hearth; the family followed. This *amphidromia*, or running around, placed the child under the protection of the household gods.

On the tenth day the father, before witnesses, formally recognized the child as his own and committed himself to name, rear, and educate it. A boy was often named for his paternal grandfather; the name always signified some good omen. Pericles means "very famous"; Alcibiades, "son of the strong one"; Socrates, "strong to save"; Plato (a nickname), "broad-shouldered"; his real name was Aristocles, "the best." Megacles means "great fame."

For seven years the child of well-to-do parents remained in the care of his nurse. She fed him from a clay bottle with a clay nipple; later she pre-chewed his food. When he misbehaved, she threatened him with

TERRACOTTA TOYS AND VASE,
5TH CENTURY B.C., BRITISH MUSEUM;
J. J. O. WEBB

Mormo, who ate bad children, or with Empusa, a hobgoblin who changed into fearful shapes. If this failed, she applied the sandal. Like their elders, Athenian children delighted in games—hide-and-seek, tug-of-war, blindman's buff, trick or treat, ducks and drakes, jackstones. They shook rattles, soared on swings, spun tops, tossed balls, rolled hoops. They cuddled toy animals and played house with clay dolls with jointed limbs, dollhouses, and toy dishes.

At seven, while boys went off to school, girls remained with their mothers and learned what the child-wife in Xenophon had learned: not much. The growing boy's constant companion was his pedagogue (child-leader), who taught him manners— to rise and be silent in the presence of his elders—and reinforced instruction with the rattan or strap. In school the child took physical training, learned to play the lyre and to write with a stylus on wax tablets. He later wrote on papyrus with a reed pen, did arithmetic and geometry, but usually studied no foreign language or science. The Sophists, who taught science, and Plato, who taught mathematics, were innovators. The student memorized hundreds of lines of poetry, chiefly Homer.

At 18 an Athenian youth came of age and was enrolled in his *deme* or township. Attica had more than 170 demes; even if your family moved away you enrolled in its original township: "Megacles, son of Hippocrates, of Alopece (Foxborough)." To celebrate the occasion the new citizen gave a drinking party, and cut and dedicated a lock of his hair. His next two years belonged to the state. He enrolled in a cadet corps, made pilgrimages to the shrines, did light garrison duty in Piraeus, then patrolled the frontiers of Attica—serious business in wartime.

Birth, education, marriage—finally death and the all-important ritual of burial or cremation. Women washed the dead man, anointed him with oil, dressed him in white, and put a wreath, often of gold leaf, on his head. They intoned a dirge; hired mourners wailed. The funeral procession, accompanied by flute players, took place before sunrise, that the corpse might not pollute the sun's light. They buried with the dead man those things he might need in afterlife: arms, armor, tools, containers for food and drink. He even carried money—an obol on his tongue—to pay Charon's ferry fare across the Styx!

THE THREE GREEK COMMANDMENTS were "Honor the gods; help your friends; adorn your city." When Pericles built the Parthenon, he honored Athena Parthenos, Athena the Virgin, patron of the city; he gave work to his fellow citizens; and he created something, as Plutarch wrote centuries afterward, "in a short time for all time, with a bloom of perpetual newness."

Pericles' political enemies carped at the expense. Money contributed by Athens' allies for the common defense, they said, had been squandered to deck the virgin goddess like a scarlet woman. Pericles rejoined that as long as the allies got

"ATHENA, *Triton-born, guide our city," prayed Pericleans. This bronze of their patron— goddess of war and wisdom, arts and sciences—lay amid the ruins of Piraeus after Romans sacked the port along with Athens in 86 B.C. She emerged in 1959, seven feet tall in her long-plumed Attic helmet, gazing "gray-eyed" through semiprecious stones.*

the defense they paid for, how he spent the surplus was none of their business. The critics, of course, are dust, the temple a possession for eternity.

Pericles beautified Athens and Attica with many other buildings: the Propylaea, or gateway to the Acropolis; the theater of Dionysus and a music hall, the Odeon of Pericles, beside it. He embellished the Hall of the Mysteries in the holy city of Eleusis. I use the Parthenon as the finest example of his effect on Athens' architecture. The task of building it called for impressive organization and technique. Pericles inspired it, Athens' allies paid for it, Pericles' friend, the sculptor Phidias, supervised it, a board of citizens inspected it and kept accounts.

Let us imagine Phidias going over the accounts with Ictinus and Callicrates, the architects, in 432 B.C., near the end of the 15-year project. Available funds for the year amount to 24 silver talents, roughly equivalent to $100,000 today. Out of this Phidias has to buy marble, bronze, ivory, gold, ebony, cypress. He has to pay quarrymen, carters, carpenters, stonecutters, assistant sculptors, as well as ivory workers, goldsmiths, and painters who work on Athena's statue; ropemakers for rope to hoist the stone; and crews to strengthen the ten-mile road from the Pentelicus quarries over which oxcarts have hauled thousands of tons of marble.

TINY TEMPLE *of Athena Nike (Victory), dreams in the night. Athenians erected it on a corner of the Acropolis during a lull in the Peloponnesian War. Like its neighbors, it wears iron-streaked marble from Mount Pentelicus, ten miles away, where workers square blocks with a sighting gauge perhaps familiar to their ancestors.*

Building the Parthenon, Pericles' architects subtly curved stones to counteract optical illusion. The floor arches slightly lest it seem to sag. Architraves, beams atop the Doric columns, follow suit. Columns lean in and back so they will not look splayed. Built up of drums locked in hairline joins and fluted to trap shadows, they swell two-fifths of the way up to look straight; corner columns are slightly thicker. Metopes, carved slabs beneath the sculpture-rich pediments, or gables, vary in size to look square from below. The Parthenon rose between 447 and 432 B.C.—a perfect union of science and art, a prayer in stone for all ages.

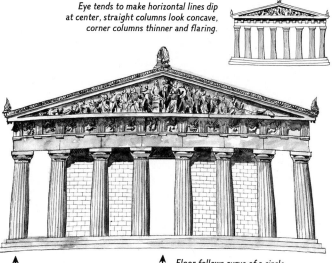

Eye tends to make horizontal lines dip at center, straight columns look concave, corner columns thinner and flaring.

Floor follows curve of a circle with three-and-a-half-mile radius.

Lines projected from corner columns would converge a mile and a half up. Drawings are distorted for emphasis.

143

PAINTING FOR NATIONAL GEOGRAPHIC BY LOUIS S. GLANZMAN. OPPOSITE: ONE OF BRITISH MUSEUM'S "ELGIN MARBLES," COLLECTED IN EARLY 1800'S BY LORD ELGIN, WHO SPENT A FORTUN

144

Phidias pays his skilled workmen one and a half to two drachmas a day—about 35 cents—and fires them for slow, wasteful, or damaged work. But he does not often fire a man. Like the craftsmen who later built medieval cathedrals, the Athenians are driven by piety and patriotism. Even the animals catch the enthusiasm. One driver tells of a mule, turned loose after a hard stint, who refused to rest, but kept trotting along with his teammates as if encouraging them. And Athena looks after her own. When a worker fell from a high scaffold and his life hung by a thread, the goddess appeared to Pericles and prescribed treatment which healed the man.

Reports of the citizen inspectors show how they have barred price gouging and payroll padding, how they have kept men and materials flowing in steadily to maintain a smooth pace. Pericles wants the temple finished in time for this year's Panathenaic festival. When the job is done, Phidias must sell surplus material: extra scaffolding, gold not needed for plating Athena's statue. He is glad he made the gold plates removable. By weighing them, he can account for every ounce delivered to him.

On every side of the Parthenon, Phidias' sculpture sings the glory of Athena. Here she springs fully armed from the forehead of Zeus, freed by Hephaestus, who stands by with

PANATHENAIC PROCESSION *climbs the Acropolis, bearing a new robe to adorn the ivory-and-gold Athena Parthenos in the Parthenon. Sculptor Phidias immortalized this crowning civic and religious event on the temple frieze: young men on spirited horses (below), magistrates, gift-bearing maidens, musicians, sacrificial animals.*

his double ax. Here she competes in miracles with Poseidon for guardianship of the city. Poseidon strikes a rock with his trident and a salt spring gushes forth (guides will show the very spot). Athena creates the first olive tree and wins Athens.

Along Phidias' frieze appears the pulsing, human world of the city itself. Here 400 figures of men and women and 200 of animals represent the Panathenaic procession, bringing a new sacred robe to the statue of Athena. Though 40 feet in the air, the figures were carved to seem at eye level. Look at them now in the British Museum and you can see how the actual procession lined up and moved. The figures almost come alive, among them, perhaps, Megacles himself.

The long lines form. Young cavalrymen, beautifully unmilitary in broad-brimmed hats, try to control restive horses. One heads the wrong way; others trot, canter, and halt, half a dozen abreast in irregular groups, while the bearded marshal tries to quell their typical high spirits and put them in some order. Next come four-horse chariots, each with a long-robed charioteer and a young warrior. Then follow elders, musicians, bearers of offerings. As the procession turns the corner of the temple, sacrificial animals appear. Keats wrote of them:

> "Who are these coming to the sacrifice?
> To what green altar, O mysterious priest,
> Lead'st thou that heifer lowing at the skies,
> And all her silken flanks with garlands drest?"

At last the sculptured marchers make their presentation to Athena in the presence of other gods. Lame Hephaestus appears again, leaning on a stick. Young Eros shields his mother Aphrodite from the sun with a parasol. Citizens gather too, and grave magistrates. A man hands the folded robe to a little boy in the culminating moment of Athens' religious life.

Phidias depicted men, human and humane. Looking at them, you hear an echo of Pericles' words: "Fix your eyes on the power of Athens . . . make yourselves her lovers, and, when you find her a great city, remember that men won that greatness for her. . . ."

*I*N 429 B.C., PERICLES DIED. Wartime overcrowding in Athens spread plague, and the austere leader succumbed. His passing was as though the spring had gone out of the year. But it had been a glorious springtime, on which men have looked back in admiration ever since. It is the tragedy of Western history that cultures which produce such men and such art have always so brief a flowering. The Age of Pericles lasted little more than 30 years.

The war with Sparta finally snuffed out the golden spark, just as another war had fanned it into life in 490 B.C., when a band of stalwart Athenians faced the hosts of Persia on the plain of Marathon, between the mountains and the sea.

LIKE GIANT TREE TRUNKS *rooted in sacred soil, the Parthenon's columns have withstood the storms of 24 centuries. Pericles' temple to the virgin Athena became a church to the Virgin Mary, later a mosque. Gunpowder stored by Turks and exploded by Venetians' cannon shattered the temple in 1687. Restored by Greeks with American aid, the fluted columns still reflect the glow of Athens' golden age.*

Leonard Cottrell *reawakens fields of battle and shrines
of gods in the land "Where grew the arts of war and peace."
Heroes and poets guide him as he treads in past and present,*

Seeking Scenes
of Grecian Glory

W HEREVER I JOURNEY in the labyrinth of Greek history, my road inevitably takes me to some intersection of past and present. The road
may twist and dip along stark ledges or cleave a fertile valley. It may lead
to the triumph of Marathon, the valor of Thermopylae, the mystery of Delphi, the majesty of Olympus. Whatever the road, whatever the destination,
there comes a moment when I stand, like Agamemnon, "neither in water
nor on dry land," poised between myth and history, enthralled by the
timelessness of Greece.

"The Persians encamped over there, near their fleet," the young Greek
army officer was saying as we stood at Marathon. He swept his hand toward
the sea. "Our Greek hoplites were there, nearer Mount Pentelicus." He
scanned the plain, shading his eyes against the afternoon sun. "We left our

Silhouette of courage, Leonidas the Spartan holds the pass of Thermopylae; Farrell Grehan

MACEDONIA

THRACE

XERXES' ARMY
480 B.C.

Xerxes' Canal

+ Mt. Athos

Hellespont

Olympus +

Troy

THESSALY

XERXES' FLEET
480 B.C.

Aegean Sea

Cape Artemisium

Thermopylae
480 B.C.

Delphi

Thebes

Euboea

Cyme

Sardis

PERSIAN EMPIRE

IONIA

G R E E C E

Plataea
479 B.C.

Corinth

Marathon
490 B.C.

Salamis
480 B.C.

Athens

Mycale +
Miletus

Delos

Sparta

X Battles

0   100

STATUTE MILES
DRAWN BY LISA BIGANZOLI
GEOGRAPHIC ART DIVISION

*"REJOICE, WE CONQUER!" gasps
a courier bearing news to Athens
that Darius' Persians have
been defeated at Marathon.
Exhausted, he falls dead.*

*Ten years later, in 480 B.C.,
the Persians again invade, led by
Darius' son Xerxes, who scourges
the Hellespont in fury when
storms wreck his span of ships.
The army crosses and, supplied
by a fleet, marches unchallenged—
until Thermopylae. Over the bodies
of valiant Spartans, the Persians
tramp south and burn Athens.*

*But they lost their fleet
at Salamis, their army at
Plataea, and, wrote Herodotus,
"departed with altered minds."*

stockades and advanced, shield to shield, spears ready, chanting the paean of battle. . . ." As I listened, past and present blurred. The 20th century? It could have been 490 B.C., for the captain at my side spoke as if he himself had fought in the battle. We stood atop a grassy mound—the grave of Athenians who fell here, a monument guarded and groomed by the Greek Army. On the plain before us Greek fought Persian in a war that would decide whether Greece would die as a conquered province of an Asian empire—or live to bestow her glory upon ages to come.

The Persian empire, surging out of Iran, stretched from Egypt to India by 500 B.C. As the empire thrust westward, outposts of Greek civilization fell: the cities of Ionia, the isle of Cyprus, the lands of Thrace and Macedonia. When Ionian Greeks revolted in 499, two Greek cities, mainland Athens and Eretria on the island of Euboea, sent help. By 490 Darius, the Persian emperor, had stamped out the Ionian uprising. Now he launched from Samos a seaborne army—complete with "horse landing craft"—that island-hopped across the Aegean. After seizing Eretria, the Persians landed an estimated 20,000 infantry and cavalry near the plain of Marathon, 25 miles north of their objective, Athens.

Darius, "the great king, king of kings . . . king of this great earth far and wide," ruled a rich, disciplined realm whose subjects approached him on their knees. Greeks would not even kneel to their gods. They so cherished freedom that they could not form a nation. Though united by language and worship and traditions, they clustered in small city-states such as Athens, Corinth, Thebes, and Sparta, each fiercely independent. And not all Greeks saw the Persians as enemies. Hippias, the man who guided the invaders to Marathon, once had ruled Athens.

When the Persians landed, Athens dispatched a runner, Pheidippides, to Sparta to summon long-pledged aid. He covered the 140 miles in two days, but he raced in vain. For the famed fighters of Sparta, celebrating a festival of Apollo, could not go to war during that holy time.

Unwilling to risk waiting for Sparta, Athens hastily mobilized militia, and her general Miltiades gave the order: "Take food and march." Joined by some 600

150

citizen-soldiers from the Boeotian town of Plataea, the 10,000 Athenians encamped at the south end of the plain, flung up a crude stockade, and awaited attack for several uneasy days. Then the Persians re-embarked their cavalry and some of their troops and marched the rest south along the Bay of Marathon.

Miltiades perceived the foe's strategy: While the Persians on the plain checked or defeated his army, the amphibious force would sail around Cape Sounion and land before defenseless Athens, in danger of betrayal by pro-Persian politicians. Only a double miracle could save Athens — and Greece: victory at Marathon against a superior, professional army, then a swift march back in time to defend the city.

"Miltiades knew," my Greek narrator resumed, "that the Persians were strongest in the center, where they massed their archers, and weakest in the wings. So he placed *his* weakest troops in the center, his strongest in the wings. His idea, you see, was to envelop the enemy by crushing the Persian wings. Then he could wheel in on the exposed flanks of the Persian center."

The Greeks swept across the plain, surprising the foe and thwarting archers

PAINTING FOR NATIONAL GEOGRAPHIC BY TOM LOVELL

accustomed to slower targets. "They were the first Greeks . . . who charged their enemies at a run," reported Herodotus, great historian of the Persian Wars. The Greeks routed the enemy wings, then attacked from three sides "and followed after the Persians in their flight, hewing them down, till they came to the sea." A myth relates that the pastoral god Pan, who could stampede cattle, helped by *pan*icking the Persians. In hand-to-hand combat on the beach, the Greeks captured seven ships. The rest of the flotilla escaped and headed for Athens.

Sunburst signals, apparently from a polished shield, flashed on Mount Pentelicus toward the Persian ships. Suspecting that this reflected a plot in Athens, the Greeks made a forced march back to the city. The sight of them arrayed for battle along the shore at Phalerum, the old port of Athens, turned back the Persian fleet.

Most Greeks hailed Marathon as glorious proof of their invincibility. But Themistocles, an Athenian statesman, warned that the Persians would return. Like Winston Churchill in Britain between world wars, Themistocles went unheeded by the masses and was mocked by political opponents. The rich fought his plan for a tax-financed navy, preferring the self-supported citizen army.

Then a lucky strike at the silver mines of Laurium, on the tip of Attica, fattened the Athenian treasury with royalties. Themistocles urged the Assembly of Citizens to spend the windfall on a navy instead of dividing it among the people. His speech had effect. Within three years the city launched 200 ships of a new class— the trireme, a galley propelled by three banks of oars.

ACROSS THE AEGEAN, meanwhile, the Persian empire was conscripting men, ships, and arms for a land-and-sea invasion of Greece. In 481, Xerxes, successor to his father's throne, massed these forces on the Asian shore of the Hellespont. Athens, Sparta, Corinth, and Aegina responded by forming a defensive league that would eventually include 31 city-states. But most Greeks, awed by Persian might, favored neutrality or even alliance with the invaders.

From the deck of a ship in the Dardanelles, the ancient Hellespont whose waters separate Europe from Asia, you can see capes jutting out from either shore to form the strait's narrowest stretch. Here Xerxes bridged the channel with boats. His Egyptian subjects, renowned as the world's best ropemakers, produced the great bridge cables. (A sample of their craft has been excavated in an Egyptian quarry: rope 18 inches in diameter attached to a 70-ton block of stone.) Sod covered the mile-long plank roadway and high screens lined it so that animals crossing on it would not shy at the seething current.

Across the Hellespont in 480 tramped an army that ancients numbered in the millions and modern scholars in the hundreds of thousands. Some 1,000 ships paralleled the army's march, landing men and supplies as the invaders headed westward through Thrace, Macedonia, and Thessaly. The fleet traversed a canal Xerxes had ordered cut through the Mount Athos peninsula. He must have paid

MODERN GREEK WARRIORS *guard the mound that enshrines 192 Athenians. They fell where, in Byron's words, "The mountains look on Marathon—and Marathon looks on the sea." Marathon runners—and a 26-mile, 385-yard Olympic event—honor the original messenger.*

AT THE PASS OF THERMOPYLAE *a Persian tide surges along the shore and breaks against Greek courage. Bronze-helmed Leonidas slashes under a hail of arrows. Gulf of Lamia no longer hems the mountains. But Persian arrowheads pointed scholars to the spot where, attacked from the rear by traitor-guided foes, Spartans went down fighting.*

PAINTING FOR NATIONAL GEOGRAPHIC BY LOUIS S. GLANZMAN. OPPOSITE: FARRELL GREHAN

PAINTING FOR NATIONAL GEOGRAPHIC BY MELBOURNE BRINDLE

SALAMIS

for the work in gold darics (named for Darius). A 300-coin cache has been found there.

Ahead of the army went ambassadors who demanded token tributes of earth and water, symbols of submission. In Thrace a tribal king's six sons marched with the Persians. After the war their father had them all blinded. Athens and Sparta refused to submit; Xerxes did not even bother sending emissaries. A decade earlier, when Darius had done so, these cities had given the Persians their earth and water by casting the messengers into pits and wells.

I crossed the Turkish-Greek frontier and followed the probable coastal route of the invaders to Kavalla, a delightful fishing port. Whitewashed houses terrace the hills above the snug harbor, where yachts tug gently at anchor. Here almost certainly Xerxes' ships found shelter.

The Persians lived off the land. But unlike the Greeks,

*Athens' "wooden wall," a crescent
of triremes armed with "brazen
beaks," smashes the Persian fleet
at Salamis. Xerxes, enthroned
under a canopy, watches from the
slopes of Mount Aegaleos.*

*Themistocles (above), father of
Athens' navy, lured the invaders
into the strait formed by a finger
of Salamis and the mainland.
Wave-lashed, unable to deploy,
the Persians died "like mackerel."
Triumphs at Salamis and at Himera
in Sicily (page 100) saved the
Greek world from being crushed
between Persia and Carthage.*

they were great meat eaters, so their fleet maintained food
dumps holding beasts for slaughter and stores of salt meat
of every kind. The depots also had piles of papyri for paper-
work—a military feature alien to Greeks.

Xerxes' troops crossed a rugged land of mountains and
plains laced by great rivers that become fierce torrents in
winter. In this outer fringe of ancient Greece, people still
seem more Turkish or Slavic than Greek, the men hard-
faced, the women proud and lovely.

Place names have so changed that I could only assume I
stood on the correct vast plain upon the coast of Thrace
where Xerxes assembled and numbered his army. I imagined
him riding along the ranks in his golden chariot, inspecting
the mightiest force the world had yet seen.

Here were Persian warriors in leather jerkins and fish-
scale armor, high-booted Phrygians, Mysians bearing
sharpened stakes, wooden-helmeted men of the Caucasus,
Scythians in pointed caps, Iranians behind tall wicker
shields, an Arabian camel corps, ass-drawn chariots from
India—and Ethiopians in lionskins who brandished stone-
headed clubs and spears tipped with gazelle horn.

The exotic horde marched on toward Athens, "drinking
rivers dry," ravaging the land. But this slave army, said
Herodotus, marched under the lash. And ahead lay a pass
called Thermopylae, defended by a band of freemen.

As the Persian emperor, with "half the world at heel,"
marched into northern Thessaly, an allied Greek army under
Spartan command advanced against the invaders. The
powerful Corinthian fleet sailed north to harass Persian
ships and cut off vital supplies from the Persian armies.

Bay of Eleusis

Mount Aegaleos

Athens, 7 miles

GREEK FLEET

PERSIAN FLEET

Saronic Gulf

Psyttaleia

The Greeks held a superb defensive position, the pass of the Hot Gates—Thermopylae—where the coastal road, flanked by mountain, sea, and hot mineral springs, narrowed to a path some 50 feet wide. Leonidas, the Spartan king who commanded the Greeks, held the pass with about 7,000 troops, including his own 300-man royal guard, all fathers of sons. If a guardsman fell, his name would live.

Xerxes, enthroned near the pass to watch his men pour through, laughed at a scout's report of vain Greek warriors bathing and preening on the eve of battle. But a Greek, serving Xerxes, heard the report and understood: The troops were Spartans, ritualistically preparing to die. "O king!" he exclaimed, "now are you face to face with . . . the most valiant men in Hellas."

While the Spartans awaited attack, Herodotus wrote, one of them remarked that the Persian archers' arrows would fly so thickly they would darken the sky. "So much the better," his comrade replied. "We can fight in the shade."

For three days a storm raged off Euboea, where part of the Greek fleet sheltered. Caught at sea, hundreds of Persian ships sank. As the storm died down, Xerxes hurled wave after human wave, including his vaunted guard, the ten thousand Immortals, against the pass. But Leonidas' troops, who manned an ancient wall, would not yield.

As night fell over the second day of battle, a Greek traitor led a Persian force along a mountaintop trail to outflank the pass. Leonidas learned of the treachery in time to send away most of his army. His Spartans, with some Boeotians, stayed as a doomed rearguard. "Have a good breakfast, men," tradition reports his words. "We shall dine tonight in Hades!"

Next morning, while the night marchers fell on the Greek flank, Leonidas led his men over the wall for a last, spear-shattering charge. Now, recounts Herodotus, they fought

GRAPES WARMED *by the Attic sun gave Athenians wine to trade for grain a lean soil would not grow. Resin sealed porous amphoras, perhaps creating the Greek taste for* retsina, *resin-flavored wine.*

Winepress dance of satyrs evokes Dionysus, god of wine. Celebrants, the Bacchae, reveled in orgiastic mystery rites, named for mystai, *tight-lipped initiates in the cult. The rites are still a mystery.*

DETAIL OF ATTIC AMPHORA, 6TH CENTURY B.C.; ROYAL MUSEUM OF ART AND HISTORY, BRUSSELS. ABOVE: ATTIC VINEYARD; MICHAEL KUH

"with their swords, if they had them, but if not, with their hands and teeth."
Leonidas fell. Spartans, rallying round his body, enshrouded it with theirs.

Where the highway from Lamia crosses a plain beside the sea, I saw a Greek
warrior gleaming in the sun (page 149). Immortal in bronze as he is in legend,
Leonidas still defends Thermopylae. Atop a nearby knoll I read inscribed words
of the poet Simonides: "Tell them in Sparta, passerby, that here, obedient to their
orders, we lie." The eminent archeologist Spyridon Marinatos told me he had
pinpointed this site after digging up hundreds of Persian-type arrowheads.

The Persians surged through the pass and into the heart of Hellas, burning the
land. Meanwhile, the Greek navy, battered by battles off Artemisium at the north

The Greek and his gods: Olympus lodged an earthy pantheon

"THEN SHE CAUGHT UP a powerful spear, edged with sharp bronze...and descended in a flash from the peaks of Olympus." Thus, Homer relates, the goddess Athena leaves her father Zeus and his consort Hera in their celestial home (right). With Hermes in winged cap, she sets off to arrange the homecoming of Odysseus.

Atop 9,570-foot Olympus, cloud-veiled above fields of poppies (opposite), ancient belief placed gods who sipped nectar, ate ambrosia, and counciled and cavorted in eternal springtime. King of this Hellenic heaven was Zeus. Romans called him Jupiter—*Diu-pater*, "God the Father." His philandering made the title literally true.

Zeus and a train of masculine deities had swept out of the north with Achaean invaders. These virile gods of a nomadic people found Grecian fields guarded by earth goddesses, and they merged with the local nymphs in divine amours. The celestial family tree groaned under the weight of their fruit: Muses, Graces, Fates, Furies, Gorgons, nymphs, harpies. The variety was endless, for ancients saw spirits in a river, a wind, a bird. Zeus often took the guise of a bull, symbol of potency; Hera was cow-eyed, Athena owl-eyed, centaurs half horse, satyrs half goat.

Homer and the Boeotian poet Hesiod codified this deluge of deities. They surrounded Zeus with a bickering, status-seeking court that mirrored those on earth. Homer depicted the arrogant Olympians following the pursuits of his aristocratic audience. Ares made war, Apollo music, Aphrodite love. But the gifted smith Hephaestus, who ignobly did useful labor, emerged as lame and repulsive.

The gods provided man no moral code, only a reason for the whims of his fate; offered no reward for virtue; and shrugged at sin. But they reacted furiously to *hybris*, presumptuous pride. When Prometheus stole the gods' fire, Tantalus fed them human flesh, and Ixion tried to seduce Hera, each was punished—not for immorality but overweening gall.

By ritual and sacrifice, Greeks sought to woo the gods' favor. They invoked divine sanction for oaths, marriages, every major enterprise. Temples studded the land and cult festivals salted the year. At Athens' Great Dionysia in March freed prisoners joined in the celebration. The Aphrodisia in early April erupted in a romping homage to the goddess of love. During summer's Cronia (like the Saturnalia of the Romans), slaves sat down with their masters to feast.

Oracles and sibyls (women gifted in prophecy) drew many suppliants. Pilgrims at Corinth listened in awe to a disembodied voice; it came from a priest concealed below the altar. Men all over the Greek world sought Apollo's wisdom at Delphi. Homer's war god at Troy had mellowed into mankind's benevolent adviser. No one could presume to learn his fate from such an oracle, but he might get an answer to a specific problem.

Impiety was dangerous but doubts could not be stilled. Herodotus, comparing other religions, questioned some Greek myths. Xenophanes rejected the idea that gods resemble men, pointing out that if lions could draw, their gods would look like lions. He favored a single, supreme deity. Euripides assailed the gods for "deceit, cruelty, and immorality." Olympian religion tended to become an empty ritual. But the Eleusinian Mysteries, honoring Demeter, goddess of growing things, and her daughter Persephone, promised what Homeric religion had neglected—resurrection and eternal life. For some years this cult rivaled Christianity.

Still Greek mythology lived on in art, drama, and poetry. Its noble themes, rousing tales, delightful fancies have given the gods immortality.

THE DIVINE FAMILY OF TWELVE OLYMPIANS		
Greek deity		Roman equivalent
Zeus	King of the Gods	Jupiter
Hera	Marriage	Juno
Poseidon	Sea	Neptune
Hades	Underworld	Pluto
Hestia	Hearth	Vesta
Apollo	Light, Music	Apollo
Athena	Wisdom	Minerva
Aphrodite	Love and Beauty	Venus
Ares	War	Mars
Hermes	Travel, Trade, Thieves	Mercury
Artemis	Youth and the Hunt	Diana
Hephaestus	Fire, the Divine Smith	Vulcan

CORN POPPY (PAPAVER RHOEAS), SENTINELED
BY WHITE MIGNONETTE (RESEDA ALBA)

ASPHODEL (ASPHODELUS MICROCARPUS)

CYCLAMEN (CYCLAMEN PERSICUM)

ROOTED IN MYTH, *Grecian wild flowers bloom with the rainbow
radiance of the goddess Iris and the tragic brevity of the youths
Narcissus and Hyacinthus. Ghostly asphodel (whence our name
"daffodil") crowned Persephone and carpeted her underworld realm.
Scarlet anemones sprang from the blood of Adonis and the tears
of Aphrodite; the goddess healed Hector's wounds with oil of roses.
Corn poppy and reseda also doctored ills. The sleep of death
came from hemlock, white-flowered relative of our parsley.
Aristotle's pupil Theophrastus was Father of Botany, and after
2,300 years Greek still names our flora: Tragopogon (goatsbeard),
heliotrope (turning to the sun), chrysanthemum (golden flower).*

tip of Euboea, slipped away to the island of Salamis off Athens. When the Athenian admiral Themistocles met with other naval commanders in Salamis, they could look across the mile-wide narrows and in the distance see Athens in flames.

As the Persians had slashed and burned their way southward, Athens evacuated its mothers and children to Troezen in the eastern Peloponnesus and its elders across the channel to Salamis, leaving only a token force behind. Abandoned dogs howled in the city. One, legend claims, swam to Salamis and died on the beach. A long promontory there, Cynosura ("dog's tail"), immortalizes the animal, said to have been the pet of Pericles' family.

Oil refineries, factories, clanging shipyards, the glare of furnaces fringe the Gulf of Salamis today. Steel-plated ships in scarlet priming paint banish the ghosts of wooden triremes that smashed Xerxes' galleys to matchwood and filled the reddened strait with Persian corpses.

Themistocles lured the Persians into the narrows by sending a slave to Xerxes with the tale that the squabbling, demoralized Greek fleet was about to flee north through the Salamis Strait and scatter. The emperor quickly deployed his thousand ships. Aeschylus says he sent some to block escape by way of the north end of the strait, and ordered the rest into the south end of the channel at dawn, certain he would catch the Greek galleys still drawn up on the beaches.

Xerxes placed his throne on a hill overlooking Salamis and proudly watched his ships filling the strait from shore to shore. But as Themistocles had expected, a morning ground swell funneled through the strait, transforming the Persian array

162

SPIDER OR HORSESHOE ORCHID
(OPHRYS FERRUM-EQUINUM)

ROCKROSE (CISTUS SALVIFOLIUS)

SALSIFY (TRAGOPOGON PORRIFOLIUS)
CROWN ANEMONE (ANEMONE CORONARIA)

ALL PHOTOGRAPHS BY FARRELL GREHAN

into a maelstrom of flailing oars and careening ships. Out of the calm waters in the island's lee came a crescent of Greek galleys, outnumbered three to one but stroked by men chanting "the deep-toned hymn, *Apollo, Saving Lord.*" Here were the sons of Hellas, joined to save their land. Aeschylus, veteran of the battle, re-created it in his play *The Persians.* He told how the Greeks' bronze-sheathed rams smashed into the Persians "till hulls rolled over, and the sea itself was hidden, strewn with their wreckage, dyed with blood of men. The dead lay thick on all the reefs and beaches, and flight broke out. . . ."

Bearing news of the Salamis disaster, messengers sped across the Aegean, rode the Royal Road from Sardis to Susa, and galloped along the highways that linked the satrapies of the Persian empire. "Neither snow, nor rain, nor heat, nor gloom of night stays these couriers from the swift completion of their appointed rounds," wrote Herodotus. His description of this pony express became the unofficial motto of the U. S. Post Office. The following summer the Persian messengers had more bad news to spread: An army of some 100,000 Greeks had wiped out the last of the invaders in a battle at Plataea in the hills south of Thebes.

IN UNITY the Greeks had found strength. And Athens had found inspiration to lead the Greek world—though her people had returned to the embers of their city and had lost everything. Everything but freedom. Within 30 years, under Pericles, they would rebuild Athens more gloriously than ever before.

What had given the Greeks a sense of national pride and cultural unity? Split

163

HERE SPOKE THE ORACLE, *voice of Apollo at Delphi.*
Kings and commoners puzzled over its mystic rantings rendered into verse.
But graven on this fourth-century B.C. *temple were words*
all could understand: Know Thyself *and* Nothing in Excess.
Plutarch, famed first-century A.D. *biographer, native to*
nearby Chaeronea, presided as a priest here many years.

MERLE SEVERY, NATIONAL GEOGRAPHIC STAFF

by geography and jealousy into feuding city-states, they had combined against the invader. Was it merely to defend their homes? To seek a deeper answer, I turned in my personal odyssey from scenes of battle to shrines of unity.

My first pilgrimage took me through the birthplace of Greece—Thessaly. Here roamed the ancestors of the Mycenaeans, the "first Greeks in Greece." Paleolithic remains found here date to 20,000 B.C. or earlier. Myths swirl through this vast, fertile plain and its surrounding wall of mountains. An archeologist friend once took me to the little town of Farsala on the plain of Thessaly, where we stood on a Mycenaean mound and watched women wash laundry in a concrete tank that caught the spill of a stream. "That stream, I believe, was where Thetis dipped her infant son Achilles, holding him by the heel," my friend said.

Homer's *Iliad* calls Achilles ruler of Phthia. Mythology adds the tale of his mother, an immortal, trying to make him invulnerable by dipping him in charmed waters. Could Pharsalus be a corruption of Phthia? But the name of this stream, Letheos, disturbed me. "I thought Thetis dipped Achilles in the Styx," I said.

My friend explained. "Only two rivers flowed from Hades, the Styx and the Lethe. A pardonable slip by the bard who told the story. No?"

I gazed at the laundrywomen and pictured the baby Achilles, soaked except for one dry tendon that bears his name—where a fatal arrow finally struck.

Mount Olympus, crowning the myth-haunted plain, was the birthplace of the gods. From the twisting Kozani-Larisa road one sees it jagged against the eastern sky. That uneven crest, like a cockscomb, looked to the ancients like divine thrones. On those pinnacles they saw the gods ruled by great Zeus, who dispatched rainbows as his messengers and hurled thunderbolts of wrath.

But to hear the will of the gods Greeks journeyed, as I did, to Delphi, their most sacred shrine. Northward from Athens I drove, past vineyards and olive

166

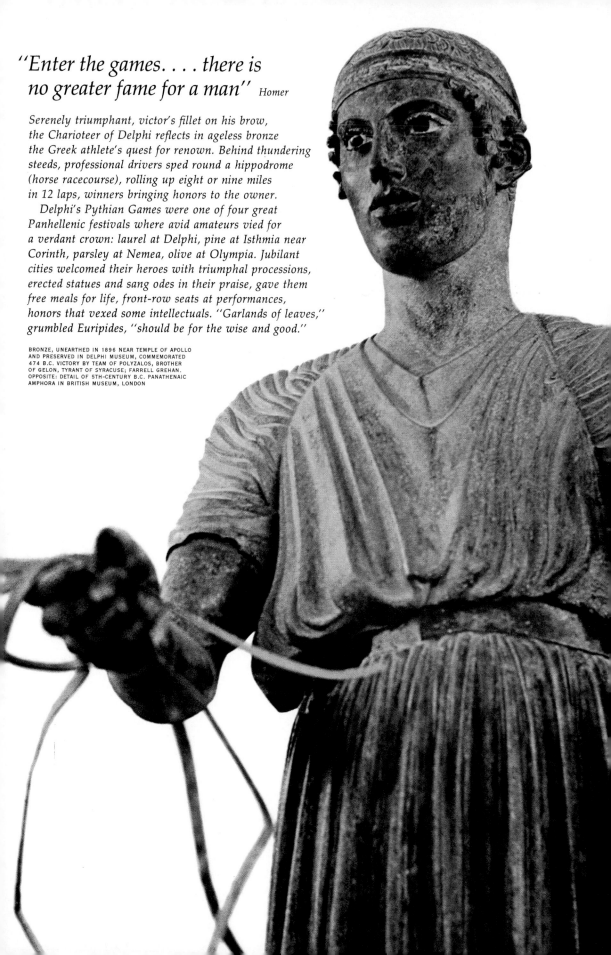

"Enter the games. . . . there is no greater fame for a man" Homer

Serenely triumphant, victor's fillet on his brow,
the Charioteer of Delphi reflects in ageless bronze
the Greek athlete's quest for renown. Behind thundering
steeds, professional drivers sped round a hippodrome
(horse racecourse), rolling up eight or nine miles
in 12 laps, winners bringing honors to the owner.

Delphi's Pythian Games were one of four great
Panhellenic festivals where avid amateurs vied for
a verdant crown: laurel at Delphi, pine at Isthmia near
Corinth, parsley at Nemea, olive at Olympia. Jubilant
cities welcomed their heroes with triumphal processions,
erected statues and sang odes in their praise, gave them
free meals for life, front-row seats at performances,
honors that vexed some intellectuals. "Garlands of leaves,"
grumbled Euripides, "should be for the wise and good."

BRONZE, UNEARTHED IN 1896 NEAR TEMPLE OF APOLLO
AND PRESERVED IN DELPHI MUSEUM, COMMEMORATED
474 B.C. VICTORY BY TEAM OF POLYZALOS, BROTHER
OF GELON, TYRANT OF SYRACUSE; FARRELL GREHAN.
OPPOSITE: DETAIL OF 5TH-CENTURY B.C. PANATHENAIC
AMPHORA IN BRITISH MUSEUM, LONDON

groves and through dusty villages. Nearing Thebes, I shared the potholed road with rattling trucks, chromed tourist buses, donkeys, women trudging under heavy loads, and a sputtering motorbike with a hunter, gun slung over his shoulder.

Beyond Thebes—once capital of Athens' rival state Boeotia, and scene of Sophocles' *Oedipus Rex*—beyond Levadhia, the road climbs through sparsely settled land. I recalled a spot where the past had come to life for me once before, and I halted to look again. Far below, between the heather-covered valley slopes, a small bridge appeared at the junction of three dirt roads. The scene had not changed since my tourist bus stopped here years before and with charming authority the woman guide ordered us out. Pointing to that junction, she said, "That is where Oedipus killed his father."

It must look much as it did to Sophocles when he wrote of young Oedipus, destined to kill his father and marry his mother. Trying to flee his inexorable fate, Oedipus comes to a crossroads where a chariot blocks his way. He angrily strikes and kills its passenger, an old

FARRELL GREHAN. RIGHT: PAINTING FOR NATIONAL GEOGRAPHIC BY TOM LOVELL

man. Later he marries Jocasta. As King of Thebes, he seeks to end a plague by cleansing the city, only to find that it is he who befouls Thebes. The old man was his father, Jocasta his mother. Unwittingly, he has fulfilled his destiny.

In the ancient theater of Delphi, near the crossroads "that drank my father's blood," you experience that searing instant when Oedipus realizes his guilt. By skillful timing, at the very moment the sun sinks behind the hills Oedipus tears out his eyes—"Why should I see whose vision showed me nothing sweet to see? What can I see to love?" In those darkening moments you come closer to the spirit of Greek tragedy than anywhere else on earth.

Delphi, its Sacred Way winding uphill past treasuries erected by various city-states, rests in the laps of the gods —on a ledge of Mount Parnassus high above a plain carpeted by more than a million olive trees. Twin crags, the Shining Rocks, guard the Sanctuary of Apollo. Here to its renowned Delphic Oracle came seekers of prophecy. They revered the words that came from Apollo's priestess, some carefully chosen, celibate, middle-aged peasant. Her title, Pythia (inquiring one), stemmed from the monster serpent

Ionian Sea

•Olympia

Gulf of Corinth
•Delphi

PELOPONNESUS

Corinth•/Isthmus
of Corinth

•Sparta

Epidaurus•

Athens•

—N→

Aegean Sea

Cape Malea

PELOPONNESUS, *a rocky hand clutching at Crete,
is tethered to the mainland by an isthmus at its thumb.
Here ships rolled over a four-mile roadway, avoiding
Odysseus' dread Cape Malea and slicing 200 stormy
miles off their passage from sea to sea. Commanding
the strategic crossroads stood Poseidon's city Corinth,
enriched by tolls and trade, extolled for Aphrodite's
"maidens whose embrace welcomes many strangers."
Athens' threat to Corinth's communications with her
colony Syracuse helped spark the Peloponnesian War.
Razed by Romans in 146 B.C., refounded by Caesar
in 44 B.C., the city spread its splendors beneath
the frowning citadel of Acrocorinth (right).*

PAINTING FOR NATIONAL GEOGRAPHIC BY H. M. HERGET. UPPER: MERLE SEVERY, NATIONAL GEOGRAPHIC STAFF

that Apollo killed here. In a trance, perhaps induced by narcotic herbs, she sat on a tripod and raved. Priests enriched themselves by translating her incoherent cries into cadenced prophecies.

The Pythia's answers were usually framed by crafty men who commanded the best intelligence service in the Hellenic world. They were always ambiguous. When Croesus, King of Lydia, asked whether he should war on Persia, he was told: "If Croesus attacks, he will destroy a great empire." He did—his own. Priests prudently issued pro-Persian oracles when Persia seemed to be winning, but hedged their bets on the eve of the Battle of Salamis by giving Athenians a two-edged prophecy: "... flee from your houses and city" and "Yet shall a wood-built wall ... be ... a stronghold for thee." (Themistocles, who may have bribed the priests, said the wooden walls were the ships at Salamis.) And when asked to find a treasure, the Oracle gave a lasting formula for diligent search: "Leave no stone unturned."

STRUGGLING THROUGH Athens' outskirts in search of the main road toward Corinth and the Peloponnesus, I reflected on the contrast between old and new in Greece. Unlike much of western Europe, where past and present mingle harmoniously, Greece is aggressively modern. The typical village is an agglomeration of concrete structures. Isolated farms or estates are rare. The peasant walks to town, driving his livestock before him, meets with friends in a *taverna*, and talks the evening away.

But as I drove through mountains that had walled the old city-states, I could sense intimations of the past. I saw people farming every foot of rocky Peloponnesus soil and recalled what a Greek collaborator had told Xerxes when the king wondered if Thermopylae would be defended: "Want has at all times been a fellow dweller with us in our land, while Valor is an ally whom we have gained by dint of wisdom and strict laws."

The road corkscrews up a high mountain barrier. Olive trees and vines give way to pines and scrub until I am hemmed by cliff and crag. Then the road, more softly curved, swirls downward. Vines and olives reappear as I descend into a lush river valley and cross a fertile plain. Such land shaped Greece. Tribes settled behind mountain walls, and tribal

ATTIC RELIEF, 4TH CENTURY B.C.; NATIONAL MUSEUM, ATHENS

"Whatever house I enter, I shall come to heal"

The Hippocratic Oath

Sleeping in a sanctuary where sacred snakes slither, a patient dreams that Asclepius, god of healing, treats him. Aristophanes has serpents lick blindness from Plutus' eyes (page 127); annually renewing their skins, snakes symbolize the art of healing. Doctors' emblem is still the caduceus, Asclepius' snake-entwined staff.

Pilgrims flocked to shrines at Epidaurus, Cos, Pergamum. Proper diet, exercise, and baths prepared them for hypnotic dream-healing that produced "divine" cures.

Born on the Aegean island of Cos about 460 B.C., Hippocrates, a physician's son, saw the parade of patients to the Asklepieion, or center of healing. Time, he reasoned, cured more effectively than temple sacrifice; disease arose not from godly interference but natural causes; best preventive was the wholesome life. Father of Medicine, he based diagnosis of illness on case histories, and in prognosis forecast its course. He prescribed diets more than drugs (sold by a pharmakopoles) and cured with enemas, emetics, hydrotherapy. Ethics of the Hippocratic Oath yet endure.

Greeks founded biology, physiology, and anatomy; linking bodily ills and the psyche, they pioneered in psychiatry. Athenians had tax-financed medicare, Romans subsidized hospitals. Greek doctors prospered in Rome. "They have conspired to kill us all," griped Cato the Elder, "and ... charge a fee for it."

171

domains evolved into states. At the heart of each state grew a fortified city—
Athens in Attica, Thebes in Boeotia, Argos in Argolis, Sparta in Laconia. When a
city-state, or *polis*, established a colony, the polis became a mother- or *metro*-polis.

Religion bound together the peoples of these contentious city-states. The first
Greek-speaking invaders of Greece, whose upsurge coincided with the beginning
of the Mycenaean age, brought to the Hellenic world such gods as Zeus and his
nagging wife Hera. And just as newcomers merged with local tribes, so Zeus
merged with tribal deities—folklore reconciled this by having him carry on scan-
dalous amours with local nymphs. Minor kings and queens began to trace their
lineage back to Zeus. Though the tribal dynasties remained independent, they
thus developed a religious unity, building not only temples to the gods of their
cities but shrines revered by all Greeks.

Now, driving past rolling pastures, I neared one of the greatest shrines, Olympia. Here men worshiped Zeus and Hera in Doric temples—and in the stadium
of the sacred Olympic Games. Gray temple columns rise among the pines that

172

FROM HARBORS *like Nauplia's, seiners have sailed since days when Athens' fish bell brought shoppers scampering for the fresh catch. Greek ships plied the Hellespont lifeline with Black Sea cargoes of salt fish, iron, timber, and grain.*

extend to the sparkling Alpheus, named for a river god. The plain has been sacred at least since Mycenaean times, and Hera herself probably replaced a mother goddess once worshiped here. Amid acres of toppled columns and shattered pediments, I could see where Zeus had been enthroned in his temple. His statue of gold and ivory, the masterpiece of Phidias, was one of the Seven Wonders of the World.

Aided by a guidebook written by Pausanias, a Greek traveler in the second century A.D., archeologists found the studio of Phidias, complete with tools and terracotta molds used in creating the statue. He and other sculptors worked here, preserving in stone the grace of Olympian athletes.

Every four years, certainly from 776 B.C. and probably before that, Greeks from every part of the Hellenic world gathered for the Olympic Games. Warring city-states honored a sacred truce during the festival. For a week, Greeks mingled as brothers, and city-states forgot their other rivalries to cheer on native sons they had proudly sent to win wreaths at the Games.

I stood where the athletes took their oaths, swearing to Zeus that they would

"Coins...well minted...ringing clear" Aristophanes

*Owl of Athena ruled the roost among coins in the Hellenic world.
Athens' tetradrachm (4 drachmas) was standard far and wide.
The Latin word* pecus *for cattle, which sired* pecunia, *money,
reminds us that men once gauged worth by cattle: Homer valued
Menelaus' armor at nine oxen. Traders used ingots (page 69)
as tender. Lydians bartered with lumps of electrum, a variable
gold-silver alloy from Asia Minor rivers; but deals bogged
down as sellers warily assayed each lump. So 7th-century Lydia
stamped them to attest value, and coinage was born (egg shape
opposite). Lydian King Croesus' pure gold coins (right) gained
greater currency, quickened trade, helped make him fabulously rich.*

Coinage soon crossed the Aegean. Greeks, who spent iron obols,
or spits (bottom), by the drachma *or handful of six, kept the same
names and ratio in their new mintage. Aegina's silver turtle was
Europe's first coin, turning into a tortoise when the island's navy lost sway.
Coiner's art achieved elegance in Syracuse nymph; triskelion touts that city's
claim to rule tricornered Sicily. As each polis proudly struck its coins, money changers
set up tables in the market; banker means "tableman." Saving in a* fiscus *or money
basket was sound fiscal policy before banks. Now archeologists withdraw such hoards
with interest. Once shy of silver, Athens minted silver-faced coppers like U. S. coins today.
Aristophanes fumed: "debased, barbaric tender—this new-fangled copper trash."*

play fair. And I saw the statue plinths upon which disgraced cities had inscribed
the names of oath-breakers. In the stadium, I saw the grooved marble starting
blocks where sprinters dug in their toes. I walked the grass-covered banks where
40,000 or more spectators sat, swatting flies.

I imagine the all-male crowds were not much different from fans at a modern
sports event. Old-timers probably recalled the good old days: "Remember Milo of
Croton? Why, he could eat a bullock in a day. Carry one, too. Started out lifting it
when it was a calf. He could hold a pomegranate in his fist — uncrushed, mind you —
and nobody could snatch it from him. There was a wrestler!"

Wrestlers used holds still seen. But the *pankration* (all-strength) combined boxing, wrestling, stomping, and finger-breaking. In one match, a man died as he won.
His body got the victor's crown. In A.D. 67 Nero, an unlikely Olympian, made a
farce of the games. When he tumbled from his chariot in a race, his competitors
tactfully halted; under the eyes of his 5,000 bodyguards the corpulent emperor
won. He also waddled off with crowns for best singer, lyre player, and herald.

T HE WAVERING NOTES of a shepherd's pipe rose from a fold in the Peloponnesian
hills. Sheep bells tinkled a faint, answering chorus. Here near Epidaurus, shrine
of "unceasingly gentle" Asclepius, god of healing, I found a gentle, friendly land.
At a wayside taverna a child offered me a posy of wild flowers. I was a stranger—
xenos. But the child knew that xenos also means guest.

Epidaurus lies at the head of a cool, sheltered valley. I approached through
hills that rose steeply, fold upon fold. My road wound past olive groves and
small villages, each with its Byzantine church. In this green valley of many
springs stood the greatest temple of Asclepius, a healer whom Pluto, god of
Hades, blamed for a population slump in the realm of the dead. Pluto complained
to Zeus, who thereupon killed Asclepius with a thunderbolt. But the "blameless

DR. PAUL MACKENDRICK, *consultant for this book, studies a Syracuse decadrachm. Coins yield clues to kings, cults, conflicts, commerce.*

physician" endured as a god himself. His daughter Hygeia, goddess of health, bequeathed us hygiene.

Ailing pilgrims slept on the skins of sacrificed animals in a dormitory with cubicles, whose foundations can still be seen. At night, the god appeared and prescribed for their illnesses. No doubt a priest impersonated Asclepius, and probably his powers of suggestion effected cures.

In the Epidaurus museum I saw testimonials: votive offerings, some of them models of the afflicted limb or organ. Archeologists also unearthed here inscriptions recording the healing of ailments ranging from baldness and pockmarks to blindness, ulcers, and aches in the *hemikrania*, "half of the skull," our throbbing "migraine."

I left the museum and climbed a piny slope to the magnificent theater of Epidaurus (page 124), financed from temple fees. I could understand why the Greeks raised a theater on a site dedicated to the god of healing. For is not drama itself a form of therapy? And where else in all Greece can one find such soothing beauty? From the top row you can see, above the pines and olives, the distant gleam of the sea.

What you glimpse from Epidaurus is the Saronic Gulf, an inlet of the Aegean that washes the northeastern shore of the Peloponnesus. The name means Pelops' island, honoring Zeus' grandson, the grandfather of Agamemnon. Indeed, since 1893 this huge fragment of Greece technically has been an island. In that year a four-mile canal, begun with a golden spade by Nero A.D. 66, was completed through the isthmus that links the peninsula to the mainland.

Ancient Corinth commanded the isthmus and became one of the wealthiest cities in Greece. Ships bearing goods between the Aegean and the Ionian seas were hauled on rollers, later on wagons, along a *diolkos* — "drag-through," or roadway. Its rutted pavement came to light in 1956.

Corinth today offers no hint of its former grandeur, for the modern city, rebuilt after a 1928 earthquake, lies about four miles from the ruins of ancient Corinth. To get there, you drive past vines whose grapes became the sweet, seedless raisins of *Corinthus* — later just plain "currant."

Corinthian love of luxury and pleasure, infamous in the city's seventh-century B.C. heyday, shocked St. Paul nearly 700 years later. "I speak to your shame," he admonished Corinthians. Guides point out the plinth where they say he spoke. Grecian Corinth survives in the Temple of Apollo's columns. Destroyed by the Romans, then rebuilt and embellished, the city lost most Greek traces. But Romans still told of the notorious priestesses of Aphrodite, whose studded sandals spelled out in the dust of the street, *Follow Me!*

"*Apollo, Delos is dearest to thy heart*"

Homer, Hymn to the Delian Apollo

I CROSSED the great Lacedaemonian plain, home of the Spartans, whose austere ways sharply contrasted with the wealth and high living in Corinth. The good life so preoccupied the Corinthians that they frequently hired warriors to fight for them. And the militaristic Spartans so disdained commerce that, instead of coins, they issued heavy rods of iron that discouraged trade—and idle shopping. Yet, in the fifth century B.C., these two city-states would find something in common: hatred of Athens.

Virtually nothing remains of ancient Sparta. The fifth-century historian Thucydides noted that the city was drab

PAINTING FOR NATIONAL GEOGRAPHIC BY H.M. HERGET

and lacked even walls. "Her ramparts," he wrote, "are her men." I quickly left the crowded streets of the modern market town of Sparta and headed for the splendid Byzantine ruins of nearby Mistra. From its slopes I looked out across the fertile plain ringed by mountains that formed the heartland of the austere Spartan breed.

Ancients told the story of two outsiders invited to dine in a Spartan barracks. One took a sip of the formidable black broth and, putting down his spoon, whispered, "Now I know why the Spartans do not fear death."

In the eighth century B.C., the Spartans, descendants of

WINDS OF PROSPERITY *filled the sails of Delos. Legendary birthplace of Apollo, the Aegean treasure island drew throngs of gift-bearing pilgrims to his temple, later treasury for the Delian League against Persia. Athenian sea power turned the alliance into an empire on a collision course with Sparta's Peloponnesian League. Triremes and high-prowed merchantmen crowded the harbor as cargoes of three continents enriched traders. Free port and slave market under Rome, Delos died after pirate attack in 69 B.C.*

177

"He is best who is trained in the severest discipline"

King Archidamus II of Sparta

Dorians, fanned out from their city in the center of the plain, defeating the older inhabitants and denying them citizenship. These *perioikoi*, "dwellers around," joined the helots, subject people forced into serfdom, in toiling for the Spartans, who thus could pursue their sole profession: war.

Trained only for battle, a young Spartan knew but one home, his barracks, one family, his unit. He could wed at 20, carrying off his bride. His word for marry also meant "seize." The husband's married life was furtive until he became a father. Even then he commuted daily between bed and barracks, taking his simple main meal in his mess hall.

In Sparta, celibacy was a crime. Street gangs of women beat up bachelors. Unmarried men and girls might be thrust into the same dark room, where all groped for mates. Spartans, wrote Plutarch, "sometimes had children by their wives before ever they saw their faces by daylight."

"Sparta is hardly famous for chaste women," Euripides agreed. "They're always out on the street in scanty outfits, making a great display of naked limbs. In those, they race and wrestle with the boys." In his *Andromache*, Athenian scorn of Sparta flames into hatred for these "specialists in evil." The play was inspired by a war that unfolded—and ended—like a Greek tragedy.

The Peloponnesian War, which bled Athens, Sparta, and

much of Greece from 431 to 404 B.C., ironically resulted from an attempt to unify the Greeks against another Persian invasion. In 478, after the Persians had been driven from mainland Greece, Ionian-Greek states in Asia Minor united under Athens. The alliance took the name Delian League from its headquarters on Delos, smallest island in the Cyclades and in my view the most lovely.

From populous, fashionable Mykonos, I crossed to virtually uninhabited Delos. Blue waves lapped the stones of the ancient harbor as we moored our small boat. I walked toward temple ruins across a carpet of wildflowers, anemones bloodred in lush grass that summer soon would scorch. To my right rose a rocky hill, its lower slopes creased by long-silent streets. Near shore, through a forest of columns turned gold by the sun, I followed in the footsteps of pilgrims who came to worship Apollo and his sister Artemis.

Lonely Delos was once considered so hallowed that no one could be born or buried on it. The aged, ill, and expectant were taken across a narrow channel to another island, Rhenea. Hillside homes of wealthy merchants rose in a later era.

From a free association of autonomous states, the Delian League eventually evolved into an Athenian empire. In 454, the league treasury was moved from Delos to Athens. By 448, Athens was collecting dues from league members by force.

ONLY THE STRONG SURVIVED *in Sparta,*
where elders hurled unfit babies from cliffs
and 7-year-old boys left home to learn war.
In a training "herd," youths bedded on rushes,
hardened unwashed bodies by drills and savage
games, learned to steal food. In legend, a lad
who hid a stolen fox under his tunic let it rip
him open to avoid the crime of getting caught.
Poets lauded the warrior "biting his lips to stifle
the pain." Recruits slew any helot (state serf)
elders thought would cause trouble, and risked
death by flogging before Artemis Orthia, whose
altar "reeks with human blood." Hoplites at 20,
they ate meager rations at common mess,
faced exile if they got fat. When, in tight ranks,
they marched to war, Spartan mothers
bade them, "Return with your shield or on it."

CLOAKED SPARTAN WARRIOR, 6TH CENTURY B.C. BRONZE; J. P. MORGAN COLLECTION, WADSWORTH ATHENEUM, HARTFORD. DRAWINGS BY WILLIAM H. BOND, GEOGRAPHIC ART DIVISION

Pericles used this extortion to finance Athens' golden age. Aggressive trade policies helped— but they hurt the commerce of Corinth.

Corinth appealed to Sparta, and Sparta invaded Attica "to war with the Athenians for the liberation of Hellas." For ten years the war was a stalemate. Athenian ships raided the Peloponnesus and kept open the port of Piraeus, linked to Athens by Pericles' Long Walls. Sparta ravaged Attica, but could not topple Athens.

Then plague, probably measles, or typhus from Egypt, swept Athens; "dying men lay one upon another," noted Thucydides. Pericles died —and with him all but a gleam of the golden age.

Cleon, Pericles' successor, told Athens "the empire you hold is a despotism . . . established by reason of your strength." The city that had nurtured the best in man began to stand for the worst. When the little island of Melos refused to be an ally, Athenian envoys proclaimed the new policy: "The powerful exact what they can, the weak yield what they must." The men of Melos were slain, the women and children enslaved. But the island left a monument. In 1820, the Venus de Milo (page 24) was found there.

Athens was lured into her catastrophic campaign against Syracuse by Alcibiades, one of

FARRELL GREHAN

"THE CITY IS WELL FORTIFIED *which hath a wall of men instead of brick," said Spartan King Lycurgus. Taygetus range, above modern Sparta (opposite), helped guard the garrison city on the Eurotas River amid Laconia's plain. To improve the breed, the laconic lawgiver "ordered the maidens to exercise themselves."*

Today's schoolgirls heed the ancient decree on Homer's "island Kranae," where Paris and Helen found a "bed of love" after fleeing Sparta. Vineyard tillers at nearby Gytheion, Sparta's port, evoke the helots bowed over the sod in perpetual slavery and fear so that the military elite might not put hand to any work but war.

180

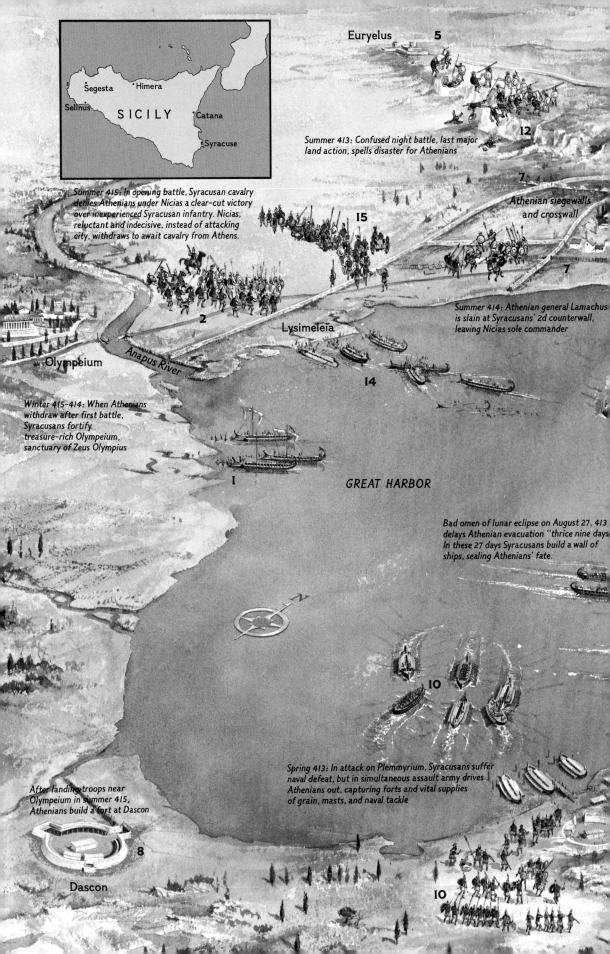

Euryelus 5

Summer 413: Confused night battle, last major land action, spells disaster for Athenians

12

7

Athenian siegewalls and crosswall

7

Summer 415: In opening battle, Syracusan cavalry denies Athenians under Nicias a clear-cut victory over inexperienced Syracusan infantry. Nicias, reluctant and indecisive, instead of attacking city, withdraws to await cavalry from Athens.

15

2

Lysimeleia

Summer 414: Athenian general Lamachus is slain at Syracusans' 2d counterwall, leaving Nicias sole commander

14

Olympeium

Anapus River

Winter 415-414: When Athenians withdraw after first battle, Syracusans fortify treasure-rich Olympeium, sanctuary of Zeus Olympius

I

GREAT HARBOR

Bad omen of lunar eclipse on August 27, 413 delays Athenian evacuation "thrice nine days." In these 27 days Syracusans build a wall of ships, sealing Athenians' fate.

10

After landing troops near Olympeium in summer 415, Athenians build a fort at Dascon

Spring 413: In attack on Plemmyrium, Syracusans suffer naval defeat, but in simultaneous assault army drives Athenians out, capturing forts and vital supplies of grain, masts, and naval tackle

8

Dascon

10

Map inset:

SICILY

Segesta Himera

Selinus

Catana

Syracuse

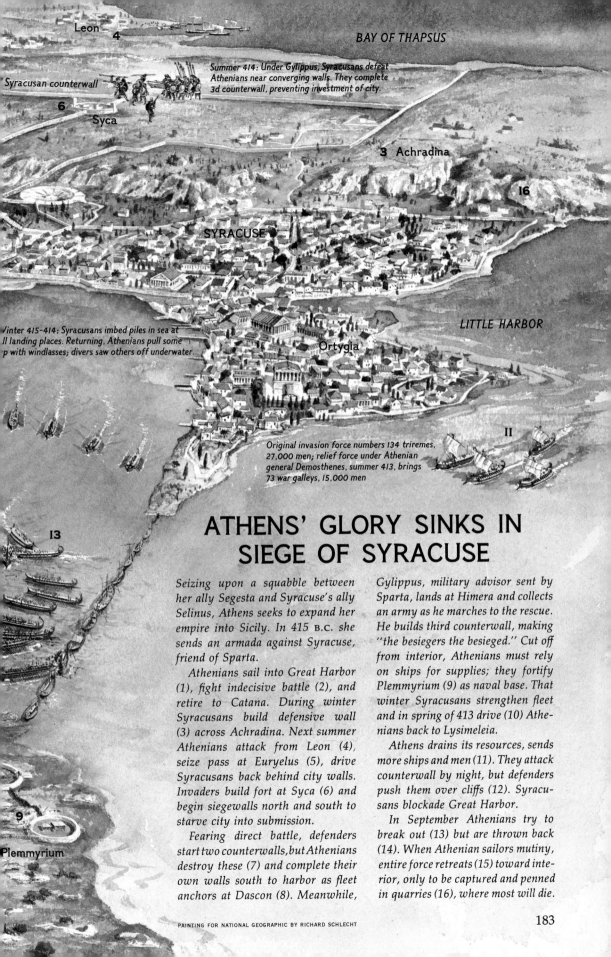

Leon **4**

BAY OF THAPSUS

Summer 414: Under Gylippus, Syracusans defeat Athenians near converging walls. They complete 3d counterwall, preventing investment of city.

Syracusan counterwall

6

Syca

3 Achradina

16

SYRACUSE

LITTLE HARBOR

Winter 415-414: Syracusans imbed piles in sea at all landing places. Returning, Athenians pull some up with windlasses; divers saw others off underwater.

Ortygia

Original invasion force numbers 134 triremes, 27,000 men; relief force under Athenian general Demosthenes, summer 413, brings 73 war galleys, 15,000 men

II

13

9

Plemmyrium

ATHENS' GLORY SINKS IN SIEGE OF SYRACUSE

Seizing upon a squabble between her ally Segesta and Syracuse's ally Selinus, Athens seeks to expand her empire into Sicily. In 415 B.C. she sends an armada against Syracuse, friend of Sparta.

Athenians sail into Great Harbor (1), fight indecisive battle (2), and retire to Catana. During winter Syracusans build defensive wall (3) across Achradina. Next summer Athenians attack from Leon (4), seize pass at Euryelus (5), drive Syracusans back behind city walls. Invaders build fort at Syca (6) and begin siegewalls north and south to starve city into submission.

Fearing direct battle, defenders start two counterwalls, but Athenians destroy these (7) and complete their own walls south to harbor as fleet anchors at Dascon (8). Meanwhile,

Gylippus, military advisor sent by Sparta, lands at Himera and collects an army as he marches to the rescue. He builds third counterwall, making "the besiegers the besieged." Cut off from interior, Athenians must rely on ships for supplies; they fortify Plemmyrium (9) as naval base. That winter Syracusans strengthen fleet and in spring of 413 drive (10) Athenians back to Lysimeleia.

Athens drains its resources, sends more ships and men (11). They attack counterwall by night, but defenders push them over cliffs (12). Syracusans blockade Great Harbor.

In September Athenians try to break out (13) but are thrown back (14). When Athenian sailors mutiny, entire force retreats (15) toward interior, only to be captured and penned in quarries (16), where most will die.

history's most audacious scoundrels. Ward of Pericles, friend of Socrates, rake, reveler, general, he led a disastrous expedition to Sicily but was called home to answer charges of sacrilege. Instead he fled to Sparta, where he seduced the queen. Athens condemned him to death. So did Sparta, for his double-dealing. Alcibiades promptly defected to the Persians but turned on them. Fickle Athens restored his command. He won some victories over Sparta, then his fleet lost a battle while he was away. He fled to a stronghold on the Hellespont, later died in Phrygia, slain, says one account, by the avenging brothers of a wronged maiden.

In 405 B.C., a Spartan fleet built with Persian money sailed into the Hellespont and was challenged by the Athenian armada. The Spartans refused to engage in battle, and the Athenians sailed back to their anchorage at Aegospotami. This went on for days—the Athenians offering battle, then going ashore for food. One day the Spartan admiral, Lysander, struck while his foes were eating. The skilled Athenian seamen were overwhelmed. Athens' lifeline to the Black Sea, along which had flowed grain, fish, iron, and timber, was cut. Starving, Athens fell in 404, a naval giant paradoxically toppled by a land power.

The Spartans were urged by their allies to kill all the men of Athens. They refused, for they remembered Marathon.

THE SUN'S LAST GLINT touched the Parthenon, and evening shadows fell across Athens as I entered the Agora. Here one thinks of Socrates, stifling in the oppressive air of postwar Athens. Enemies finally answered his probing questions with a charge of "corrupting the minds of the young." In 399 B.C., a 70-year-old veteran of the very war that had so sadly changed his city—Pericles' city—he was sentenced to die. Friends offered escape, but he would not break the laws of his beloved polis even though they were used against him. Indeed he welcomed the hemlock; it would set his soul free.

"The sun is still upon the mountains . . . no need to hurry," implored a companion. But, Plato tells us, he "quite calmly, and with no sign of distaste . . . drained the cup."

Through Plato and Aristotle, his light kept burning—as did that of Athens. She bowed to Hellenic unity under Philip of Macedonia, who looked upon her as the "Theater of Glory." In 337, she sent delegates to the congress of states at Corinth, where Philip preached his crusade against Asia. Athens' brilliance touched Philip's son through his tutor, Aristotle. The young man then set out to conquer and to illumine the entire world. His name: Alexander.

LINKED BY A GOLDEN AGE, these men lived Athens' triumph and tragedy. Herodotus (lower) traveled widely seeking causes of East-West conflict and recounted the Persian Wars "so . . . the past may not be blotted out . . . by time." Dubious claims he annotated with "I do not believe it."

Athens lost a general and the world gained a historian when Thucydides (upper) was exiled for losing a battle in the Peloponnesian War. Taking a leaf from Herodotus, he recorded that war "as a possession for all time." He depicted the infamy of Alcibiades, whose siren song of Syracusan conquest became an Athenian dirge. An aristocratic playboy, Alcibiades (center) defected to Sparta and then to Persia before rejoining Athens.

Crammed into Syracusan quarries (opposite), 7,000 survivors of Athens' proud 40,000 faced death or slavery. But Greek masters freed some who charmed them with Euripides' verses!

The World of Alexander

In a dogged 25,000-mile quest Helen and Frank Schreider follow from start to finish Alexander the Great's

Epic March to the Ends of the Earth

USK DROPPED SWIFTLY over Delphi. The springtime sun slanted across the valley, highlighting the ruins of the ancient treasuries and the theater, splaying fingers of shadow from the columns of the Temple of Apollo. When the last tourist departed, Helen and I slipped into the enclosure. As darkness fell and moonlight filtered through wind-riffled pines, we settled back among the stones and let our imaginations re-create a centuries-old drama. It is the year 336 B.C. A blond, beardless young man hastens unannounced toward the Oracle, long famed for its prophecies. He brushes aside outraged priests — the day is unfavorable for oracles — and demands a revelation of the seeress, through whom Apollo speaks. She refuses, but the youth drags her into the temple. "My son," she cries at last, "thou art invincible!"

Aral Sea

Amu Darya

(Oxus)

U. S. S. R.

CHINA

Alexander weds Roxane, daughter
of Sogdianan nobleman, 327 B.C.

• Tashkent

Leninabad

Khodzhent
Alexandria Eschate

Samarkand
Maracanda

SOGDIANA

A S I A

PPE

Meshed

Balkh
Bactra-Zariaspa   Mazar-i-Sharif

Khawak Pass
11,650

Chitral
Ayun

Indus

KASHMIR

HINDU KUSH

Kamdesh

BACTRIA

Nawa Pass
6,000

Lawarai Pass
10,230

Dir

HIMALAYAS

Kabul

GANDHARA

Herat
Alexandria Areion

Khyber Pass
3,500

Peshawar

Taxila

Mangla Dam

Attock

AFGHANISTAN

Ghazni
Alexandria

Bucephala

Beas

Alexandria
Kandahar

Jhelum

Chenab

Alexandria Prophthasia

Qala-i-Kang

Ravi

Harappa

Battle of the Jhelum, 326 B.C.

(PERSIA)

P A K I S T A N

Indus

I N D I A

BALUCHISTAN

Mohenjo-Daro

Gumbaz

Pura
Iranshahr

Bampur

Bela

ndar Abbas

Karachi

Probable coastline
in Alexander's time

ROUTE OF NEARCHUS

Arabian Sea

Alexander's fleet sails for home, 325 B.C.

To rule well, first be ruled, Aristotle taught a royal pupil

That is all the answer he desires, Alexander replies in the account by the Greek biographer Plutarch.

A new king on a shaky throne, 20-year-old Alexander of Macedonia well knew the psychological advantage of a favorable response from the Oracle. For the next 13 years he fought to make that prediction come true. He ventured farther and won more than any conqueror before him, casting a giant's shadow both in history and in legend as Alexander the Great.

IN THE MIDDLE of the fourth century B.C. the Persian Empire stretched from Asia Minor to India, from Egypt to what is now the U.S.S.R. It was the greatest empire the world had yet seen. A century and a half had passed since Persia's hordes had invaded Greece and burned Athens. Though the Persians had been driven back to Asia Minor, Greek militants still preached vengeance. But war demanded unity and Greece remained fragmented in rival city-states, exhausted by the Peloponnesian War.

Into the vacuum rode Philip II from the northern kingdom of Macedonia, intent on uniting Greece and invading Persia. A master in the art of war, he developed the celebrated Macedonian phalanx—rank upon rank of infantrymen with shields closely joined and spears more than twice as long as those of their foes. Shock troops—skilled horsemen of Thessaly and Macedonia—flanked the solid phalanxes.

As Philip rolled south, the Greeks resisted. In Athens orators denounced the northerner; Demosthenes' eloquent

FATHER OF LOGIC, *Aristotle went to Pella at Philip's request to teach his son Alexander how to live "a noble life." The lad absorbed politics, science, a love of Homer's epics—and perhaps lighter lessons. "The flute," once wrote the sage, "is not an instrument which has a good moral effect; it is too exciting."*

Aristotle (to whom tradition wrongly gives a lisp) split science into specialties that still stand. Biology intrigued him most; from Asia Alexander sent him plants and animals to study. Aristotle saw a porpoise born, decided it was no fish; 2,000 years later science proved him right.

Philip's Macedonian capital slumbers under a Greek town as diggers bare a suburb (above, left). There dog and hunters bag a stag in a pebble mosaic (opposite) signed "Gnosis made it."

thunder still echoes in our word "philippic." The decisive clash came in 338 at Chaeronea, northwest of Athens. Philip commanded on the right wing while his 18-year-old son Alexander led a cavalry charge from the left. They wheeled and chewed up the Greek center. All Greece save Sparta now submitted, and Philip was free to lead a united force against Persia. When an assassin's knife cut him down, young Alexander made his father's dream his own.

What kind of man was this Alexander, whose trail linked three continents, who could boldly defy—as he had at Delphi—sacred conventions of his time?

A hero-worshiper, he was himself a hero on a grander scale than even Homer conceived. The single decade that brought him from youth to death took him beyond the known boundaries of civilization. Though his epic empire broke up in less time than it had taken him to win it, in death he achieved the ultimate ambition of his hectic life: He joined the demigods in the realm of legend.

Leading one of history's most aggressive fighting forces, he conquered Asia Minor, circled the eastern Mediterranean, seized its maritime provinces, and thus neutralized the Persian fleet. In a series of brilliant battles he destroyed the power of Darius III, the Persian king, and took his lands and titles for himself.

He might have stopped then, rich in glory and plunder. But his thirst for fame and his questing spirit drove him on. For seven more years he fought his way from mountain to mountain, from city to city, all the way to the valley of the Indus, as his troops turned sullen and mutinous. In time he brought them back to Babylon, which saw his death and the breakup of his subjugated but unreconstructed

HELEN AND FRANK SCHREIDER, NATIONAL GEOGRAPHIC STAFF (ALSO FAR LEFT). BRONZE BUST OF ARISTOTLE, NATIONAL MUSEUM, NAPLES; SCALA

empire. He had conquered all. He had unified nothing. Yet the tumult of his passage had stirred together widely scattered cultures.

Here was our quarry: an incandescent spirit combining unequaled leadership with courage to confound every adversary and an occasional brutality to puzzle historians from his time to ours. Conditioned for conquest by Philip, schooled in logic by Aristotle himself, inclined toward recklessness by his violent and passionate mother Olympias, Alexander was prepared, as perhaps no other man has ever been, to dominate his world.

STATELY RHYTHMS *of Macedonia stir a memory of Alexander, whose name lives in the legends of every land he crossed. Macedonian women, myth says, rushed into a seesaw battle to help their men; a grateful Alexander allowed them to adopt this helmet-shaped headdress. Matrons wear black, maidens white.*

Helen and I would seek his track in the mountains of Macedonia, the deserts of Egypt, the snowy Hindu Kush, the steppes of central Asia, and the wastes of Baluchistan. In a blue Land-Rover, named Bucephalus after his favorite mount, we drove from Delphi to Pella, Philip's capital near Thessaloniki, where Alexander spent much of his youth.

Nea (New) Pella crowns the slope where the ancient city stood. In fields of wheat, cotton, and tobacco, excavations have revealed columned palaces and brilliant mosaics. Created with the wealth Alexander won, they reflect the life he lived. In one, Alexander with field cap and cape fights a lion. In others, a charioteer quells wild-eyed horses, and hunters attack a stag. "These may be the palaces of Alexander's generals, built soon after his death," our guide told us. Philip's palace may lie on the west side of the present village.

At Pella's school we watched children carrying bright balloons in a relay race; many were blond and fair-skinned, as he was. Quintus Curtius Rufus, Roman biographer of Alexander, describes him as strong and well-proportioned, though not tall, with endurance "beyond belief."

Near us a boy galloped his horse through the green spring wheat. He rode bareback, as did Alexander, and the horse had a white blaze on his forehead, as did Bucephalus. We thought of that day when Alexander, barely in his teens, tamed the fiery stallion, whose name means "bullheaded." The horse had been offered for sale to Philip, but when trainer after trainer failed to mount the wild, nervous creature, Philip despaired of him.

"I can manage this horse," said Alexander, turning Bucephalus toward the sun. The horse, no longer aware of his own frightening shadow, calmed immediately. The prince mounted and mastered him. With tears of pride Philip cried out: "O my son, look thee out a kingdom worthy of thyself, for Macedonia is too little."

Alexander left Pella on a bright spring day in 334 B.C., leading 30,000 foot soldiers and 5,000 cavalry across fields ablaze with yellow mustard and blood-red poppies. Supplies followed, and with them botanists, geographers, and professional "steppers" to measure distances, for Alexander went forth not only to conquer but also to study, survey, and understand the new world he was entering. He plunged into his venture with the exuberance of youth and the confidence of a god. He never returned.

Alexander covered the 300 miles from Pella to the Dardanelles in 20 days and bivouacked at Sestos on the western shore. From a ridge above the town we looked across into

Asian Turkey. Below, olive groves shelved steeply down to the straits Alexander knew as the Hellespont, Greek Sea.

As his troops boarded the galleys that would carry them across to the enemy domain, Persian satraps mustered an army strengthened by Greek mercenaries at the Granicus River, two days' march inland. Alexander left the ferrying to his general, Parmenion. Taking the helm of a galley himself, he steered south to Troy. His most treasured possession was a copy of Homer's *Iliad*, given him by Aristotle. Alexander deemed it the "perfect portable treasure of all military virtue and knowledge" and slept with it beside his dagger under his pillow.

His journey to Troy became a plea for favor from his hero Achilles and a ploy to obtain a potent symbol of good luck. Legend tells us that he exchanged part of his own armor for a sacred shield from the Trojan War, Greece's first recorded invasion of Asia, nearly a thousand years earlier. Then he headed north to meet the enemy.

THE GRANICUS RIVER, today the Kocabas, waters a region of rolling farmland. In lowland fields baggy-trousered women stoop to plant seedling rice. On the hills spring wheat gleams like wind-rippled silk, and fat cattle graze in lush pasture. Drained by irrigation, the river flows in a brown trickle. Alexander found it a torrent, the Persian army spread along its bank near the present town of Biga. Parmenion urged caution.

"I should disgrace the Hellespont should I fear the Granicus," Alexander declared.

Shouting for his men to follow, he spurred his horse into the river. Arrows and spears rained down on them, but the speed and fury of the assault carried the Macedonians across. Persian horsemen rushed the Companions, Alexander's elite cavalry, hoping to slay the king and end the fight. Conspicuous in white-plumed helmet and splendid buckler, Alexander charged ahead. He met the concerted attack of two nobles, lost part of his helmet to one's battle ax, was saved from the other's sword thrust by his friend Black Cleitus.

The Persians broke and fled.

Victory at the Granicus gave Alexander a firm foothold in Asia. The main body of the Persian army, still more than

EASTWARD TO EMPIRE: *The Hellespont behind him, 22-year-old Alexander splashes onto Asian soil. Landing uncontested, he flung his spear into the ground, signifying intent to humble Persian might. His start in 334 B.C. was auspicious. Armed with a sacred shield from Troy, he led his men to victory at the nearby Granicus River.*

PAINTING FOR NATIONAL GEOGRAPHIC BY TOM LOVELL

1,000 miles to the east, posed no immediate threat. But the Persian fleet, numerically superior to the Greek navy, controlled the seas. Alexander determined to break Persia's sea power by overrunning its maritime provinces. He turned south toward the Mediterranean.

Spreading word that he came as a liberator, not as a conqueror, Alexander found many of the cities, established centuries earlier by Greek immigrants, ripe for revolt. At Ephesus the people stoned the Persian officials and welcomed the Macedonians. In city after city Alexander restored democratic government and remitted taxes. When asked why he did not reap more tribute from so rich an empire, he replied, "I hate the gardener who cuts to the root the vegetables of which he ought to cull the leaves."

With hardly a skirmish he marched to Miletus, the leading city of Ionia. There a large Persian garrison held out to await help from the Persian fleet, but the Greek fleet arrived first and blockaded the harbor.

We found it difficult to imagine any fleet at Miletus. The twisting Maeander (Menderes) River has silted up the bay and extended the coastline until even from the hill above the ruins of the theater, built about A.D. 100, we saw only a blue glint of the sea that once lapped the stones at our feet.

After a brief siege Alexander took Miletus, then stormed

198

the large Persian garrison at Halicarnassus. Within seven months the Macedonian army controlled the coast.

All through southern Turkey the past forms a backdrop for the present. A road now follows the rugged shore where Alexander marched. It passes through Izmir, ancient Smyrna, where the fragrance of roasting lamb pervades vine-garlanded streets and the swoosh of jets counterpoints the gentle clip-clop of horse-drawn carriages at sunset. South of Izmir the road winds past rock coves where fishing villages drowse in the sun and sponge divers spread their pungent harvest to dry.

We camped beneath cliffs honeycombed with tombs, and in pine forests beside streams flowing past ancient walls. Near an old Greek theater at Kas we listened to a *saz* player twang melodies on his two-stringed instrument. At Aspendus Turkish actors in a Roman theater performed Sophocles' masterpiece, *Oedipus Rex*.

Near Phaselis, where Alexander rested his troops, a boy hitched a ride with us. "I am studying English," he offered.

"Perhaps you can help us," I said. "Is there a market nearby where we can buy some food?"

He nodded. "You can get some at my village."

Soon he signaled me to a stop, and I followed him along a path between stone-walled compounds. We entered a courtyard where a girl milked a cow under an apricot tree and a woman stooped over a round earthen oven.

"My home," the boy announced.

"But I thought we were going to a market."

"Please. Wait." He vanished into the wooden house. Soon he was back with eggs, tomatoes, peppers, and green onions. His mother brought a hot disk of whole-wheat bread and a bowl of yogurt. I reached for my wallet.

"No," he said, "you are my guest."

My young friend helped me carry the food back to the Land-Rover. We found it surrounded by villagers. A rugged, mustachioed soldier opened a path for us. As we drove off, he handed Helen a rose.

SPRING FOUND ALEXANDER marching to Gordium to rendezvous with fresh troops. We climbed from the coast and followed his route across the high Anatolian plateau, where today thousands of acres of poppies make Turkey one of the leading producers of medicinal opium.

Women moved among the shoulder-high plants, harvesting the drug. They slit the waxy green pods and scraped the dried juice from older slits into wooden trays. One of the

Coast of wonders sired brilliant minds, mighty monuments

On Asia Minor's fertile doorstep Greek culture bloomed centuries before Alexander arrived. Migrating across the Aegean about 1000 B.C., Greek settlers, spurred by contact with Near Eastern civilizations, fathered Hellenic philosophy and science. They learned to shape monuments of marble while motherland Greeks still worshiped in wooden shrines.

Here rose three of the Seven Wonders of the World. Alexander gazed on the great colonnaded tomb of King Mausolus—immortalized in "mausoleum"—at Halicarnassus, now under modern Bodrum (above). Crusaders mined the stones to build the castle of St. Peter, which still commands the harbor. A 100-foot Colossus—the sun god

Helios in bronze—guarded nearby Rhodes in the 3d century B.C. Ancients also ranked Ephesus' Temple of Artemis as a Wonder.

Greeks in Asia spun epics and sang short poems set to music of the lyre. Lyrics of Sappho burn with passion for her schoolgirls on the isle of Lesbos. Smyrna, today Izmir (below), claims Homer.

So does Chios. Halicarnassus sired Herodotus, Father of History. Anaxagoras of Clazomenae brought Ionian philosophy to Periclean Athens. Thales of Miletus was "first to inscribe a right-angled triangle in a circle, whereupon he sacrificed an ox." Pythagoras of Samos gave his name to a geometric theorem. Physicians still swear by Hippocrates of Cos.

On an eagle rock Alexander's successors built Pergamum, regal city rich in sculpture and learning. It processed skins for writing—the charta pergamena we know as parchment. In the 2d century B.C. bizarre Attalus III, who grew his own poison plants, willed the kingdom to Rome.

women broke open a pod filled with tiny white seeds and offered it to Helen.

"No, thank you," Helen said, stepping back.

Amused, the woman opened her kerchief-wrapped lunch and pulled out a loaf of bread. It was sprinkled with black. "*Aynı*—the same," she laughed. When dried, the white specks become the black poppy seeds of the baker.

At Gordium a few mounds and crumbled walls mark the site where fabled King Midas once held court. Here—so goes the story—stood a famous chariot, its pole tied with an intricate knot. Whoever could untie it would be lord of Asia. Alexander severed the knot with one sword stroke.

From Ancyra—present Ankara, capital of Turkey—the young conqueror's route led us southeast across Cappadocia to the Cilician Gates in the Taurus Mountains. Today, horns blaring, buses and trucks try to drive three abreast on the new two-lane road through the pass. In Alexander's day the defile was so narrow that two loaded camels could not travel it side by side.

Properly defended, the pass could have kept Alexander from reaching the coastal plains along the northeast corner of the Mediterranean. But he stormed it in a night attack and marched on to Issus, near the present Syrian border.

In a hovering helicopter Helen and I looked out on the battlefield of Issus, where Alexander first confronted Darius in person. There, on a narrow plain beside the sea, the smaller Greek force outmaneuvered the larger Persian army.

Bristling with spears, the Macedonian infantry drove forward. Alexander and the Companions charged at the Persian horsemen. The enemy front collapsed and Alexander raced on toward Darius himself. The King of Kings turned and fled, leaving behind his family and harem.

That night, as Alexander dined in the opulence of Darius' tent, he remarked, "This, it seems, is

ANATOLIAN WOMEN *pitch wheat amid cones of Cappadocia in Turkey's Goreme Valley. The proud province never completely bowed to Alexander; his men had to fight to keep Cappadocian communications open. Nature honed the region's spires from volcanic debris; in them ancients hollowed homes with stone stoves and divans. Refuges for early Christians, they now shelter Moslem farmers.*

HELEN AND FRANK SCHREIDER, NATIONAL GEOGRAPHIC STAFF

To spur his army Alexander recounted feats of Xenophon and the Ten Thousand

FORCED to fight at Issus, Alexander's men faced a foe stronger than Persia: fear. He set before them an example of Greek spirit braving Persia's overwhelming odds 68 years before. Xenophon, disciple of Socrates, warrior, gentleman farmer, essayist, and historian, immortalized it in his *Anabasis*, "the march up country."

Xenophon joined 10,000 Greek mercenaries, hungry veterans of the Peloponnesian War, who hired on with a Persian army in 401 B.C. Cyrus the Younger led them from Sardis, lusting for the throne of his brother Artaxerxes II. The two clashed at Cunaxa, near Babylon. Cyrus fell, his army broke up, and the Greeks were stranded amid foes 1,500 miles from home.

Refusing to lay down arms, they headed up the Tigris toward Trapezus, Greek colony on the Black Sea, long sailed by grain ships. Artaxerxes' forces hounded them, lured their officers into truce talks and slew them. Leaderless, demoralized, the Greeks drifted toward surrender. "Rely upon our arms," Xenophon pleaded; "we have—the gods willing—many fair hopes of deliverance." Just then a soldier sneezed—a lucky omen. Xenophon was elected general. Instead of a mob, startled Persians now met an army, pledged to fight for the common good.

On they marched, Persians at their heels. Slingers met cavalry attacks but aimed only at riders; Greeks later sat the riderless mounts. When arrows dwindled, Greeks taunted Persian archers at long range, then harvested shafts that fell short. Seized village larders filled their kettles. On through lands of the Kurds, on through the mountains of Armenia Xenophon led. But not by decree; each plan faced a vote in this polis in motion, this "epitome of Athens set adrift in the center of Asia."

Fierce tribesmen rolled boulders on them in narrow passes. Snowdrifts mired them; some went snowblind or lost toes to frostbite. Xenophon shared their trials, once quit his horse to march in a grumbling soldier's place.

One day shouts rang from the van: "*Thalassa! Thalassa!*"—"The sea! The sea!" Four wintry months from Cunaxa, survivors embraced each other, goal in sight, their foe shamed by an outnumbered band of Greeks.

As Alexander's tale ended, his outnumbered men "crowded round . . . and cheering him to the echo bade him lead on without delay."

royalty." But of all the spoils, he kept for himself only a jeweled casket in which to carry his treasured *Iliad*.

Alexander continued south between mountains and Mediterranean to Tyre in Lebanon. He found this key naval base and commercial center a proud, high-walled city on an island half a mile from shore. He left it in humble ruins on a peninsula. When the Tyrians refused him entry, Alexander built a 200-foot-wide mole, or causeway, to the island.

After seven months of laboring on the mole under a rain of stones and arrows, the Macedonians rolled their catapults within range of the east wall. Shipborne rams battered the south wall. Tyre fell, and the Persian fleet, left without a port, became Alexander's.

Drifting sand has widened Alexander's mole, and an asphalt road leads across it to the harbor where once Tyrian galleys anchored. Small boats puff black diesel fumes into the still air. Fishermen mend blue nylon nets on the quay or sip coffee and smoke water pipes while they listen to wailing music on the radio.

At Tyre Alexander received a message from Darius, suing for peace. Darius offered one of his daughters in marriage, 10,000 talents (a weight of gold worth 300 million dollars today), and all the territory west of the Euphrates, one-third of his empire. Alexander consulted his staff. "Were I Alexander," Parmenion advised, "I would accept."

"So would I, were I Parmenion," Alexander replied. He was now determined to take all of Darius' empire. Continuing down the coast he found the Egyptians ready to accept

"Fighting among the foremost . . .
he got a sword-wound in the thigh"

Plutarch

Braving javelins at Issus, bareheaded Alexander gallops lance in hand toward Darius, who flees in his chariot (opposite). Threading the Cilician Gates, where headlights now paint a river of fire (left), Alexander had pushed along the narrow coastal plain toward Syria. When Persians poured from a pass at his rear, he wheeled toward Issus.

His cavalry pawed the dust at each flank; phalanxes held the center, with ranks so tight that long spears from the fifth bristled beyond the first. Trained to stand firm while other units maneuvered, phalangites often heard taunts as "men who do not fight." Here they swept in with the lightly wounded Alexander to help rout the horde hemmed in by hill and sea. Darius escaped through the dusk-darkened pass. Road and rail now thread it; American jets howl past a 12th-century fort guarding this Turkish gateway to the plain of Issus.

HELEN AND FRANK SCHREIDER, NATIONAL GEOGRAPHIC STAFF. OPPOSITE: POMPEII MOSAIC IN NATIONAL MUSEUM, NAPLES, COPIED FROM LOST 4TH CENTURY B.C. GREEK PAINTING; SCALA

STORMING DEFIANT TYRE, *main base of the Persian fleet, Macedonians exploit a breached wall in 332 B.C. When Alexander started a causeway to the island-city, defenders harried his workers with missiles, fire ships, even frogmen who cut underwater cables. Floating catapults and battering rams finally cracked the citadel. Here, shielded from burning arrows by a hide tent, spearmen reach the opening and drop a long gangplank. They slaughtered 8,000 Tyrians, sold 30,000 into slavery. The causeway, widened by sand drifts, still links Tyre to the Lebanese mainland (above).*

him as Pharaoh. At Memphis he sacrificed to the gods and gazed on the great pyramids, one of the Seven Wonders of the World. Then he sailed down the Nile to the sea. At a place "admirable for . . . a city" he founded Alexandria.

HELEN AND I stored our Land-Rover in Beirut and flew to Cairo. Joined there by Fauzy Abd El Hamid, a jovial Egyptian journalist, we drove toward Alexandria on the delta road. On both sides spread fields green with millet, wheat, cabbages, alfalfa, and cotton. Then, across a salt lake, we saw the tall buildings of the greatest and most enduring of the many cities Alexander founded.

For more than a thousand years, through Greek, Roman, Christian, and Moslem occupation, Alexandria's universities, libraries, and museums drew scholars from all over the East. Though still a favorite resort of Egyptians, the city has lost its old international flavor. As one Alexandria businessman told us: "Now Cairo is the hub of Egypt. Alexandria is like an empty stage."

The Greek historian Arrian relates that while Alexander was laying out his city he felt "an overmastering desire" to visit Ammon, the famous Oracle at Siwa Oasis, some 300 miles southwest. With considerable difficulty we located a taxi driver willing to tackle the desert trip in his Mercedes. He sighed with relief when the date palms, ponds, and green fields of Siwa blossomed from behind a butte.

We found the oasis overflowing with Egyptian engineers and social workers bent on instilling national consciousness in the long-isolated desert people. Teachers had even persuaded a few fathers to send their daughters to school.

Blue-shrouded matrons fled from our cameras into the warren of mud-walled alleys. But the maidens were more cooperative. Most of them were under twelve and had been collecting trousseaus since they were five or six; girls marry young at Siwa. Each wore a silver charm on a chain around her neck as a symbol of virginity.

One group of them was sitting in the shade of a date palm, singing. We asked Fauzy to translate. He grinned. "It's a calypso, Siwa style. Few taxis ever come here. The girls think it's great." The song went:

> We won't marry the boy with a camel
> Nor even the one with two donkeys.
> We're going to marry the boy who comes
> To take us away in a Mercedes.

When Alexander arrived at Siwa, he was greeted by the chief priest of Ammon, or Amun, an Egyptian deity whom the Greeks equated with Zeus. The priest addressed Alexander as the "Son of Ammon" and led him to the Oracle.

"He set out for Ammon . . . hoping to learn about himself" Arrian

Acclaimed as Pharaoh in Egypt, Alexander plunged into the Libyan Desert to query the Oracle of Ammon at Siwa Oasis (upper). Searing sands had swallowed 50,000 Persians on a similar trek,

HELEN AND FRANK SCHREIDER, NATIONAL GEOGRAPHIC STAFF

but Alexander's legendary luck held. Rain slaked raging thirsts. Ptolemy, the Macedonian general who later ruled this land, told how two talking serpents led the way across drifting dunes.

From the Oracle Alexander sought word of his future and—some said—of his past, for his mother claimed that Zeus, not Philip, had fathered him. He "received the answer his soul desired." Horned Alexander, on a Thracian coin of the third century B.C., *reflects belief in his kinship with ram-horned Ammon, whom Greeks identified with Zeus. Time has toppled Ammon's temple. Remote Siwa harvests its dates, and an eight-year-old, soon to wed, stitches her trousseau (opposite).*

From the inner sanctuary of the temple priests brought forth a golden bark bearing a ram-headed figure of the god adorned with precious stones. In the movements of the figure's head and body the priests read the answers to Alexander's questions. Though he never disclosed those answers, he left Siwa well satisfied. Word spread that he had been told he would rule all lands.

Alexander returned to Tyre, rested his troops, then marched swiftly northeast to where Darius waited with a reinforced army. We also left Egypt and, once again in our Land-Rover, took up the trail across the rich, rolling wheatland that today makes Syria one of the few Arab countries capable of feeding itself. It was a fertile land in Alexander's day too. But he found it burned black by the Persians in an unsuccessful effort to delay his troops.

The Iraqi army was more successful in delaying us. Barely inside Iraq, near Mosul, we were stopped by a roadblock of soldiers. This was the country of the Kurds, the fiercely

209

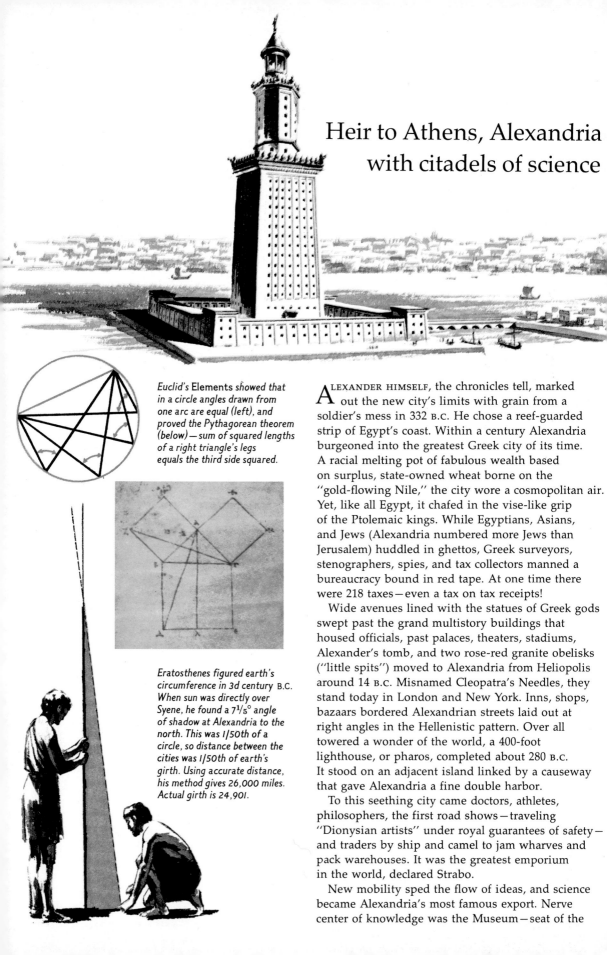

Heir to Athens, Alexandria with citadels of science

Euclid's Elements showed that in a circle angles drawn from one arc are equal (left), and proved the Pythagorean theorem (below)—sum of squared lengths of a right triangle's legs equals the third side squared.

Eratosthenes figured earth's circumference in 3d century B.C. When sun was directly over Syene, he found a 7$\frac{1}{5}$° angle of shadow at Alexandria to the north. This was 1/50th of a circle, so distance between the cities was 1/50th of earth's girth. Using accurate distance, his method gives 26,000 miles. Actual girth is 24,901.

ALEXANDER HIMSELF, the chronicles tell, marked out the new city's limits with grain from a soldier's mess in 332 B.C. He chose a reef-guarded strip of Egypt's coast. Within a century Alexandria burgeoned into the greatest Greek city of its time. A racial melting pot of fabulous wealth based on surplus, state-owned wheat borne on the "gold-flowing Nile," the city wore a cosmopolitan air. Yet, like all Egypt, it chafed in the vise-like grip of the Ptolemaic kings. While Egyptians, Asians, and Jews (Alexandria numbered more Jews than Jerusalem) huddled in ghettos, Greek surveyors, stenographers, spies, and tax collectors manned a bureaucracy bound in red tape. At one time there were 218 taxes—even a tax on tax receipts!

Wide avenues lined with the statues of Greek gods swept past the grand multistory buildings that housed officials, past palaces, theaters, stadiums, Alexander's tomb, and two rose-red granite obelisks ("little spits") moved to Alexandria from Heliopolis around 14 B.C. Misnamed Cleopatra's Needles, they stand today in London and New York. Inns, shops, bazaars bordered Alexandrian streets laid out at right angles in the Hellenistic pattern. Over all towered a wonder of the world, a 400-foot lighthouse, or pharos, completed about 280 B.C. It stood on an adjacent island linked by a causeway that gave Alexandria a fine double harbor.

To this seething city came doctors, athletes, philosophers, the first road shows—traveling "Dionysian artists" under royal guarantees of safety— and traders by ship and camel to jam wharves and pack warehouses. It was the greatest emporium in the world, declared Strabo.

New mobility sped the flow of ideas, and science became Alexandria's most famous export. Nerve center of knowledge was the Museum—seat of the

lit the Mediterranean
and a wonder of the world

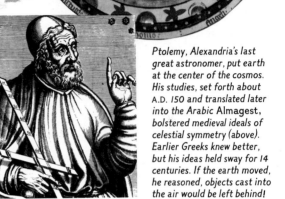

Ptolemy, Alexandria's last great astronomer, put earth at the center of the cosmos. His studies, set forth about A.D. 150 and translated later into the Arabic Almagest, bolstered medieval ideals of celestial symmetry (above). Earlier Greeks knew better, but his ideas held sway for 14 centuries. If the earth moved, he reasoned, objects cast into the air would be left behind!

Muses—built by Ptolemy I. Great men learned and taught at the observatory, botanical and zoological gardens, the famed Library with its half-million scrolls, the schools of medicine, mathematics, and astronomy. Here Jewish scholars translated the Old Testament into Greek; Aristarchus of Samothrace collated the Homeric texts; Aristarchus of Samos deduced that the earth spins on its axis and turns round the sun; and Hipparchus of Nicaea divided the year into 365¼ days. Archimedes (page 101) studied here, and here came Herophilus, who dissected condemned prisoners and held that the brain, not the heart as Aristotle had taught, is the site of intelligence; Eratosthenes, head of the Library, whose description of the globe hinted at a "new world"; and Euclid, "most successful textbook writer" in history, whose *Elements* of geometry were taught 2,000 years.

Truly a city of the world, this shining cosmopolis enlightened Rome, nurtured early Christian scholars, enriched ages to come.

Marvelous machines of Alexandria evolved as toys. Hero hooked a windmill to an organ (right) "so the pipes will play when the wind blows," but centuries passed before windmills did real work. Archimedes held engineering vulgar, yet fathered devices that still serve. His endless screw (below) lifts water to fields for Egyptian farmers (left). At Syracuse in 212 B.C. his ingenious grapples and "burning glasses" to set ships afire with sunrays raised havoc with the fleet of the Romans, who slew him. Perceiving the enormous potential force of the lever and fulcrum, he had boasted: "Give me a place to stand, and I will move the world."

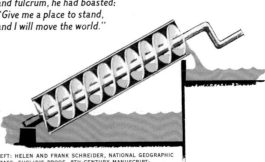

LEFT: HELEN AND FRANK SCHREIDER, NATIONAL GEOGRAPHIC STAFF. EUCLID'S PROOF, 8TH-CENTURY MANUSCRIPT; BODLEIAN LIBRARY, OXFORD. ASTROLOGICAL CHART, C. 1247; BIBLIOTHÈQUE NATIONALE, PARIS. PTOLEMY FROM BETTMANN ARCHIVE. HERO'S WIND ORGAN, COURTESY VALENTINO BOMPIANI

independent tribesmen of the highlands. "My men have orders to search every car for arms," an Iraqi officer explained. "Mind you, there's no problem now. Still, we have to be careful." He escorted us to Mosul, where we were given a pass and—to assure that we would have no trouble with the "pacified" Kurds—an armed escort to Faysh Khabur, where Alexander crossed the Tigris to face Darius.

The Persian king's best hope of stopping the seemingly irresistible Macedonians lay in his scythed chariots. To give them every chance, he leveled the plain near Gaugamela, east of Mosul. When Alexander saw the freshly prepared ground he thought Darius had undermined it to trap the Macedonian cavalry.

We climbed a knoll at Gaugamela. Below us flocks of sheep churned the dust into a brown cloud. To the north lay the long, low hill from which Alexander may have first seen the campfires of the Persian host. Plutarch describes the voices coming from the Persian camp as "the distant roaring of a vast ocean."

Alarmed at the enemy multitude, Parmenion proposed a night attack. Alexander would have none of it. "I will not steal a victory," he countered. He was not boasting. He wanted to break the Persians' fighting spirit in a head-on battle; a surprise attack might give Darius an excuse for losing. Alexander and his army got a good night's sleep. By contrast, the Persians, fearing precisely what Parmenion had advised, kept watch all night and faced the dawn weary from lack of sleep.

Alexander marched his phalanx obliquely to the right, throwing the Persian line off balance. Darius countered with cavalry charges, then loosed his chariots, curved blades flashing on their wheels. According to plan, Alexander's ranks parted. Unable to turn quickly, the chariots raced through, and the Macedonians dragged horses and drivers to the ground. Darius again launched his cavalry, exposing a gap in his line. Ever alert for such an opportunity, Alexander formed the Companions into a wedge and plunged straight for Darius. The Persian king, seeing his guard of Greek mercenaries and Indian elephants crumble, abandoned his chariot and weapons and fled on horseback.

Elsewhere the battle was going badly for the Macedonians. Outflanking some units, overrunning others, the Persians seemed to be winning the day—until they learned that Darius had deserted them. As at Issus, Persian resistance collapsed.

The battle won, Alexander's weary troops may have thought the war over. But

as long as Darius remained free, Alexander meant to pursue him. The fleeing monarch had gotten a good start eastward into the mountains, and for the moment Alexander was content to wait. He marched south to Babylon on the Euphrates, whose people surrendered almost eagerly, and rested his troops for a month.

We found it difficult to evoke the glory of Babylon from what remains of it today. Walls that Herodotus described as more than 300 feet high, and so wide that two chariots abreast could race atop them, have vanished. The glazed tiles that adorned its buildings glisten in museums across the globe. The Hanging Gardens, another of the Seven Wonders of the World, are now mud-brick platforms devoid of a single blade of grass. But in the reduced-scale, beautifully reconstructed Ishtar Gate, a semblance of King Nebuchadnezzar's grandeur lives on.

While in Babylonia, Alexander appointed a Persian as governor, the first step in his plan to unite victors and vanquished in a stable empire. Then, eager to collect the treasures that waited in the coffers of central Persia, he set out toward what is today Iran.

The terrain we crossed in his pursuit could have changed little since he passed. Squat villages of sun-baked brick trembled in perspective-distorting heat waves. Clumps of grass loomed as large as trees. Camels walked on wavering legs above pool-like mirages.

For a while we paralleled a Bedouin wedding procession. The black-masked bride peered from a swaying shelter on her camel. When we stopped, the caravan leader galloped toward us. I slammed the Land-Rover into gear: Arabs are touchy when strangers look at their women, even from afar. But all he wanted was water.

HONEYMOON PALANQUIN *hides a Bedouin bride (right). Distorted by a mirage, the Iraqi caravan wobbles on liquid legs; heat waves mirror the bellies of the lead camels. Sweeping through Syria, Alexander pressed toward "wide and wasted country" for a showdown with Darius.*

"So they continued beating and battered, with no quarter given"

Arrian

We shared what we had. The caravan moved on. We followed, while I photographed from atop the moving Land-Rover. Suddenly the sheik unslung his rifle—and posed!

Alexander hurried on toward Persepolis, along the way collecting booty recorded by historians as 180,000 talents in coin and bullion, gold and silver vessels, jewels and rich furnishings. But greater treasure lay undiscovered beneath the land he plundered. Today drill rigs sprout from the eroded brown landscape. They pump more than five million barrels of crude oil a day, making Iran one of the largest producers in the Middle East.

Alexander and his men wintered in luxury at Persepolis, the splendid ceremonial capital of the Persian monarchs.

Encouraged by his drunken colleagues, Alexander burned the palaces of Xerxes in revenge against that king, who had put Athens to the torch 150 years before.

In spite of this act of epic vandalism Persepolis retains more of its original splendor than any other city on Alexander's route. In exquisite bas-reliefs, as crisp today as when they were first chiseled in stone, soldiers march across the walls in precise formation. Bulls and lions fight in stylized fury. And on the grand staircase of the Apadana, or audience hall, the people of ancient Persian provinces bring offerings in silent tribute.

Surely Alexander studied these reliefs with as much interest as we did. Half the peoples represented were already

SPEAR-STUDDED *phalanxes and charging horse squadrons dissolve into a melee as one of history's most decisive battles boils to a climax near Irbil (Arbela), Iraq, in 331 B.C. Facing scythed chariots and Persia's finest troops on a field of Darius' choice, Alexander routed the King of Kings, who continued fleeing to the end of his days.*

This crammed Renaissance canvas gives trees and heights to the dry plain of Gaugamela and includes the capture of Darius' family (at right), which occurred at the Battle of Issus.

"BATTLE OF ARBELA" BY JAN BRUEGEL, 1602, IN THE LOUVRE; GIRAUDON

TIME'S BACKWATER *buoys boatman in the Tigris-Euphrates marshes; rolled mats for trade nearly swamp his high-prowed* mashuf. *Sumerians, Babylonians, Persians, Arabs bred his tribe. Living in a world of reeds, the Madan make of 20-foot stalks vaulted homes Alexander would recognize.*

From Gaugamela his men swaggered south; opulent Babylon "pampered" them "for 34 days." Skirting the marshes, to Susa they sped, draining Darius' winter capital of some 50,000 talents of silver—perhaps $100 million today. Past mud-hut hamlets like the one above they marched in bitter cold to the Persian Gates, a strongly held pass in the Zagros range. Flanking maneuvers and a slashing attack panicked defenders, who "threw themselves over the cliffs." Ahead, easy prey, lay Persepolis.

subjugated. But to win all Persia, Alexander would have to conquer the rest. His greatest efforts were still to come.

I**N THE SPRING** of 330 B.C. Alexander marched north to Ecbatana, Persia's summer capital, now Hamadan. His object: the capture of Darius himself. But the Persian fled through the Caspian Gates, a pass over the Elburz Mountains. The Macedonian pursued him, averaging an extraordinary 36 miles a day. When he caught the straggling baggage train, he found Darius dead, murdered by his own disillusioned generals. King of Persia at last, Alexander marched to Zadracarta, modern Gorgan, to assume not only the title but the pomp of an Oriental monarch.

From Gorgan we plunged into the vast Turkoman steppe, stretching east of the Caspian Sea and north of the Elburz Mountains. The nomads' wicker-and-felt *yurts*—tents that looked like halved tennis balls—studded the undulating plain. Through the perpetual blanket of dust we occasionally glimpsed a ghostly horseman clad in flapping sheepskin, the living image of the nomads who once fought Alexander.

In the fourth century A.D. some unknown king built a 100-mile-long barrier to keep those nomads out. Medieval Persian poets attributed the wall to Alexander; parts of it still stand; Turkomans call it (Continued on page 223)

DRUNK WITH WINE AND RICHES, *victors sack sacred Persepolis.*
Persia's kings ruled elsewhere, came here to dazzle gods with splendor,
to win favor with rites that echo in folk festivals today. "Avenge Greece,"
cried Alexander, hurling the first firebrand. Cedar beams blaze while looters
drag out treasures, even rip silver rings from drapes. "As soon as sleep
had restored his senses," wrote Curtius, Alexander "regretted what he had done."

PAINTING FOR NATIONAL GEOGRAPHIC BY TOM LOVELL

Persia, "long steeped in luxury," drew strength from more than gold

The treasures of Persepolis, said Alexander, would burden 5,000 camels and 20,000 mules. Chroniclers tell of heaped bullion, regal robes, "furniture designed not for use but for luxurious display," even a golden grapevine fruited with gems. Such spoils freighted the conquerors' wagons, overflowed their homeland's coffers — thus sparking a runaway inflation — or vanished under the dust of ages.

In 1877, villagers near the Amu Darya, Turkistan river known to ancients as the Oxus, began to peddle finds from a site none would disclose. Experts dubbed the hoard the Oxus Treasure, dated most of it to Persia's prime in the two centuries before Alexander.

Now these and other masterworks evoke an empire that outshone any the world had known. Pious Mede parades on a plaque of gold; his forebears ruled early Persians — and wore history's first long trousers. Winged ibex, a vase handle in silver and gold, recalls a demonic beast feared by men of Parsa, the district whence Persians under Cyrus the Great seized the Medes' empire in 550 B.C. Darius I extended it to the edges of India and Europe.

Satraps, or governors, ruled the realm's 20 provinces, collected tribute, kept order. Inspectors — "eyes and ears of the king" — kept tabs lest satraps gain the power to revolt. Roads, built for wheels, linked the empire.

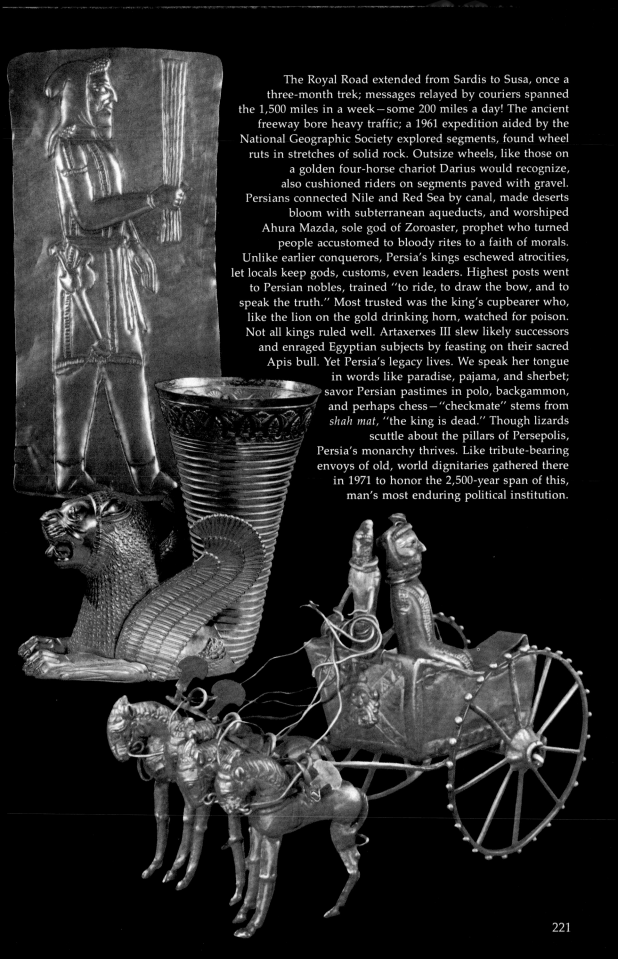

The Royal Road extended from Sardis to Susa, once a three-month trek; messages relayed by couriers spanned the 1,500 miles in a week—some 200 miles a day! The ancient freeway bore heavy traffic; a 1961 expedition aided by the National Geographic Society explored segments, found wheel ruts in stretches of solid rock. Outsize wheels, like those on a golden four-horse chariot Darius would recognize, also cushioned riders on segments paved with gravel. Persians connected Nile and Red Sea by canal, made deserts bloom with subterranean aqueducts, and worshiped Ahura Mazda, sole god of Zoroaster, prophet who turned people accustomed to bloody rites to a faith of morals. Unlike earlier conquerors, Persia's kings eschewed atrocities, let locals keep gods, customs, even leaders. Highest posts went to Persian nobles, trained "to ride, to draw the bow, and to speak the truth." Most trusted was the king's cupbearer who, like the lion on the gold drinking horn, watched for poison. Not all kings ruled well. Artaxerxes III slew likely successors and enraged Egyptian subjects by feasting on their sacred Apis bull. Yet Persia's legacy lives. We speak her tongue in words like paradise, pajama, and sherbet; savor Persian pastimes in polo, backgammon, and perhaps chess—"checkmate" stems from *shah mat*, "the king is dead." Though lizards scuttle about the pillars of Persepolis, Persia's monarchy thrives. Like tribute-bearing envoys of old, world dignitaries gathered there in 1971 to honor the 2,500-year span of this, man's most enduring political institution.

Alexander's Wall. To learn what we could about it, we searched out American anthropologist William Irons in a remote Turkoman settlement. We found him in a yurt and were invited in by his host. Shoeless, we sat on felt mats around a fire and drank tea; smoke filtered through a hole overhead. After a supper of rice, lamb, onions, and hot bread, Bill Irons translated as the father of the family spoke. Looking at the old man's wispy beard and his eyes reflecting the red embers of the fire, we felt we were listening to an itinerant storyteller of long ago.

"You know, Alexander had two horns growing from the sides of his head. But he didn't want anyone to know about them, so he wore his hair long. Only his barber knew, and he was sworn to secrecy. But the barber just had to tell. He whispered his secret into a well. Soon reeds grew from the well, but whenever anyone made a flute from them, no music came out, only the words, 'Alexander has two horns.'"

"What about the wall?" we prompted.

"Well, Alexander had two sons. He divided his kingdom between them. They were always arguing about the boundary, so Alexander built the wall to separate them."

As Alexander marched east from Gorgan, he learned that Bessus, the Persian general who had plotted Darius' murder, had fled to Balkh in what is now northern Afghanistan. Proclaiming himself King of Persia, Bessus began raising another army. Alexander saw this as rebellion and set out to nip it.

Driving over Alexander's route, which later became the old Silk Road between

TURKOMAN NOMADS *tenting near the Caspian Sea preserve the timeless craft of rug making. They spin wool from their sheep, dye it, and weave it on a loom that crowds a yurt. Families long treasured individual designs; one red dye came from a scale insect, kermes, which gave us "crimson."*

Rugs adorned palaces in Babylonia and Egypt. In Cyrus' tomb at Pasargadae Alexander found the gold funeral couch resting on rich carpets, perhaps of felt or flat weave. Persia's pile rugs, hundreds of knotted strands per square inch, first won renown eight centuries later.

Prized Persians get a spring cleaning (right) in the hot mineral pool at Rai, near Teheran. From here—ancient Rhagae—the Macedonians pursued Darius east through the Caspian Gates to the Turkoman steppe—to find him dying in a cart, stabbed by his own men. Now Alexander became King of Kings. But the regicide Bessus lived on to plague him as pretender to the Persian throne.

HELEN AND FRANK SCHREIDER, NATIONAL GEOGRAPHIC STAFF

China and Arabia, we measured our progress by the caravansaries. These fortified hostels were spaced about every 17 miles, the average distance a camel train could travel in a day. Mud ruins in a dusty brown sea, they lie deserted now. Trucks roaring past spew black diesel fumes and grind the old Silk Road into a tortuous washboard that left us quivering for hours after we camped each night.

Near today's Iranian-Afghan border, Alexander learned of a revolt to the south and postponed his pursuit of Bessus. Speed, mobility, and surprise, three aces in his deck of military tricks, quickly settled the uprising. He left a garrison in control and ordered the founding of another Alexandria. We know it as Herat.

HELEN AND FRANK SCHREIDER, NATIONAL GEOGRAPHIC STAFF

Herat looks, sounds, and smells much as it did when it served as a great trade center for merchants from China, India, Arabia, and Africa. Plodding camels grumble under heavy loads. Silk merchants reel thread in dim little stalls. Nightingales sing in wooden cages. Turbaned men string peppers into crimson chains. Women in veils and tentlike skirts wander from stall to stall, haggling before buying.

While at Herat, Alexander heard of more uprisings and continued southward. Following his route through south-

ALONG A DESOLATE TRACK
the authors speed from sunset's parting glory toward night and Meshed, Iran. Trodden by Alexander, the route later gained fame as the Silk Road. Aristotle wrote of thread spun from cocoons of "a great worm which has horns." Dazzled by China's silk, imperial Rome paid 12 ounces of gold for a pound of it.

225

west Afghanistan, we drove for a while over a newly built road, then along a track twisting between jagged, reddish mountains. Near Qala-i-Kang, Alexander quelled an uprising of a different sort, the first of many within his ranks. For some time he had been drifting away from his Macedonians. To them the conquered Persians were no better than slaves. But Alexander, continuing his efforts to win their friendship, appointed Persians to high office and himself wore Persian dress.

At the same time he grew distrustful of his old friends. Hearing rumors of a plot against his life, he ordered the army to try Philotas, one of his ablest generals. On the flimsiest of evidence, Philotas was executed. Macedonian custom decreed the same fate for kinsmen of a traitor. Though he spared other relatives, Alexander ordered the murder of Philotas' father, loyal old Parmenion.

Most of the summer and fall of 330 Alexander campaigned in southern Afghanistan. In December he reached the Kabul Valley, only to find his pursuit of the usurper Bessus blocked by snow-mantled mountains higher than any he had ever seen. He decided to await spring before crossing 11,650-foot Khawak Pass.

We too arrived in Kabul in December and set about arranging a trek over the pass. But it was Ramadan, the month when no Moslem may eat, drink, or smoke

CRUMBLING CITADEL *of Herat—*
often battered, often rebuilt by
Arab, Turk, and Mongol invaders
—still guards this ancient
caravan center and provincial
capital of Afghanistan.
Alexander fortified the site
(he named it Alexandria Areion)
while mopping up in central Asia.
Between here and the Hindu Kush
he founded three more Alexandrias.

Flowing chaderis *(opposite)*
hark back to turbulent times
when strong men stole women.
Husbands and fathers kept
wives and daughters in purdah,
hidden behind walls or shrouded
against prying eyes in public.
Today purdah's pleats may mask
nylons, miniskirt, even blue jeans!

HELEN AND FRANK SCHREIDER, NATIONAL GEOGRAPHIC STAFF. OPPOSITE: ROLAND MICHAUD, RAPHO GUILLUMETTE

between sunup and sundown. We could find no one to guide us until Bob MacMakin, an American resident of Kabul who speaks the local language, came to our rescue. Bob and his wife Mary took us through the Afghan capital's bazaars to buy what we needed. We parked near new office buildings and dodged a few camels that were dodging limousines. At the Green Door Bazaar—all the shops have green doors—we found sheepskin jackets and hats. A veiled woman strode by, wearing what looked like a pleated tent. The tent parted; underneath she wore high heels, nylon stockings, and a miniskirt.

W E LEFT OUR LAND-ROVER and hired one with a driver to take us as close to the pass as possible. Next morning we headed north with the MacMakins for the snowy barrier of the Hindu Kush—Killer of Hindus. At Dasht-i-Rewat, 100 miles from Kabul, Bob found four men with pack horses to take us over the Khawak Pass. A mile

227

beyond the village we set up two small tents and crawled into sleeping bags. The men and horses joined us next day.

Describing Alexander's crossing of the Hindu Kush, Curtius wrote: "The army . . . in this absence of all human civilization, endured all the evils that could be suffered, want, cold, fatigue, despair." As we emerged from our tents before dawn into a cold, blue, wind-whipped world, we began to understand the Macedonians' plight.

Soon after we started up the foot-wide trail, Helen and I realized that a year of following Alexander by car had not conditioned us for following him on foot over a mountain in midwinter. At 8,000 feet we were gasping for breath. By noon we reached the snow line. The trail became icy and treacherous. Before dark we came upon a crude stone hut with a flat mud-covered roof. We waited at a respectful distance while Ghulam Zubair, our chief packer, spoke to the man of the house. Without hesitation he offered the shelter of a small storeroom and stable.

Morning found us stiff, but hot tea, eggs, and bread improved our outlook. We resumed the trail, now along the icebound Khawak River. At one ford my horse stumbled in hip-deep water. Desperately trying to stay on, I grabbed a cinch rope, but I could feel it giving, feel myself sliding into that icy water. I saw a flash of red-striped robe, a whiskered face under a turban as my horse wrangler, Mohammad Mirza, dashed into the stream, grabbed the bridle, and swiveled the horse into shallow water.

It took only seconds to lead horse, load, and thoroughly unnerved rider to shore, but Mohammad was already crusted with ice. When I thanked him, he grinned and shrugged. "It doesn't matter," he said. "I am used to this. Besides, I am an Afghan."

That day we made only three miles instead of the expected ten, stopping at a village where the aged chief welcomed us. We gave the village guesthouse a four-star rating. We had an oil-drum stove, dung patties for fuel, and felt pads on the floor. Warm and dry and full of packaged spaghetti, we sprawled on the floor and studied the map. With any luck, we should make the summit the next day.

Writing of the Khawak, Curtius says, "The unusual cold of the snow caused the death of many. . . . It was especially harmful to those who were fatigued. . . ."

EVERY STEP A STRAIN *in the knife-edged air, the Schreider party slogs over 11,650-foot Khawak Pass in the Hindu Kush. Rather than round the range, Alexander crossed here to cut off the evasive Bessus. "Now we know why Alexander's men mutinied," the authors quipped.*

HELEN AND FRANK SCHREIDER, NATIONAL GEOGRAPHIC STAFF

Fatigue was our constant companion that next day. Above 10,000 feet, climbing steeply, we gulped air so cold it seemed to sear our lungs. We took turns riding one lightly loaded horse, and grabbed other horses' tails to help us along on foot. Ever so slowly we neared the summit. And then the horse Helen was riding stepped into a drift-concealed hollow, throwing her into deep snow.

". . . When they struggled to rise again, they could not do so. But they were roused from their torpor . . . for there was no other cure than to be forced to go on."

The Afghans rushed to Helen's side and gently helped her up. They urged her to mount again, but she knew she must walk, and walk quickly, to keep from freezing.

At the summit I looked back down the trail and imagined Alexander's army strung out, an antlike stream, each soldier weary, wondering where he would sleep.

No village guesthouse awaited us that night. At dusk we stopped at the first trailside shelter and blessed the old amir, Abdur Rahman, who almost a century before had built these dome-shaped huts to protect travelers on the pass.

Two days later we reached a village on the far side of the Hindu Kush. We had covered 47 miles in five days—and gained a new appreciation of what it must have been like to travel through this country in Alexander's day.

After returning by truck and bus to Kabul, Helen and I recrossed the Hindu Kush in Bucephalus. Again we picked

HEFTING A HEADLESS CALF *in the no-holds-barred Afghan pastime, buz kashi, a rider breaks across the field at Mazar-i-Sharif. To score, he must carry the "ball" round a pole and drop it in his goal circle. Scions of superb horsemen who fought Alexander in Bactria, players flail at each other with whips, hands, and feet. The fallen rebound, whip in teeth, to remount for the fray (opposite).*

Matching them in fury but not trappings, Alexander rode bareback. The saddle enters Western history in 4th century A.D., *stirrups in the 6th. From Bactria he marched north, rafted the Oxus River, finally captured Bessus. Alexander hung a wooden collar on him for killing a king, paraded him naked, cut off his nose and ears, and shipped him to Ecbatana where he was torn limb from limb.*

HELEN AND FRANK SCHREIDER,
NATIONAL GEOGRAPHIC STAFF
OPPOSITE: MARC RIBOUD, MAGNUM

"Alexander when he saw [Roxane] fell in love with her" Arrian

HELEN AND FRANK SCHREIDER, NATIONAL GEOGRAPHIC STAFF

SAMARKAND BRIDE *serving guests evokes Alexander's marriage to Roxane, Bactrian maiden "of remarkable beauty." Alexander spent two years subduing Sogdiana and Bactria after conquering Maracanda—today's Samarkand.*

Sacked by Genghis Khan in 1221, this seat of Arab culture flourished in the following century under Tamerlane, who made it the capital of his empire. He built lavish gardens, palaces, and shrines whose glory is recalled in the radiance of Mazar-i-Sharif's Blue Mosque (opposite). If a colored pigeon lands in the square, Moslem legend says, it immediately turns white.

up Alexander's trail and followed it north and west to Balkh, a once-great caravan center, now a mere village surrounded by mud-walled ruins. Bessus had fled Balkh as Alexander approached, but the Macedonian made it his headquarters for two years while he pursued the pretender and subdued the wild tribesmen of the Oxus River, today the Amu Darya.

These hard-riding nomads were the toughest adversaries he had yet faced. We saw a sample of how tough they might have been at nearby Mazar-i-Sharif, present capital of Balkh Province. Today, as in Alexander's time, northern Afghanistan breeds horses famed for their power and speed. They need both to compete at *buz kashi*, the national sport and surely one of the roughest in the world.

We watched some 30 horses and riders warm up. The horses were handsomely caparisoned with leather and bright brass, the men in velvet jackets, red for one team, green for the other. "Buz kashi literally means 'goat drag,'" our guide explained. "But now they use a calf—a dead one, of course."

Two circles chalked on the playing field formed the goals for each team. At the referee's whistle the headless carcass was dropped in the middle of the milling horsemen. One man in red grabbed a leg and lifted the 120-pound carcass with one hand. A Green rider grabbed another leg. Red and Green rode across the field, lashing each other. The Red swerved, broke Green's hold, and slid the carcass into the circle.

For two hours it went on. Horses grew sudsy with sweat, the men bloody. The rewards for such torture must be great, I remarked. "Not really," our guide said. "Prestige is the reward. Families will spend half their savings to buy a good buz kashi horse. These men play to win, just for the honor."

SEARCHING FOR BESSUS, Alexander's army took five days crossing the Oxus on rafts of tents stuffed with straw. We took considerably longer. No foreigner may cross this border river into the Soviet Union. The only way we could get over was to fly from Kabul to Tashkent, capital of the Uzbek S.S.R.

There the tourist agency director questioned our itinerary, which included Samarkand and Leninabad. "Samarkand is on the tourist list," he said. "But why do you want to go to Leninabad?" I replied that Alexander founded a city near there and called it

STAIRSTEPS OF PLENTY, terraced fields of wheat descend to the Kunar River near the Afghan-Pakistan border. Farmer's rifle bespeaks the region's heritage of violence. Alexander fought fierce tribes here, and sent back to Macedonia oxen "of unusual beauty and size . . . to work the land."

HELEN AND FRANK SCHREIDER, NATIONAL GEOGRAPHIC STAFF

Alexandria Eschate — Alexandria the Farthest. "Leninabad," he replied firmly, "is not on the list."

So, with an Intourist guide, we set off for the 200-mile trip to Samarkand. West of Leninabad we picked up Alexander's trail again. Crossing the Oxus, the Macedonians captured Bessus, who had been betrayed by his lieutenants. Alexander ordered him tortured and executed. But new leaders arose. Alexander took Samarkand, then moved northeast.

Somewhere in here — no one knows where — Alexander demanded the surrender of an impregnable height called Sogdiana Rock. The defenders laughed: "Find soldiers with wings." By night some 300 Macedonians scaled it with ropes, using iron tent pegs as pitons. At dawn Alexander called, "Come see my flying soldiers."

The Sogdians surrendered. Among them was Roxane, daughter of a nobleman. As a prize of war she already belonged to Alexander, but he gallantly married her.

Although Alexander occupied Samarkand, no sign of his presence remains. Instead, the city reflects the taste of its 14th-century conqueror, Tamerlane, who brought artisans from every Moslem country to make this the world's most beautiful city. From Samarkand, whose blue-tiled mosques and tombs echo the glory of "the Jewel of Islam," Helen and I flew back to Kabul.

In early summer of 327 B.C. Alexander marched east from the Kabul Valley into what is now Pakistan. His goal was daring indeed: to add India to his empire. He took with him an entourage that, in the seven years since he had left

OPEN-HEARTED, *open-faced Kalash Kafir carries flour from a communal grist mill in remote northern Pakistan. Her isolated tribe retains customs found nowhere else in these mountains; they call to mind ancient ways of far-off Greece.*

Kafirs—"Infidels" to Moslem neighbors—make wine and in a vanishing art carve effigies to honor the dead (opposite). To the horseless Kalash tribe wooden horses mark prestige. Dancers circle a fire (upper), slipping sedately right and left to drum and reed pipe in an age-old rite. Tufted helmets of cowrie shells resemble those of Greek dancers on page 194.

Macedonia, had swelled to 120,000. It included thousands of Persian horsemen and camp followers.

Alexander himself had changed. He drank more and frequently exploded in bursts of temper. In one he murdered Black Cleitus, the friend who had saved his life at the Granicus. He was ruthless with those who opposed him. In spite of this, he retained the loyalty of his men.

SOMEWHERE ON THE EDGE OF INDIA Alexander encountered a strange people who claimed descent from Dionysus, Greek god of wine. Their government resembled that of the Greeks. Possibly the Persians had exiled Greeks from Asia Minor to this part of their empire.

From these people, legend says, descended the pagan Kafirs who still live in the mountains between Pakistan and Afghanistan. Helen and I set out to find them. At Kamdesh, once a Kafir village now converted to Islam, the

people told us that across the border in Chitral we might find other Kafirs—the Kalash—who made wine and carved images to adorn their wooden graves.

Helen and I exchanged excited glances. Curtius mentions wooden sepulchers and wine. Was it possible that in this sea of Islam there remained a tiny island harboring traces of Greek culture even older than Alexander?

THE MACEDONIANS left Afghanistan via the Nawa Pass. We entered Pakistan through the Khyber Pass to the south. At Peshawar we found the road to Chitral State closed by snow. But we could fly to the town of Chitral, hire a jeep to Ayun, then walk 18 miles to the Kalash villages.

Like a jagged wound, the Brumboret Valley slashes into the Hindu Kush. The path that threads its boulder-strewn sides is too steep even for mules. Here, and in the nearby Rumbur Valley, live the Kalash Kafirs.

We crawled along icy ledges and crossed the green Brumboret River countless times on trembling bridges made of two narrow planks pegged together in the middle and weighted at the ends with rocks. Then the valley broadened; wooden houses, their fronts carved in geometric designs, stood among cedar and mulberry trees on the hillsides.

We heard a musical tinkle and saw three Kalash women with bells hung from their belts. Their hands and faces were lightly tattooed. They wore black robes and tufted black headdresses covered with cowrie shells. We stared at those headdresses; we had seen similar ones in Greece.

Up the path stood a crudely carved figure with a pointed helmet like those we had seen on the walls of Persepolis. We passed a graveyard, and there they were, as described by Curtius: wooden sepulchers, lying in a grove of trees.

When we met with the village elders, we sat on chairs. Nowhere east of Turkey, except here and at Kamdesh, had we found villagers using chairs. The elders' beretlike hats resembled those in mosaics at Pella and on coins of Alexander's time. Our guide translated as we asked question after question. Did they know of Alexander? They did not. Yet they made wine, and the women danced at night around the fire, as ancient Greeks had done, and as neighboring Moslem peoples do not. The Greek-like elements of Kalash culture, coincidental as they may have been, combined into a picture suggesting antiquity, isolation, and, conceivably, kinship with the strange folk Alexander visited.

We arrived back in Chitral on a balmy Himalayan day. Since heavy snows had put Chitral's runway out of service, we decided to climb over the Lawarai Pass toward Dir,

PRIEST-KING OR GOD FROM MOHENJO-DARO, NATIONAL MUSEUM OF PAKISTAN, KARACHI; JOSEPHINE POWELL. OPPOSITE: HELEN AND FRANK SCHREIDER, NATIONAL GEOGRAPHIC STAFF

Exotic lands awaited Alexander across the fabled Indus

Persia's vast empire now his, he invaded "the land of the Indians" on a bridge of boats similar to that near Attock, Pakistan (opposite).

Some 2,000 years earlier great cities throve in this fertile valley. History forgot them; not until the 1920's did diggers begin uncovering Mohenjo-daro and Harappa with their lattice of streets, granaries, baths, sewage systems, and mighty walls of kiln-dried brick. Like Egypt and Mesopotamia, this third pioneer river civilization developed irrigation, pictographs, crafts, wheeled vehicles. It was first to cultivate cotton. Indus centers traded by sea with Sumer. About 1500 B.C. Aryans swept in from the north with their god Indra.

Alexander found Indians tall and dark, clad in white tunics, beards dyed red, purple, or green. Arrian reported that "no Indian . . . is a slave." Naked sages mused under banyan trees. Warriors with scimitars and longbows went to battle to the beat of drum and cymbal. Taxila, a "prosperous city," greeted Alexander royally and joined him in war on a neighbor, King Porus.

where we could get a ride back to Peshawar. After a jouncing drive in a battered jeep and a three-hour hike, we reached a teahouse crowded with porters waiting to carry loads over the pass. At dawn we started up an almost vertical ravine. Our porters, shod in thong-wrapped hides, seldom slipped. But our rock-climbing shoes skidded on the icy trail, slowing our progress.

Our usually cheerful guide, Abdul Samad, began to fret. "We must hurry. We must reach the top before the sun makes the snow heavy. Two years ago 80 people died here in an avalanche."

Descending to a village-lined valley in Pakistan's Dir State, we noted that every man carried a gun. "Mr. Frank," Abdul cautioned, "please lower your eyes. Mrs. Helen, don't take pictures of women. This is the land of blood feuds. Men have been killed for smaller things than looking at another man's wife."

"Well, the men don't seem to worry about looking at me," Helen said.

Abdul smiled. "That's different."

IN THESE MOUNTAINS Alexander took town after town, though defenders contested every hill. But weariness was beginning to tell. He had subdued Asia Minor in a year and a half; it took him nearly a year to capture an area in Pakistan smaller than Connecticut.

In 326 B.C. he crossed the Indus on a bridge of boats built by his engineers. Over a similar bridge near the same spot we followed Alexander to Taxila.

The king of Taxila welcomed him, and Alexander refitted for the conquest of India and a pitched battle against King Porus at the Jhelum River.

LAST GREAT BATTLE: *Macedonians crush army of King Porus at the Jhelum River. "Maddened by the disaster," wrote Arrian, the Indian's elephants collided "with friends and foes alike."*

PAINTING FOR NATIONAL GEOGRAPHIC BY TOM LOVELL

We hurried on to the Jhelum, a mere stream now, its water diverted and impounded by the colossal Mangla Dam, part of the largest irrigation scheme in the world. Swollen by spring rains, the Jhelum that Alexander faced was not even fordable. He ordered boats brought overland from the Indus. Across the Jhelum stood Porus with 35,000 infantry and cavalry, and 200 elephants.

After a series of feints Alexander ferried his forces across the river under cover of a night thunderstorm. Hours of bloody battle followed. Then Porus' elephants bolted, and the Indians retreated in wild disorder. When Porus surrendered, Alexander asked how he would like to be treated. "Like a king," Porus replied. Admiring a gallant foe, Alexander restored the Indian to his throne.

At the Beas River, just inside present India, Alexander faced a real mutiny for the first time. His homesick men, unnerved by the fierce fight against Porus, concerned by reports of even greater armies ahead, refused to go on. Alexander summoned his officers and tried to rally them. Silence greeted him. Then Coenus, a faithful general, rose, removed his helmet, and addressed Alexander:

"O King, I speak not for those officers present, but for the men. . . . Those that survive yearn to return to their families, to enjoy while they yet live the riches you have won for them. . . . A noble thing, O King, is to know when to stop."

Angered and disappointed by the speech, Alexander sulked in his tent for three days. When at last he bowed to the will of his men, they rejoiced. "Alexander," they said, "has allowed us, but no other, to defeat him." He led his men back to the Jhelum to begin the journey home.

T HE HUGE ENTOURAGE started downriver in the fall of 326 B.C., part of the army marching along the banks, the rest embarking in a fleet of nearly 2,000 vessels. "It was very remarkable," recounts Arrian, "to hear . . . the noise of the rowers, when all together they raised their rowers' chanties. . . . Those Indians . . . to whom the clamor of the oarsmen and the beat of the oars reached, came also running down to the bank and followed, singing their own wild songs."

Rather than backtrack, Alexander chose a southward course. The trip along the Jhelum, Chenab, and Indus Rivers took nine months as the army fought from city to city. During one siege, Alexander, impatient with halfhearted fighting, pushed into the town with only three bodyguards. When his army breached the walls, it found the men hovering over their fallen king. Beneath the sacred shield he had taken from Troy eight years before lay Alexander with an arrow in his lungs.

For days he remained semiconscious. When he was carried by boat to his camp,

Alexander turned back, but his legend persists

N OT KINGS nor stubborn geography could stay this hero, pictured weeping by the Indus "because there were no more worlds to conquer." Homesickness of his soldiers did. Checked, he chose the long way back, exploring the Indus to the Arabian Sea, courting death storming yet another citadel. Panic gave way to joy when troops saw that their wounded leader still lived (left).

Idolized by his men, hailed as divine in lands he won, Alexander passed into the legends of three continents. Central Asia worshiped him as Iskander, founder of cities (one, Bucephala, honored his horse). Chiefs in Turkistan claim descent from him; Afghan mothers frighten naughty children with tales of Iskander. Persians called him son of Darius; Egyptians, son of the last Pharaoh, Nectanebo. Early Christians portrayed Jesus in his likeness; Ethiopia made him a saint, and Islam enrolled him as a prophet. Mogul art shows him in a diving bell seeking the sea's secrets. Medieval Europe depicted him as a knight of chivalry.

Romans, first to call Alexander "the Great," held themselves heirs to his empire and ambitions. Augustus wore Alexander's head on a signet ring, emulated his deeds and divinity.

Buddha owes his image to Alexander's march. No artist presumed to portray "The Enlightened One." Later, inspired by statues Greeks brought to Gandhara, a region astride the upper Indus, sculptors created Buddha in the image of Apollo (below). They clad him in flowing chiton, gave him wavy hair and topknot, classic cut of eye and curve of lip— but added to his forehead the Oriental third eye, which emits spiritual light.

the men thought he was dead. But he raised his arm in greeting, and when they saw him helped onto his horse, they shouted for joy.

At the Arabian Sea, Alexander sent part of his forces by ship along the coast. With the rest he marched west across the Baluchistan desert. Helen and I gave long, hard thought to this part of our journey. Should we return by sea, or follow Alexander overland? Our maps showed few roads, most of them mere camel tracks. We faced 1,100 miles of almost uninhabited wasteland.

But we had followed Alexander too long to give up now. In Karachi, Pakistan, we stocked up on food, water, and gasoline. On a windy morning we headed west.

Arrian writes that the suffering of the army on this march was so extreme that discipline fell to an all-time low. Soldiers broke open the royal stores, butchered the transport animals for food, burned the baggage wagons for fuel, even abandoned most of their booty.

Traveling in March, we found the heat bearable. But the terrain was just as forbidding as in Alexander's time— bleached, wind-swept earth and salt-encrusted mud flats, glistening silver in the pale, dust-filtered sunlight.

Often we plowed through deep silt in four-wheel drive and gas-gulping lower gears. Wind pelted the Land-Rover with abrasive sand and obliterated all tracks. To protect the engine, we sometimes stopped to let sandstorms pass. We traveled for hours without seeing a living thing, neither tree nor bird nor animal. Each night we camped wherever the darkness found us, with only the wind for company.

Throughout this terrible march Alexander remained the peerless leader. When his scouts found a little water, enough for only one man, they brought it to their king.

GREATNESS *shows in Alexander's sharing 60 days of suffering in the burning Baluchistan desert. Offered a helmetful of precious water when his men had none, he emptied it on the ground.*

He had hoped to set up supply depots for his fleet, sailing along the coast. But guides lost their way, pack animals sank in sand, men died of thirst. At Pura, survivors reached a royal road to Persepolis. The authors found only this rocky wasteland (opposite), once almost lost the Land-Rover in a flash flood.

Alexander thanked them, Arrian writes, and "poured it out in the sight of all . . . the whole army was so much heartened that [it seemed] every man had drunk. . . ."

But on one occasion too much water caused as much grief as too little. A flash flood in a stream drowned most of the camp followers; the troops barely escaped.

At Pura, Alexander found food and water and set off on the royal road to Persepolis. Today that road lies buried and forgotten beneath desert sand and rocks. An hour after leaving nearby Bampur we were slithering through clinging mud along the Bampur River. We twisted between wind-tortured tamarisk groves and rain-slashed ravines, across desert where soft sand held the wheels and clumps of spiny grass caught on the chassis. For two days we wandered westward,

245

navigating more by the feel of the land than by compass. We came to a village, the largest of several we had seen along the way. Perhaps a hundred huts stood in an oasis of date palms. All around were fields of green wheat, the only bright color in our monotonous world of grays and browns.

We knew a few phrases of Farsi, Iran's national language. With these and gestures, we persuaded a young man to guide us 20 miles to Gumbaz, the next village on our map. After an hour plowing through sand, we realized he was following no track but a beeline course. We asked about the camel trail on our map.

"Car better than camel," he grinned. "Camel go easy way. Car go over everything." After bogging down a few times, we switched to the camel track and made better time. We could find no one to lead us out of Gumbaz and decided to try on our own. Within ten miles we were stopped by boulder-studded desert. Even our faithful Land-Rover could not take such terrain. Searching for an easier way, we followed a dry wash which opened into a stretch of black gravel. Elated, we headed west. Three days later we reached a road and turned toward Persepolis.

WHEN ALEXANDER arrived at Persepolis, he found his empire in disorder. Many of his governors, both Macedonian and Persian, had exploited their positions, overtaxing the people and embezzling funds. He quickly executed the offenders. At Susa, where the Persian kings had built magnificent winter palaces, Alexander carried his union of East and West a step further with a ceremony in which 10,000 of his troops formalized their marriages to Persian women, and 80 officers married daughters of Persian nobles. He gave them all handsome dowries, and he himself, though already married to Roxane, took a daughter of Darius as a second wife.

Susa also saw the death of Calanus, a fakir Alexander had brought from India. To the king his dying words were, "We shall meet again in Babylon."

His mind full of new projects, Alexander built a fleet to explore the coasts of Arabia and Africa. He sailed up the Tigris to Opis, ancient Assyrian city where Cyrus the Persian had defeated the Babylonians in 539. Here the Macedonians' long-smoldering resentment against what they considered Alexander's Persian ways flamed into open rebellion. He had incorporated Persian units into his army and now he was sending some of his Macedonians home. His men shouted: "Send us all home. You can campaign with your father Ammon." They thought Alexander believed himself a god; they may have been right. He replied with swift execution of the leaders and an impassioned defense of his actions. Then he held a feast shared by 9,000 Macedonians and Persians.

Alexander entered Babylon for the last time in the spring of 323. Worn out by wounds, hardship, and overdrinking, he fell ill of a fever. Soon he could neither move nor speak. He was propped up and each officer and soldier filed past. He acknowledged each man with his eyes or a slight movement of his head. Within two days Alexander died. He was not yet 33 years old.

"ALL HERE WAS FRIENDLY, *and produced fruit of all sorts." Thus Arrian describes the place near Bandar Abbas, Iran (opposite), where Alexander's fleet rested after a harrowing voyage from India. The men blew bugles to scare off whales, ate camels to keep from starving, battled hairy savages who lived in whalebone houses. Temperatures here at the mouth of the Persian Gulf reach 130° F. Gold rosette adorns woman's nose.*

THOMAS J. ABERCROMBIE, NATIONAL GEOGRAPHIC STAFF

He had won an empire covering more than one and a half million square miles. He had mapped unknown territory, built cities, opened trade routes, stimulated the exchange of ideas. From the Mediterranean to the Hindu Kush, Greek became the lingua franca of court and commerce.

His vast realm survived for only a few years as the Diadochi—his "successors"—fought each other for power. Eventually the empire crumbled into city-states, small kingdoms, and three dominant powers headed by generals of Alexander's armies —Antigonus in Macedonia, Seleucus in Syria, and Ptolemy in Egypt.

WEDDING OF TWO WORLDS: *Determined to fuse the peoples of his empire "as in a loving cup," Alexander celebrates a mass marriage at Susa in the spring of 324 B.C. Here, in Persian dress, he takes Darius' daughter Barsine as his second bride; 80 Macedonian officers wait to wed Persian noblewomen, 10,000 troops to confirm their marriages. Wedding witnessed by the Schreiders near Susa (below) evokes the celebration. Alexander died the following year, but his dream of different peoples dwelling in peace in a single empire lived on. It became Rome's ideal.*

As Arrian wrote, "Alexander had no small or mean conceptions, nor would ever have remained contented with any of his possessions . . . but would always have searched far beyond . . . being always the rival, if of no other, yet of himself."

Perhaps it was that very rivalry with himself that made Alexander great. His own words to his army, as recorded by Arrian, might be a worthy epitaph: "I set no limits of labors to a man of spirit, save only that the labors themselves . . . lead on to noble enterprises. . . . It is a lovely thing to live with courage, and to die, leaving behind an everlasting renown."

PAINTING FOR NATIONAL GEOGRAPHIC BY TOM LOVELL. OPPOSITE: HELEN AND FRANK SCHREIDER, NATIONAL GEOGRAPHIC STAFF

By Emeline Richardson

Unraveling the Mystery
of the Etruscans

V IA UMBRO-CASENTINO, one of the loveliest roads in Italy and a particular
favorite of mine, follows the broad valleys through the heart of inland
Etruria, Rome's name for the ancient realm of the Etruscans. On it I pass
terraced Arezzo and lofty Cortona, towering over fields as fertile today as
in that almost forgotten yesterday when Etruscans tilled them. Southeast,
beyond Lake Trasimeno, Perugia sprawls along the Apennine foothills. To
me these ageless places are Arretium, Cortona, Perusia, in their time the
three richest and strongest cities of Etruria.

The road skirts the glittering lake, then twists southwestward into the
tumbled hills that guard Chiusi — Clusium, the Enclosed City, to the Romans.
"Lars Porsena of Clusium — By the nine gods he swore that the great house
of Tarquin should suffer wrong no more." I chant Macaulay's verse to the

Revelers enliven a tomb at Tarquinia with wine and strains of double flute and lyre; Robert Emmett Bright, Rapho Guillumette

brown goats spilling down a hillside onto the road ahead. Through these hills Porsena, King of Clusium and chief of the League of Twelve Cities, marched with all the hosts of Etruria. His army was destined to get as far as Rome and grim Horatius on the wooden bridge across the Tiber. But that tale lies farther down my road, in the first faint shadows of Etruria's twilight.

To see her dawn we must peer through veils of legend, as did the Greeks and Romans. Luckier, or more inquisitive than they, we may also peer through periscopes, probing the Etruscans' hidden tombs, or unmask their buried cities with aerial cameras. We are enticed by their curiously sophisticated art, their fine, commonsensical city plans and engineering projects. Yet much of the mystery remains. The key to their lost language eludes us, and our computers as well.

In a savage Italy the Etruscans planted seeds of civilization; to a frontier town called Rome they brought the first glint of grandeur. Later, when Rome burst forth from her Latin hills to conquer the peninsula, the Etruscan cities were her sternest enemies. But no one withstood the legions forever, and now, in the land the Etruscans had enriched, only their tombs survive. Nearly all we know about their way of life comes from their way of death. Small wonder the search for

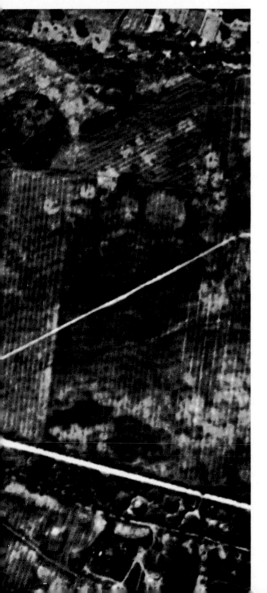

VALVASSORI. LEFT: ROYAL AIR FORCE. UPPER: MERLE SEVERY, NATIONAL GEOGRAPHIC STAFF

X-RAY OF THE PAST, *an aerial photograph exposes an Etruscan necropolis beneath fields near Cerveteri. Skilled eyes of English archeologist John Bradford (above, center) and Italian engineer Carlo Lerici (right) spot clues to hidden crypts; small, light circles reveal patches of grass dried out because they rooted in tomb roofs, not deep soil. Modern road skirts excavated area where domed sepulchers line lanes like houses in this city of the dead (upper); an entrance shows at left. Measuring variation in the soil's electrical conductivity, Lerici pinpointed some 650 tombs nearby, and mined a wealth of lore on ways of the vanished Etruscans.*

253

their tombs has gripped man's imagination for centuries.

It was at Vulci, in 1828, that the great grave hunt of the 19th century began when a plowman and his oxen crashed through the buried stone roof of a tomb. The owner of the land, Napoleon Bonaparte's brother Lucien, started a treasure hunt that unearthed more than 2,000 relics in four months. Fascinated by the discoveries, George Dennis, a British consul in Italy in the 1840's, explored lonely Etruscan sites on horseback and wrote of the worn stones and glittering treasures he had seen. Since then, thousands of tombs have been unearthed, from Spina on an ancient mouth of the Po to Salerno at the gateway to Lucania.

Many lay hidden, their mounds leveled by centuries of plowing, until recent decades when new technology came to the aid of archeology. World War II aerial photographs disclosed the ghostly outlines of tombs invisible on the ground. We have found promising leads in other aerial clues: shadows and markings revealed in the raking light of dawn or sunset, and variations in crop-growth patterns (a sparse yield may indicate a shallow layer of soil).

Like gigantic treasure maps, the photographs led archeologists to lost Etruscan "islands." But could a tomb's contents be assessed without costly excavation? Dr. Carlo M. Lerici of Milan devised an ingenious technique similar to those he had applied in probing for minerals. By sending a current into the earth and measuring differences in electrical potential at given points, geophysicists determine a tomb's size. Then a drill bores down to pierce the roof. A quick sweep, by eye and camera, through a light-equipped periscope shows whether the tomb is worth opening.

Vigorous games come to life in the places of the dead: chariot races, wrestling and boxing matches, discus hurling, and a strange sort of gladiatorial contest—a savage game of blindman's buff played by a man with his head in a sack who flails a club at a vicious dog.

As if to explain the Etruscans' love of games, Herodotus wove that theme into his account of their origin. He said they migrated from Lydia in Asia Minor. To survive a chronic famine there, they invented "the games of dice, knucklebones, handball, and many others. . . . The Lydians would play games one whole day and abstain from food, and on the next day they would eat."

After 18 years of this fun-or-fasting, the king of Lydia divided his people into two groups and cast lots as to which should remain and which should leave. Those whose lot it was to find a new land called themselves Tyrrhenians in

FED. PATELLANI FROM PIX. OPPOSITE: PAINTING OF TARQUINIA'S TOMB OF THE OLYMPICS BY PETER V. BIANCHI, NATIONAL GEOGRAPHIC STAFF ARTIST

CHARIOTS RACE *across a frescoed wall—the eye of man witnesses it for the first time in 2,500 years! Probing a tomb with tube-mounted minicamera, scientists shatter the darkness with electronic flash, revealing a find of the century. Sports-loving Etruscans looked to a fun-filled hereafter. From their duels at funeral games evolved Rome's gladiatorial combats.*

255

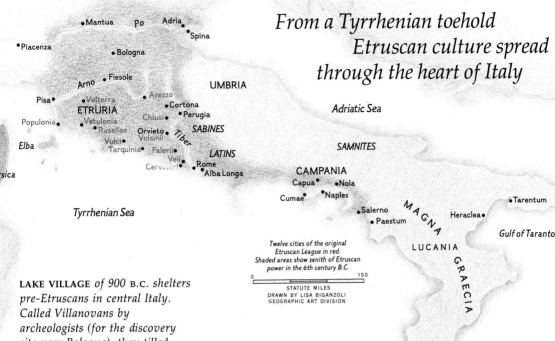

From a Tyrrhenian toehold
Etruscan culture spread
through the heart of Italy

Mantua · Po · Adria · Spina
Piacenza · Bologna
Arno · Fiesole
UMBRIA
Pisa · Volterra · Arezzo
ETRURIA · Cortona · Perugia
Populonia · Vetulonia · Chiusi
Rusellae · Orvieto · Volsinii · SABINES
Vulci · Tarquinia · Falerii
Elba · Veii · LATINS
Cervetri · Rome · Alba Longa
Corsica
CAMPANIA
Capua · Nola
Cumae · Naples
Tyrrhenian Sea
Salerno
Paestum · Heraclea
Tarentum
Gulf of Taranto
MAGNA
LUCANIA
GRAECIA

Adriatic Sea

SAMNITES

Twelve cities of the original
Etruscan League in red.
Shaded areas show zenith of Etruscan
power in the 6th century B.C.

0   150
STATUTE MILES
DRAWN BY LISA BIGANZOLI
GEOGRAPHIC ART DIVISION

LAKE VILLAGE *of 900* B.C. *shelters pre-Etruscans in central Italy. Called Villanovans by archeologists (for the discovery site near Bologna), they tilled, hunted, and fished in a land of roving shepherds.*

Urns for their cremated dead (below) reflect houses of the living—a custom shared with Rome's forebears, who dwelt in similar thatched mud hamlets in Latium. Tools and weapons went to the grave with men, jars and safety pins with women.

Villanovans smelted Etruria's copper, tin, and iron—as did the Etruscans, whose traders plied to Magna Graecia. Their legendary leader Tyrrhenus is commemorated by the Tyrrhenian Sea, their trading colony Adria by the Adriatic. "Tuscany" embodies the name Etruscan.

honor of their leader, the king's son Tyrrhenus. "After voyaging past many peoples," Herodotus continues, "they came to the land of the Ombrici where they built cities and live to this day."

Herodotus did not invent the Ombrici, or Umbrians. We know they founded Perugia (capital of the region still called Umbria) long before the Etruscans made that city their own. But the Greek historian's tale was disputed even in ancient times. Some scholars maintain that the Etruscans either came from the north or were native to the region. We cannot yet solve the puzzle of their origin by piecing together traditions of antiquity and the finds of modern archeology. Too many pieces are missing. But we do know that a new, Eastern-flavored culture suddenly burst upon Etruria in the early seventh century B.C. Many archeologists, myself included, believe this change can best be explained by the arrival of immigrants from the east.

We can read and pronounce Etruscan inscriptions—their speech seems to sputter with clicks and hisses—because they used a Greek alphabet. But, lacking an Etruscan Rosetta Stone, we can translate only a relatively few words handed down by the Greeks and Romans. The word *phersu*, painted near a masked dancer on an Etruscan tomb wall, seems related to the Latin word for mask, *persona*, and may still live in our "person."

The Greeks and Romans delighted in conversation and copiously recorded it. Alas, we search in vain for such

257

intimate records of Etruscan daily life. The 10,000 or so scraps of writing we have found are funerary and ritual. The only Etruscan books the Romans translated were the *Disciplina Etrusca,* volumes of religious lore. We can, though, evoke this silent people through their vibrant art, and we can see them in their daily lives by picturing them in the cities they built from the Po Valley in the north to the "most blessed of all plains, and . . . fruitful hills," Campania in the south.

B LESSEDLY EMPTY on the blind mountain curves, Via Umbro-Casentino begins to clog with local traffic, very local: sheep and goats, a woman carrying chickens, yokes of great white oxen, their heads hung with fly-shooing fat tassels of bright crimson wool—all obviously bound for a country fair. The big, muscle-rippling white cattle of Italy are always splendid to look at, beautiful and white enough to be descended from the strain bred for sacrifice in antiquity. Indeed, their fine red tassels put me in mind of some ancient festival with sacrificial rites and games and lively young men and women dancing to the music of the lyre and double flute. The pipes accompanied all sorts of activity; one disapproving Greek wrote that Etruscans kneaded bread and beat slaves to the same tune.

My car crawls past the procession and I begin to think of lunch and the good wine of Orvieto. And very soon it comes into view, the great mesa of Orvieto, its sheer cliffs crowned by the jumble of a medieval city. But Orvieto—*Urbs Vetus,* the Old City, to scholars of the Middle Ages—rose from Etruscan roots. And that is all

SUN-GILDED ORVIETO, *Etruscan founded and cathedral crowned, caps a mesa halfway between Florence and Rome. Streams carved such natural fortresses from tuff— hard-packed layers of volcanic ash. Craters cupped lakes like Bolsena.*

In the "land of calves," an early meaning of Italia, white oxen had sacrificial status. Etruscans also yoked them for toil, as do Tuscan farmers today.

Etruria: white oxen and golden cities "for godlike kings of old"

GENTLE SMILES, *lively gestures weave a blissful air about this Etruscan couple reclining on a couch. Tender pose atop a sarcophagus expresses a wish that the marriage last unto eternity. Ancient Greeks would recognize dress and hair styles, but a man and wife banqueting together would scandalize them.*

TERRACOTTA FROM CERVETERI (CAERE), 6TH CENTURY B.C., VILLA GIULIA; DAN McCOY, BLACK STAR

PAINTING FOR NATIONAL GEOGRAPHIC BY H. M. HERGET

we have of their great cities, the stone roots of homes and temples built of wood and sun-dried brick. Etruscans hewed homes of stone, but only for the dead.

Whatever its Etruscan name, Orvieto doubtless began as did all their cities. . . . On a day declared auspicious by priests, the city's founder yokes a bull and a heifer to a bronze-shod plow. Circling to the left, he plows a furrow around the circuit of the future city. Its prospective citizens follow him, carefully throwing inward the clods turned up by the plow. Wherever a road will enter, men lift the plow-share and carry it across the width of the roadway, breaking the sacred circle so that "those things that are necessary but unclean" can be hauled in and out.

A network of streets begins to emerge on the mesa (a favorite site in southern Etruria). Beyond the city limits will lie the tombs, usually on a facing hill across a stream. The necropolis at Orvieto probably emulates the city of the living: small houses on long, narrow blocks formed by streets that meet at nearly right angles. As the city flourishes, the streets broaden to 50-foot-wide avenues paved with pebbles. Horse-drawn carriages clatter along them. On raised sidewalks cloaked men parade their bejeweled, fashion-conscious wives. At a crossing a woman daintily lifts her ankle-length skirt and on shoes with turned-up toes minces over the gutter slosh on a row of steppingstones. Perhaps a lounging artist roguishly notes that shorter skirts are "in" this year. He will immortalize the style in a tiny carved gem.

Early Etruscans undoubtedly worshiped at sites revered by Villanovans and others who peopled this land before them. From these open-air sanctuaries evolved the typical

ETRUSCAN PROCESSION *winds to a cypress-shaded sanctuary where dancers and pipers honor the dead. Such festivals seemed wild to austere early Romans, tame to later ones. Etruscan haruspices— soothsayers who read portents in animal entrails—awed Romans, whose augurs could ask the gods only yes-or-no questions.*

A seer reads omens in a liver on bronze mirror (left, above); some 35 gods' names adorn a model liver (at right) studied by novices.

OPPOSITE: MIRROR FROM VULCI, 5TH CENTURY B.C., VATICAN MUSEUM, AND BRONZE SHEEP'S LIVER FROM PIACENZA, 3D CENTURY B.C., PIACENZA CITY MUSEUM; SCALA

Etruscan temple, described by the Roman architect Vitruvius as "heavy-headed, low, broad." Statues of terracotta (baked earth) or gilded bronze adorn the rooftree, eaves, and gables of its great spreading roof.

Some 40 miles southwest of Orvieto, and a slightly longer distance northwest of Rome, lies Tarquinia, considered by the Etruscans their oldest city. Here I love to feast my eyes on Etruria's finest frescoes in the tombs outside the walled medieval city overlooking the sea. Etruscan tradition traces Tarquinia's name to Tarchon, brother of Tyrrhenus. In the fields of Tarquinia a plowman turned up a baby with the gray hair of an old man and the gift of prophecy. Tarchon summoned the princes of Etruria to record the sayings of the earth-born child. From these spring Etruria's sacred lore: the Book of Entrails, which interpreted the liver of a sacrificial animal; the Book of Rituals, which prescribed for the founding of cities, the

263

building of temples, and the duration of life; the Book of Thunderbolts, which gave meaning to rumbles of thunder and flashes of lightning. Greeks believed Zeus hurled thunderbolts; Romans called their thunder god Jupiter. Etruscans held that nine gods had this power and only a priest could tell who flung a bolt—and why. I wondered about this once during a storm at Volterra, that majestic walled city high and lonely in northwestern Etruria. As the fitful lightning made the city apocalyptic against the surrounding black hills, I thought, "An Etruscan priest could tell me what it all meant."

B Y THE FIFTH CENTURY B.C. the Etruscans ruled wide regions of Italy. Reliable tradition puts 12 of their cities in Etruria, 12 in the Po Valley, another dozen in inland Campania. Like those of Greece, the Etruscan cities were independent states ruled by kings, later by annually elected magistrates. Wealth poured into them from iron, copper, tin, and lead mines, from farms and vineyards, from eastern trade and piracy. Greeks forever harped about piratical Etruscans, but they themselves preyed on shipping in the Tyrrhenian Sea.

Though Etruscans held the islands of Elba and Corsica for many years, they never had a true maritime empire. Their oldest cities, such as Caere (Cerveteri)

and Tarquinia, stood on hills far enough from the shore so that sea raiders could be spied in time to man defenses. Founders of earlier cities in Greece took the same precaution. Athens is sited this way; so is Corinth.

Along Etruria's coast men in towers watched not for foes but for fins. One of these "tunny towers," as the ancients called them, stood on the heights above Orbetello, once the port of Etruscan Vulci. I have often seen the descendants of Etruscan fishermen set sail from Orbetello, mast-hung lanterns glowing in the summer dusk, to gather sardines and mullet. In this timeless town you can still enjoy what must have been the feastday dishes of Vulci and Tarquinia: pork livers simmered with bay leaves, roast pork flavored with rosemary, and fish stuffed with the same pungent herb. It grows on the nearby hills, tinting them with the pale-blue blossoms called in Latin *ros marinus,* dew of the sea.

One of the Greek traders whose ships plied these waters settled in Tarquinia when a revolution in 657 B.C. drove his kinfolk from power in Corinth. His son Lucumo married an Etruscan seeress, Tanaquil. Wealthy and brilliant but snubbed as a foreigner by Tarquinian society, Lucumo yearned for the power his royal family once had known. Tanaquil, the Roman historian Livy tells us, urged him to migrate to a place "where all ranks are of sudden growth and founded on worth,

LIVING ROOMS OF THE DEAD *enshrine the pursuit of pleasure and the rhythm of routine. Banqueting couples loll on a wall in Tarquinia; a naked slave boy keeps the wine flowing, while on an adjacent fresco (page 250) musicians entertain. Etruscan women demanded luxuries and were "great wine-bibbers," ancients gossiped. At Cerveteri (left), stucco pickax, butcher knife, rope, tongs, kitchenware, and arms hang in neat array; marten, cat, duck, and dachshund-like dog shared afterlife with the dead, who reposed on stone pillows, sculptured sandals at bedside. When diggers opened tombs, air often turned bones to dust before their startled eyes.*

TOMB OF THE LEOPARDS, 5TH CENTURY B.C.; DAN McCOY, BLACK STAR. LEFT: TOMB OF THE RELIEFS, 4TH CENTURY B.C.; SCALA

GOLD FIBULA, VULCI, 7TH CENTURY B.C.; BRITISH MUSEUM, LONDON

"To the Etruscan all was alive"

D. H. Lawrence, Etruscan Places

BRONZE LANCER, PERUGIA, 5TH CENTURY B.C.; PERUGIA CIVIC MUSEUM

BRONZE DIVER, PERUGIA, 5TH CENTURY B.C.; STATE MUSEUM OF ANTIQUITIES, MUNICH

BRONZE CHARIOT, MONTELEONE, 6TH CENTURY B.C.; METROPOLITAN MUSEUM OF ART, NEW YORK

TERRACOTTA ASH URN, CHIUSI, 7TH CENTURY B.C.; CHIUSI MUSEUM

"THE QUICK RIPPLE OF LIFE," as Lawrence put it, throbs in a warrior arching to hurl a lance, in a young diver poised to plunge. Chimera, fire-breathing monster of mythology, claws the ground, set to spring (opposite). With serpent tail and goat's head thrusting from its back, the lion-faced beast existed only in the mind's eye. But an Etruscan artist breathed life into it; and when it emerged from the soil of Arezzo in 1553, Benvenuto Cellini doctored time's wounds.

Cherished possessions solaced the dead in Etruscan tombs: a parade chariot adorned with a hero getting his weapons, Greek style, from female hands; a woman's perfume flagon of bucchero—pottery fired to a gleaming black (opposite, center). In Gubbio, north of Etruscan Perugia, a potter duplicates the ancient acrobat-on-ostrich motif. Found with the flagon were five pairs of dice and silver goblets bearing the woman's name, Larthia.

The Etruscan goldsmith's art gleams in a brooch decorated with lions and sphinxes (above), and in a pendant portraying the horned river god Achelous (opposite, upper). Thousands of minute granules of gold form hair and beard.

In block-patterned dress an early Etruscan (right) stands atop her ash urn amid griffins and breast-beating mourners. Tall talisman (far right) displays a startling modern-art look.

MERLE SEVERY, NATIONAL GEOGRAPHIC STAFF

GOLD PENDANT, 6TH CENTURY B.C.;
THE LOUVRE, PARIS

BUCCHERO FLAGON, CERVETERI,
7TH CENTURY B.C.; VATICAN MUSEUM

VOTIVE BRONZE, 4TH CENTURY B.C.; THE LOUVRE

BRONZE CHIMERA, AREZZO, 4TH CENTURY B.C.;
ARCHEOLOGICAL MUSEUM, FLORENCE

MERLE SEVERY, NATIONAL GEOGRAPHIC STAFF. LEFT: TOMB OF HUNTING AND FISHING, TARQUINIA, 6TH CENTURY B.C.; SCALA

GIFTS OF EARTH AND SEA *enriched the Etruscans, who mined the craggy isle of Elba and fished Tyrrhenian waters (left). Seabirds and dolphin cavort about a boat protected by lucky eye on prow. As of old, Elba's ore goes to mainland smelters; moderns draw iron from slag the ancients discarded.*

and there is ample room for a brave and energetic man." The place she so enthusiastically described was a settlement where an ancient salt route from the Sabine Hills to the coast crossed the Tiber—a place called Rome.

ROMULUS, fabled founder of Rome, had laid out the city by Etruscan rite of plow and sacred circle in the year we reckon as 753 B.C. Myth makes Romulus the grandson of the king of Alba Longa and the circle's site as the Palatine Hill. Amazingly, archeology supports much of the tale. Alba Longa, now Castel Gandolfo, summer residence of the Pope southeast of Rome, is one of the earliest inhabited sites in Latium, realm of the original Romans. There, around 1000 B.C., lived a people who kept the ashes of their dead in urns shaped like their thatch-roofed huts. We know they later moved, for remains of their huts have been found on the Palatine and traces of their cemeteries in what became the Forum.

Soon a second people settled on the Esquiline, another of Rome's seven hills. They did not cremate, but inhumed, or buried, their dead. But the two people apparently intermarried, for evidence of the two funeral rites appears side by side in the same cemetery. The remains lend some archeological plausibility to Livy's exciting story that Rome's bachelor founders stole wives from the neighboring Sabine people.

By the time Lucumo arrived at the Janiculum Hill on the Etruscan side of the Tiber, Rome had grown into a bustling, cocky, not particularly refined town. As Lucumo stood on the hill with Rome spread below, an eagle swooped down, snatched his pointed cap, and gently replaced it the next moment. His wife called the impromptu coronation a portent of great fortune.

Free with money and kind words, Lucumo made friends rapidly—so rapidly that when the king of Rome died the people chose Lucumo to rule. He Latinized his name (actually a title meaning "king" or "prince") to Lucius and added Tarquinius to honor his hometown. History tacked on Priscus—First—to distinguish him from Lucius Tarquinius Superbus—Tarquin the Proud.

The Tarquins may be legendary personalities, but there is no doubt that Rome's Etruscan kings in their 100-year reign put their stamp on the city's history. Draining the swamps between the Capitoline and Palatine Hills, Etruscans created a new focus for the burgeoning city's life: the Forum. Here appeared the markets and lawcourts, the senate house, and the citizens' assembly. Here beat the heart of a city that would become the center of an empire and the ancient world.

Before the Etruscans came, Romans sat on bare hillsides to watch chariots race on the great course called the Circus Maximus. Etruscans ringed the track with wooden bleachers. On the Capitoline the Etruscans built their greatest monument, the 210-foot-long Temple of Jupiter, Juno, and Minerva; we can still see its cut-stone foundations under the Palazzo dei Conservatori. The temple's statue of Jupiter gave the Romans their first image of a god.

Other Etruscan symbols would endure in Rome. When Tarquin the First conquered Veii and Caere, Dionysius of Halicarnassus says, these royal Etruscan cities sent him their regalia: a golden crown, an ivory throne, an eagle-topped scepter, a purple, semicircular cloak, and bundles of axes and rods. The cloak became the toga; the axes and rods, borne by 12 lictors attending the king, became the fasces, bundles of authority that in a distant day would symbolize Mussolini's fascism.

The arrogance of Tarquin the Proud exasperated the Romans, tradition tells us. When his son Sextus ravished the beautiful and virtuous matron Lucretia, Roman nobles rebelled, expelling the Tarquins and vowing that never again would a king rule their city. The Tarquins sought aid from other Etruscan powers. Thus began Lars Porsena's march in 508 B.C. Romans reeled before his drive. The Janiculum Hill outpost fell; defenders discarded their weapons and fled into the city. Brave Horatius stayed, holding the bridge at the Tiber until his comrades could destroy the wooden span and thus save the city. Legends clash over his fate, but whether he perished there or swam to safety, he lived on in Roman hearts. He was the first Roman honored by the state with a statue in the Forum.

Driven from Rome, the Etruscans never regained prominence. The fierce Samnite

MIGHT MADE RITE *when wooing wouldn't work: Rome's legendary founders, denied wives by Sabine tribesmen, seize their daughters at a festival staged by Romulus. When kinfolk marched to the rescue, the women, won by "honeyed words," defended their abductors and proudly became the mothers of Rome.*

Their progeny, expanding Rome's dominion, fought invading Pyrrhus (above) and his elephants. Driven back to his Grecian realm in 275 B.C., he declared: "What a battlefield I am leaving to Rome and Carthage!"

"THE RAPE OF THE SABINE WOMEN," C. 1636, BY NICOLAS POUSSIN; METROPOLITAN MUSEUM OF ART, NEW YORK.
ETRUSCAN PLATE FROM CAPENA, 3D CENTURY B.C.; VILLA GIULIA.
HELLENISTIC BUST, NATIONAL MUSEUM, NAPLES; SCALA

271

SYMBOL OF ROME, *glory of Etruscan art,*
Capitoline Wolf suckles Romulus and Remus.
Myth says Mars fathered the twins; their mother
descended from Aeneas, Trojan hero celebrated
by Virgil in the Aeneid. Finding the babes
abandoned on the Tiber banks, the she-wolf saved
them. Romulus founded Rome; when Remus mocked
its sacred boundary, his twin slew him, crying:
"So perish all who ever cross my walls!"
    When Lars Porsena's Etruscans threatened Rome,
Horatius saved the day at a timber span
near the Isle of the Tiber (below), where the
Fabrician Bridge at right has stood since 62 B.C.
The Etruscans' power waned, but their rich heritage
lingered to grace the swelling city of destiny.

tribe swept them from Campania, Celts seized their cities in the Po Valley. Rome, now a republic ruled by consuls, slashed through Etruria; by 280 B.C. every Etruscan city there had either surrendered or died under Rome's sword.

Magna Graecia, the Hellenic domain along the coast from the Bay of Naples to the Gulf of Taranto, summoned Pyrrhus, King of Epirus in western Greece, to challenge Rome. He fought in vain, though he won two costly battles (henceforth no soldier would cheer a Pyrrhic victory). In the dazzle of Rome, the Etruscans flickered out.

For centuries the Forum they had built would witness the pomp of processional triumphs awarded consuls victorious in war. In purple toga, with crown and scepter, a mortal turned god for a day would ride in a chariot to the temple on the Capitoline. His face would be reddened with minium so that he looked like a terracotta image of a god. These trappings of Tarquin and his gods would gird Rome's armies as she turned to face a master warrior, sworn to destroy her.

By Gilbert Charles-Picard

The World of Hannibal

THE CHILD grasps his father's hand and in the dim temple repeats what he is told to say: He will hate the Romans; to the end of his life he will never have any other goal than the punishment of their accursed nation; he will reject both appeasement and compromise until he wins complete victory. It is a mighty oath for a nine-year-old boy, but few will live to keep a vow so well as young Hannibal of Carthage, whose name rings through the ages as the Scourge of Rome. Except for Hannibal, we would scarcely remember the North African city of Carthage or its people. Their forebears were the Semitic wanderers who settled Tyre, Sidon, Byblos, and other centers along the Levant, the eastern rim of the Mediterranean. From a shellfish they made purple dye; from a word meaning "purple" they acquired their Greek name, "Phoenician." Romans Latinized it to "Punic." Skillful seamen, they roamed far in search of trade. While Greeks in the eighth century B.C. thrust westward along the Mediterranean's north shore, founding colonies in Sicily and Italy (Magna Graecia), Phoenicians paralleled them along the south shore. One colony on Tunisia's northern bulge became the nucleus of their mercantile empire. They called it *Kart Hadasht*, "New City." Romans rendered it "Carthago" and grew to fear and hate it as a powerful rival. Of its great buildings, only meager outlines now remain; of its art, we find little more than sculptured tombstones; of its literature, nothing. We read

Hannibal, "the man for whom Africa was too small a continent," looks out upon Italy's Lake Trasimeno, scene of a mighty Carthaginian victory over Rome; Tom Allen, National Geographic staff

a few impressions by its enemies. Plautus' comedy *Poenulus* delighted Romans with its Carthaginian merchant, dubbed *gugga* (roughly, "little rat"). He shuffles onstage, earrings dangling, followed by aged slaves doubled under trashy wares. A character scoffs at his long Punic robe: "Hey, you there, without a belt!"

In the spring of 238 B.C., when Hannibal swore enmity to Rome, Carthage was recovering from the First Punic War, fought for the domination of Sicily. To challenge the swift, bronze-prowed galleys of Carthage, Rome had trained crews and built ships modeled, it is said, on a beached Punic vessel. They met the Carthaginian fleet off Sicily in 260 and dropped long gangways onto the Punic ships. Over these ramps—called *corvi* (ravens) from the beaks that spiked

ROMAN "RAVEN" *drops its iron beak into Carthaginian deck off Mylae, Sicily, in 260* B.C. *Unclad*

them into position—thundered Roman soldiers to redden the decks. Such battles humbled Carthage. In 241 B.C. the city bowed to Rome.

The Carthaginians gave up footholds in Sicily they had struggled to maintain for five centuries—since they first collided there with Greeks. Moreover, the 23-year war drained the treasury. Their unpaid mercenary army mutinied and led into savage rebellion the Libyan peasants who worked the fields. While Carthage fought for its life, Rome seized the old Punic colony of Sardinia.

Desperate for a leader to end the revolt, the ruling tribunal of Carthage, the One Hundred and Four, turned the city defenses over to Hamilcar Barca, a young general who had led the mercenaries and knew how to defeat them.

legionary sets grappling hook and leaps clear; soldiers rush across to win a sea battle with land weapons.

PAINTING FOR NATIONAL GEOGRAPHIC BY STANLEY MELTZOFF

Victorious, this Hamilcar, Hannibal's father, represented a hopeful new regime
to the nearly quarter of a million Carthaginians so long penned inside their walls.
But to the governing nobles, his popularity was odious. They summoned him and
confronted him with a heavy dossier in which jurists and hair-splitting officials
had noted various irregularities—accounting mistakes, imprudent words—the
little errors committed by a man who puts the goal before the means.

Hamilcar remembered great men of the past whom the oligarchy had destroyed.
Himilco, once victor over the Greeks in Sicily, had been dressed in a slave tunic
to confess his sins at the temples. Then, locking himself up, he had taken poison.
Bomilcar, an aspiring dictator, hung for hours in agony on the marketplace cross,
heaping insults on his enemies; Hanno the Great, who had solidified Punic gains
in Sicily, was pinned on that same cross, eyes pierced, body streaming blood.

But times were changing. Powerful friends rallied to Hamilcar and organized foes
of the oligarchy into a true opposition. They inspired the Assembly of the People,
Carthage's largest administrative body, to bar prosecution of the country's savior.

PHOENICIANS *spread westward when Assyria besieged their home cities of Tyre and Sidon and commandeered galleys like one below that sails a sea of stone. Sidonians founded Leptis Magna, Tyrians chose the outpost of Carthage as their* Kart Hadasht,

PAINTING BY PETER V. BIANCHI, NATIONAL GEOGRAPHIC STAFF ARTIST. ABOVE: RELIEF FROM NINEVEH, 7TH CENTURY B.C.; BRITISH MUSEUM. BELOW: W. ROBERT MOORE

New City. Its traders fanned out to expand ports like Gades and build new ones. Legend deifies Elissa, Princess of Tyre and the "ill-starred Dido" of the Aeneid, *as founder of Carthage. She sited it on a hill (opposite) in 814 B.C., but Libyans would sell only what an oxhide would cover. She ringed the hill with strips of hide!*

Below the Byrsa—the hill's name means "oxhide" in Greek but "fortress" in the Semitic of Phoenicia—Carthaginians dug and paved an oblong port for merchant ships and a circular naval base, now silted ponds (left). Admiral's palace crowned the central isle. From here Hannibal left for Spain.

279

The dreaded tribunal dared not defy the populace. Now in city squares and temple porticoes one heard philosophers trained in Greece praising the advantages of a wise monarchy—even, perhaps, a popular government.

THE HISTORIAN Polybius, who watched the final razing of Carthage, built us a backbone of fact about the city's wars. Aristotle described its politics. Hannibal himself told of his oath half a century after he took it; beaten and exiled, he yet looked back on its fulfillment. Archeology adds substance to our shadowy vision of Carthage. As Director of Tunisian Antiquities for many years, I watched "detectives of the past" weave each small discovery into the fabric of knowledge. But to picture the details of daily life, I must often rely on informed conjecture. Only thus can I describe Hamilcar pondering his future on that day of decision when a boy's vow shapes the world's destiny.

I imagine the father in the study of his house, probably on Mount Megara,

WARES OF THE WORLD *funnel through Carthage: Greek wine, African ivory, a caged leopard for Rome's*

today's Sidi bou Said, a headland in the Gulf of Tunis. Here the well-to-do basked
in a healthful climate: The sirocco seemed almost refreshing after its passage over the
gulf; the scorpions, subdued by the god of the wealthy, seemed disinclined to sting.
From his house, designed by a Greek as were so many good things in Carthage,
Hamilcar viewed Cape Bon, 65-mile spur of the Atlas Mountains pointing toward
Sicily. There lay quarries supplying limestone for city buildings.

Today, scholars travel to Cape Bon to study Kerkouane, the only site in Africa where
Romans did not obliterate the Punic trace. Here the landed gentry exploited
olive groves and vineyards and built spacious homes that tell us much. Judging
from them, I picture Hamilcar pacing his courtyard, sandals slapping on pink
cement. A monumental door was angled to keep people on the street from
gazing inside. Delicate Ionic columns, faced in stucco, supported galleries.
A stuccoed altar received offerings to the family gods. Benches lined the court and
its vestibule for the comfort of visitors; a large reception room with walls painted

arena, slabs of Iberian copper. Middlemen and shippers, Carthaginians exported few of their own products.

PAINTING BY PETER V. BIANCHI, NATIONAL GEOGRAPHIC STAFF ARTIST

to imitate rare marble awaited special guests. Here, and in the ostentatious dining room adjoining it, a frieze high on the wall depicted the god Dionysus (borrowed like so many things from Greece) and his followers.

Fragments of marble and blue glass encrusted the floors—except for the reception room, where a mosaic of multicolored pebbles showed a griffin attacking a stag. The monster's great wings thrashed above its leonine body as its talons and beak ripped at the prey's heaving flesh.

A bathroom opened off one side of the courtyard, small but comfortable, with a slipper-shaped tub and several handbasins attached to the outside of the bath so one could wash hands and face.

A stairway led to the next floor, domain of the women. There Hamilcar's wife (history does not divulge her name) was admiring her grandson, the little Hanno, brought for a visit by her eldest daughter, wife of the present figurehead king of the city. Grandmother and servants exclaimed at the child's strength, at the appetite with which he fed from a terracotta nursing cup with a scrap of cloth wrapped around the spout to resemble a nipple.

In the basement of the house, slaves bustled about their duties. Some baked flat cakes, light and oily, in a terracotta oven. Others cleaned fish still wet from the sea. In a palm-shaded garden, cooks turned spits above an open fire, roasting lambs and she goats spiced with aromatic herbs.

Conscious of the activity, the general yet remained deep in thought. Now that the latest peasant revolts had been subdued, the people clamored to have him elected one of the two suffetes, the magistrates who ran the city. But Hamilcar shunned politics. He could stand before his troops and find words to give them confidence for an attack. He was less at ease in the public square.

Moreover, it was increasingly clear that Carthage was no longer mistress of her own affairs. Rome, victor in that long, harrowing First Punic War, apparently did not intend to finish her off, but would never again let her thrive. The rape of Sardinia, an outrage that echoed far and wide, clearly showed that Carthage would remain a vassal and tributary to Rome forever. To make war again would be folly with only a vestige of the army left—and no fleet at all.

*H*AMILCAR KNEW that his best hope for recruiting fresh resistance to Rome and escaping the jealousy of the One Hundred and Four lay in Spain with its wealth of metals and fighting men. Hamilcar had seen Iberian mercenaries in action. What couldn't be done with them if he could give them a common goal besides quick booty! And in Gades (now Cadiz) Phoenicians had been settled longer than anywhere else in the western Mediterranean. They had sought help from their Carthaginian cousins every time Celts raided from the hills or Greeks sailed through the Strait of Gibraltar to prowl the Atlantic coast.

CARTHAGINIAN MARTS *echo in* souks *of Tunis—stall-lined alleys where smiths din, perfumes sweeten the air, and memories stir of slave trade. Vanished Carthage lies under suburban sprawl. Sightseers can reach it by tram, disembarking at Hannibal Station.*

W. ROBERT MOORE

They could hardly refuse to give help to Carthage now.
In Spain, Hamilcar would be master of his destiny,
without having to account for his actions. He could
raise an army and fashion an empire like Alexander's.
One day Rome would see him approach from the farthest
reaches of the western world with Iberians, Celts, all the
barbarians of the north behind him.

He would leave his wife at home. She was quite capable
of managing the house and administering the estates.
In a pinch she could turn to her sons-in-law for help.
One, Bomilcar, had plenty of free time. The ruling nobles
of Carthage had so reduced his powers as king of the city
that he did little else but preside over one of the councils
and receive ambassadors.

Hamilcar considered his own sons, his "lion's brood"
as a Roman later called these three future generals.
Hasdrubal and Mago—seven and five—could remain under
their mother's care, though Hasdrubal had reached the age
to quit the women's quarters. But Hannibal? At nine,
he needed a manly education. Yet no Spartan tutor
could replace a father, especially for a lad who did not
easily accept reprimands. Perhaps Hannibal
should accompany his father to Spain. Would
he not learn soldiering in camp better than
at the training ground? Then again, perhaps
he was too young.

A breeze ruffled Hamilcar's long robe.
He would have preferred a Greek general's
uniform—short tunic and purple cape
clasped at the shoulder—for the ride he
must make today, but the purpose of his
journey demanded proper attire. For he
was to make a sacrifice to his family god.

"*T*HERE WAS in their city a bronze
image ... extending its hands, palms up
and sloping toward the ground, so that
each of the children when placed thereon
rolled down and fell into a sort of gaping
pit filled with fire." Thus does Diodorus
of Sicily, writing in Caesar's day, describe
the Carthaginian rite of child sacrifice.

Those who laid their firstborn in
the fire-reddened arms of Baal Hammon,

HEART-SEARING RITUAL *sees noble
families of Carthage sacrifice their
firstborn to appease Baal Hammon
in time of crisis. Babies "pass
through the fire" as sloping hands
of the idol roll them into the
inferno in the god's temple.*

*Priest readies a child (left)
on the stele that marked its ashes.*

284

PAINTING BY PETER V. BIANCHI, NATIONAL GEOGRAPHIC STAFF ARTIST. OPPOSITE: STELE FROM CARTHAGE, 4TH CENTURY B.C., BARDO NATIONAL MUSEUM; W. ROBERT MOORE

protector of the city, received from this terrible Canaanite deity the promise
of blessings to make them forget the horror. The little victim would live forever
in the god's palace; a new descendant would take his place; miraculous harvests
would crowd the parents' fields; their ships would return with bulging cargoes.
The anguish of watching without visible emotion while flames reduced their baby
to a tiny pile of bones and ashes seemed to give them a sense of regeneration.
Now they were slaves of the god, and they felt in themselves some of the awesome

285

force which had maintained their city through so many perilous centuries. The common folk of Carthage crowded the sanctuary, or tophet, proud to be admitted to the holocaust where formerly only kings and nobles were allowed.

Later ages grew skeptical of the monstrous tales of infanticide. But in 1921 Tunisian officials stopped an unauthorized searcher from carrying off a stele — a slender tombstone a yard high, bearing the engraved outlines of a priest with a child in his arms. Diggers probed the spot where the prowler had found it and some 25 feet down came upon a necropolis amid the arches and columns of the port which the Romans eventually built on the site of razed Carthage. Here stood thousands of small steles and sandstone blocks cut in the shape of temples and thrones — all Punic monuments. Under nearly every one was an urn, roughly finished as are all Carthaginian containers, holding the ashes of a very young child. The stones were inscribed with sacrificial dedications: "To the Lord Baal Hammon, this is dedicated. . . ."

BARDO NATIONAL MUSEUM; MICHAEL SEMAK. OPPOSITE: THOMAS J. ABERCROMBIE, NATIONAL GEOGRAPHIC STAFF

SILENT STONES *mourn children of Carthage, victims of sacrifice. Queen Elissa, in legend, leaped on a flaming pyre to win favor for her city. Carthaginians enshrined the spot, built their harborside warehouses elsewhere. Here scholars found infants' ashes in urns beneath steles (left). They named the place "tophet" for the Biblical shrine near Jerusalem where idolaters passed children "through the fire to Molech."*

Clay faces of smiling gods and grimacing demons masked dancers who sought to ward off evil spirits from living and dead.

I once guided delegates from a congress on legal medicine through this tophet. Some asked that the contents of the urns be sent to them for laboratory analysis. We had to clear this request with puzzled customs' men. Regulations had not provided for this kind of shipment!

Besides the tophet, scholars have brought to light a tiny "chapel" on a plot of ground that conquering Romans left unrazed. Here, surely, was the holiest spot in Carthage—the very ground where the city's traditional founder, Elissa (whom Virgil called Dido), sister of Pygmalion, King of Tyre, stepped ashore in the ninth century B.C. Hamilcar knew grander shrines. Near the two small harbors stood the Temple of Reshef, gold plaques covering its tabernacle, and the hill called the Byrsa was crowned

287

by the Temple of Eshmoun, its many-columned portico reached by a stairway with 60 steps. Yet no shrine was so revered as the little chapel.

THE FIRST of Hamilcar's ancestors to settle in Carthage, five generations after Elissa, had passed along to his descendants his reverence for the god Baal Shamem, Lord of the Skies, and his son, Melkart. The Barcas had served them ever since. Even priests could not explain the differences between Baal Shamem and Baal Hammon except that the former did not always require human sacrifice. Hamilcar ordered victims for his sacrifice — a bull and a ram — to be ready at Baal Shamem's temple. Now he called for his horse, stepped toward the door, and was suddenly confronted by a boy. I can envision him with brown curls, his high, straight brow

288

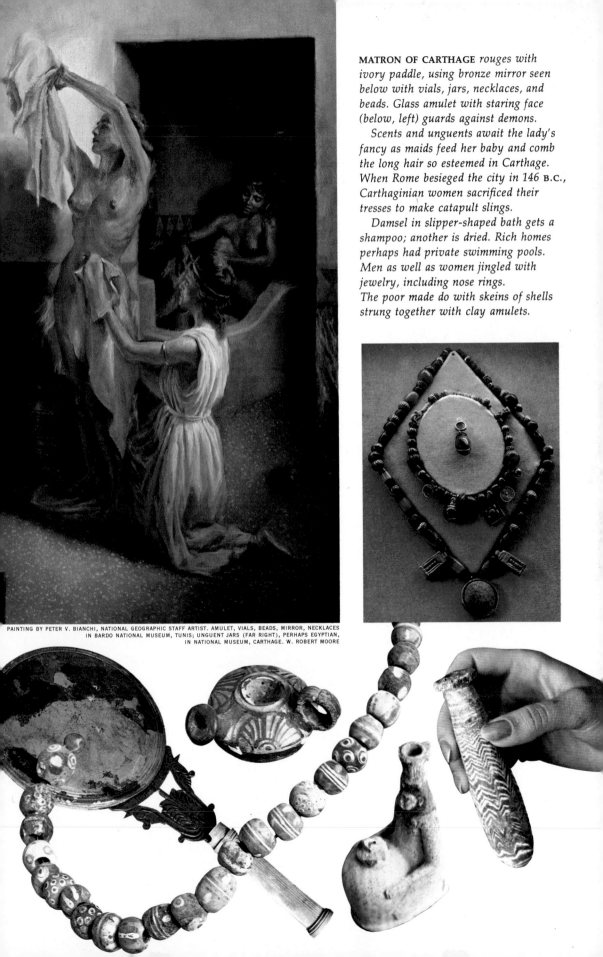

MATRON OF CARTHAGE *rouges with ivory paddle, using bronze mirror seen below with vials, jars, necklaces, and beads. Glass amulet with staring face (below, left) guards against demons.*

Scents and unguents await the lady's fancy as maids feed her baby and comb the long hair so esteemed in Carthage. When Rome besieged the city in 146 B.C., Carthaginian women sacrificed their tresses to make catapult slings.

Damsel in slipper-shaped bath gets a shampoo; another is dried. Rich homes perhaps had private swimming pools. Men as well as women jingled with jewelry, including nose rings.
The poor made do with skeins of shells strung together with clay amulets.

PAINTING BY PETER V. BIANCHI, NATIONAL GEOGRAPHIC STAFF ARTIST. AMULET, VIALS, BEADS, MIRROR, NECKLACES IN BARDO NATIONAL MUSEUM, TUNIS; UNGUENT JARS (FAR RIGHT), PERHAPS EGYPTIAN, IN NATIONAL MUSEUM, CARTHAGE. W. ROBERT MOORE

OLIVES, *a major crop in days
of Carthage, remain a staple in
Tunisia's trade. A proposed law
would have added olive oil to
every can of motor lubricant!*

*Pickers harvest green olives for
eating before winter ripens and
fattens them with oil. One tree
may yield half a ton yearly and
serve several owners. Each tends
his own branches.*

*A retired Carthaginian general,
Mago, wrote a treatise on raising
olives and other crops. Though
scorning the culture of Carthage,
Romans envied its green thumb
and translated Mago into Latin—
the only Punic author so honored.
Fragments remain in quotes by
Pliny and other Romans.*

*In Nabeul, southeast of Tunis,
potters make amphoras (above)
like those of Punic forebears. The
town lies near Neapolis, razed
by Romans along with Carthage.*

THOMAS J. ABERCROMBIE, NATIONAL GEOGRAPHIC STAFF.
ABOVE: W. ROBERT MOORE

and arching nose honoring his Tyrian forebears, his flared nostrils hinting of African strains as well. The cheeks do not quite match; the chin points a bit sharply, but the black eyes burn with an intensity astonishing in a child. Already the son has acquired the stern gaze of the father.

"I want to go with you."

Hannibal says no more, yet Hamilcar feels his god has spoken through his son. He takes the boy's hand without a word. Beyond the front door, trusted servants wait on horseback and a groom holds Hamilcar's mount. He leaps into the saddle, picks up the child, and sets him on his horse's rump.

*F*IG GROVES shade the riders as they angle down the hill from Megara. They cross a garden-covered plain with small white houses and occasionally a mausoleum, high and square, topped by a pyramid. Refugees of the Mercenary War built thatched huts here, and the road passes them—smelly shacks around which naked children, black and white, play with emaciated dogs.

To seaward, red cliffs tower over the road—clay quarries used by potters and brickmakers. Donkey caravans clog the route, baskets laden with fish, fruits, or new bricks from the freshly molded piles drying in the sun.

Hamilcar prods his mount past and into the road through Carthage's northern necropolis where stiff statues, crudely sculptured in the ancient fashion, mark the grave shafts. One has been opened, and men with block and tackle are lowering a white marble sarcophagus into it. Kilns smoke nearby; beside them potters hawk little statues and busts of Demeter, guarantor of happiness to the dead, another god the Carthaginians borrowed from the Greeks. These trinkets, purchased by families in mourning, will accompany the dead through eternity.

Beyond the cemetery gate the riders jog through a narrow street where women squabble and gossip on the balconies of multi-storied buildings and screech at the children swarming in the general's way. Then come the workshops— cramped cubicles where artisans crouch beside their displays of wares to be sold. Some hammer out copper and bronze, some cut gems. In small shops, merchants sell cloth or richly colored rugs.

A customer leaning on the counter of a drink vendor recognizes Hamilcar and points him out to the crowd. A great cheer goes up and the people gather about the party, calling out blessings and praises and shouting curses on Rome. The outriders push their horses through, making way for the general and his son. Some Campanian merchants who have just sold a cargo of their famed black pottery at a good profit sense the welling hatred for Romans and decide to duck into an alley for safety. There a lurking pickpocket relieves one of them of a fat purse!

Now up a hill the troupe rides and halts before the Egyptian-style pylons that frame the temple of Baal Shamem, a modest building several centuries old. They cross a courtyard edged by porticoes and ending in a cubelike sanctuary. Few worshipers come here, but those that do belong to the noblest families and the priest cannot complain of their gifts.

The holy man waits as his illustrious visitors approach. He has donned his vestments: round toque, linen robe, white sandals. Now he sits rereading an ancient papyrus dealing with the battles of a king of the old Phoenician city, Sidon. In these lines, almost a thousand years old, he finds a foreshadowing of the present ordeals of Carthage, and he pauses in his reading now and then to heap curses upon the enemies of his city.

A servant interrupts this pious exercise to announce Hamilcar's arrival, and the priest hurries to meet him, accompanied by sacrificer, flute and harp players, and an official observer who sees that the ritual follows the rules. Hamilcar and the holy man weigh their words, for they know this official is a spy for the ruling nobles. He will listen for a word that might enable the tribunal to implicate the general in some seditious enterprise and so discredit him.

BEARDLESS YOUTH, *delicate features captured in a bronze from Morocco, is the real Hannibal, says the author. He appears again on the lower Carthaginian coin; Hamilcar on the upper. Spain's Cartagena (lower right) shelters ships where the Barcas anchored their dream of revenge on Rome. After Hamilcar died, son-in-law Hasdrubal founded this "New Carthage." Sailboats racing past Gibraltar (below) evoke Phoenician fleets scudding past the "Pillars of Melkart" to seek fortunes in distant lands.*

COINS IN BRITISH MUSEUM. BUST FROM VOLUBILIS IN RABAT MUSEUM, MOROCCO; ROGER WOOD.
ABOVE: BATES LITTLEHALES, NATIONAL GEOGRAPHIC PHOTOGRAPHER. RIGHT: DAN McCOY, BLACK STAR

Shrewdly, Hamilcar consults a stone tablet listing the fee for each sacrifice, pays the official the required amount for a bull and a ram, and sees that his secretary collects a receipt. The spy's official duties end here. A glare from Hamilcar sends him padding away with a swirl of his robe.

Now the priest, accompanied by harp and flute, chants in the Canaanite tongue the words that will transfer Hamilcar's personality into the two animals' bodies. Young Hannibal understands little of the rite but stands firmly beside his father.

The sacrificer's ax flashes twice. Attendants carry away the two victims. No sacred banquet will follow, for this is a burnt offering—all the flesh must be consumed at the altar. The priest leads Hamilcar by the hand inside the *naos,* the sanctuary, to enter into the presence of his god. Unlike Egyptians and Greeks, Phoenicians feel it impossible to enclose divine power in an image fashioned by man. What statues they admit to their temples represent only external aspects of a deity. They look alike and never adorn the naos.

But at the entrance to Baal Shamem's sanctuary stands a transparent stone set on a golden pedestal. Though it cannot depict the god, it is considered the work of the smith god Chrusor, and Hamilcar prostrates himself before it. Hannibal imitates his father's every gesture, but hesitates to move into the sacred shadows. Thus it is that the general takes his son's hand and leads him through the vow of hatred.

The road ahead is at last clear to Hamilcar. He will cross to Spain with his young son. And should he not live to take his own revenge on Rome, Hannibal will carry it out, sweeping into Italy, a sacred vow burning in his breast.

A fiery genius conquered men and mountains to keep a vow of hate.
National Geographic's Tom Allen traces his bloody path

Through the Alps to the Gates of Rome

ETCHED IN FLAME, Hannibal shouts commands to soldiers who must think him mad. But, as ever, they obey the general who has led them to this lofty, forsaken realm. They cut and haul timber from the sparse forests and build a pyre about the massive rock that blocks their path. Elephants shy, trumpeting their fear of fire. Logs crackle in the snow. Men pour their last rations of sour wine over the rock. Acrid mist veils them as they hack at the rock with picks. Suddenly, it cracks. Hannibal has shattered the final barrier on his bold passage through the Alps.

Now he leads his gaunt men down upon Italy, his war cry "Conquer or die!" For he marches against the rock that only blood can sunder—Rome.

But on that October day in 218 B.C., Hannibal's army itself seemed conquered. "They are the ghosts and shadows of men, already half dead," a

Hannibal in the Alps "splits the very rocks asunder"; painting by Peter V. Bianchi, National Geographic staff artist

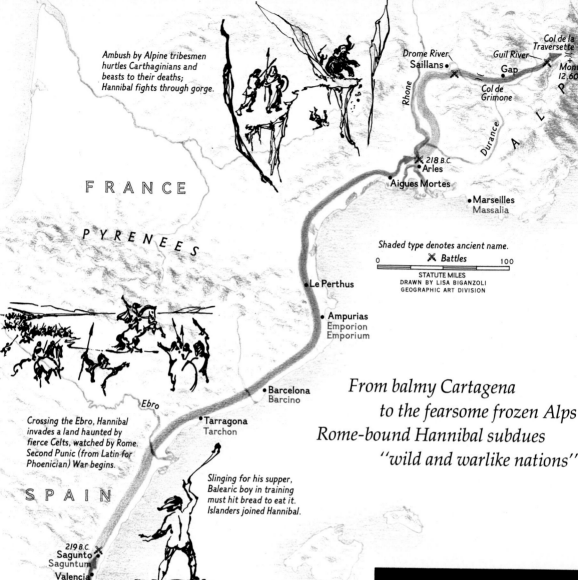

Ambush by Alpine tribesmen hurtles Carthaginians and beasts to their deaths; Hannibal fights through gorge.

Drome River
Saillans
✗
Rhone
FRANCE
PYRENEES
Le Perthus
Ampurias
Emporion
Emporium

Guil River
Gap
Col de la
Traversette
✗
Monte V
12,602 f
Col de
Grimone
Durance
A
L
P

✗ 218 B.C.
Arles
Aigues Mortes

Marseilles
Massalia

Shaded type denotes ancient name.
0   ✗ Battles   100
STATUTE MILES
DRAWN BY LISA BIGANZOLI
GEOGRAPHIC ART DIVISION

Crossing the Ebro, Hannibal invades a land haunted by fierce Celts, watched by Rome. Second Punic (from Latin for Phoenician) War begins.

Ebro
Barcelona
Barcino
Tarragona
Tarchon

S P A I N

Slinging for his supper, Balearic boy in training must hit bread to eat it. Islanders joined Hannibal.

*From balmy Cartagena
to the fearsome frozen Alps
Rome-bound Hannibal subdues
"wild and warlike nations"*

219 B.C.
Sagunto ✗
Saguntum
Valencia

BALEARIC ISLANDS

Denia

Elche
Helike

Murcia

Cartagena
Carthago Nova

On the path of conquest Hannibal traversed
the Iberian peninsula, peopled by tribes
whose imprint endures in the faces of Spain.
Matador in Madrid, pondering blood and sand,
mirrors the bronze visage of an ancient Celt.
Señorita of Valencia reflects the elegance
—and coiffure—of the Iberian "Lady of Elche."
Her stony visage came to light where Hamilcar
fell in a skirmish, defending his son Hannibal.
Celts, spreading across Iron Age Europe,
pushed south through Pyrenean passes in the
7th and 6th centuries B.C. From their union with
Iberians came the peninsula's Celtiberians.

Roman general told his troops as they braced for battle on the plains of the Po. "All their strength has been crushed and beaten out of them by the Alpine crags. . . . Snowstorms have frozen their sinews stiff. Their hands and feet are frostbitten."

These frostbitten ghosts were the survivors of a great army that had marched forth under the hot Mediterranean sun five months before. Out of the Carthaginian colonial capital of New Carthage in Iberia had streamed columns that stretched for miles: 90,000 infantrymen, 12,000 horsemen, 37 elephants, countless mules laden with the baggage of war and the colony's silver to pay for more. At their head rode Hannibal, who would never see this city again.

From here his family, the Barcas of Carthage, had ruled not only a colony but also a personal army. Hamilcar Barca, his father, had begun the conquest of Iberia but fell in battle. An assassin slew Hamilcar's son-in-law and successor, Hasdrubal, founder of the city. Hannibal, at the age of 26, took command by unanimous choice of the troops. Almost at once he prepared to fulfill the childhood vow he had made in North Africa: He would march against Rome.

I took up Hannibal's trail in New Carthage, the Spanish port whose modern name, Cartagena, preserves the memory of its founders. I would follow him along the rim of the Mediterranean, into the Alps, down the spine of Italy. And I would seek him in the ruins of Carthage, where he was born, and at the walls of Rome, where he pounded at the gates of history.

Cartagena sprawls about its huge harbor, a deep bay sentried by domed hills. From the highest, site of a Roman citadel, I looked down upon a city whose tasks have little changed in more than 2,000 years. What lured Carthaginians endures: the lead and iron of nearby mines, the bay where ships of war and trade still anchor. As I descended to the bustling streets, however, I despaired of finding a sign of Hannibal or his time. White-uniformed policemen impatiently shuffled cars, bicycles, and motor scooters. Transistor radios jangled me into the present.

"This is our oldest street," my guide said, leading me down a cobbled, tranquil

LIMESTONE BUST FROM ELCHE, 5TH CENTURY B.C., IN THE PRADO, MADRID; FOTO MAS. RIGHT: WILLIAM GREENE, PHOTO RESEARCHERS. LEFT: ALBERT MOLDVAY, NATIONAL GEOGRAPHIC STAFF. OPPOSITE: BRONZE BUST FROM BOURAY, C. 3D CENTURY B.C., IN ST. GERMAIN-EN-LAYE MUSEUM

297

lane. Along the shop-lined street wild *canarios* sweetly lamented their bondage in cages hung at curtained doorways. Mothers strolled by, savory market basket on one arm, chubby, black-eyed child on the other.

"And here are your Carthaginians," he announced, ushering me into a small archeological museum. All about lay crude buckets, ladders, hanks of rope—relics of ancient mines that conjure up scenes Hannibal could have witnessed: Slaves climb down notched-log ladders into watery pits. There they hack and claw from the soil of Iberia the metals that enrich Carthage—iron, lead, silver. Above, other slaves at wooden pulleys haul up the precious ore in leather buckets or reed bags tied to ropes of woven esparto, the tall grass that still abounds around Cartagena.

From here Hannibal turned first, as I now did, to Saguntum, a coastal settlement that stood like a Roman island in the midst of the land Carthage had conquered. I headed up the Costa Blanca, the White Coast, where gleaming sand hems dazzling sea. Seaward, the view across time and water is changeless. The Mediterranean's winds still bear to Iberia the soft warmth of Carthage. And the skies still flash memories of the once dread name Barca—Thunderbolt.

Now Sagunto, the city rises in terraces to a steep-sloped

SEARING SUN *over Saguntum kindles memories of the flaming finale to Hannibal's siege. When Carthaginians stormed walls long battered by ram and missile, the city's leaders, writes Livy, built a golden bonfire of treasure and leaped into it. Other Saguntines—Iberians and Greek colonists allied to Rome— "set fire to their own houses and burned themselves alive . . . with their wives and children."*

Stone shot unearthed here recalls Hannibal's catapults, accurate to 200 yards, with a maximum range of 500 yards. Powered by gut or hair ropes tautened by windlass, they hurled stone or concrete balls of up to 60 pounds.

Romans later rebuilt Saguntum's ramparts and theater. Conquering Arabs raised the Moorish gate in background. City's medieval name, Murviedro, came from "Old Walls." Spain calls it Sagunto.

ridge half a mile long. Stone walls, some battlemented, some breached by time and war, rim the ridge. Stones placed by Iberian hands bear others laid by Roman, Moor, and Spaniard. A theater spreads along the lower hillside. Thousands once sat here on narrow stone seats and watched provincial productions of Roman plays. Rome came to rebuild the theater, but in those dark months when Saguntum fought Hannibal, no Romans came.

By treaty, the Ebro River divided Carthage's southern Iberia from the northern Iberian land Rome nurtured as a buffer state. Some 75 miles south of the mouth of the Ebro, however, lay Saguntum, a rich protectorate of Rome.

Hannibal could not march against Rome until he wiped out this citadel that offered a sea gate to the enemy. In a bloody prelude to war, he attacked Saguntum nearly a year before he began his epic trek from New Carthage to the Alps and down upon Italy.

Abandoning the gravel road that sweeps upward from Sagunto, I climbed the ridge's flank, so sheer that in places I could not stand erect. I reached carefully for handholds; thick patches of long-needled cactus garrisoned the hill. When Hannibal's men struggled up it, writes the Roman historian Livy, "so closely were the men on either side pressed together that no missile could miss its mark."

I could envision the scene: From towers on the heights Saguntines hurl iron-headed javelins, some wrapped in flaming pitch. Hannibal charges, rashly leading his troops through a storm of spears. Suddenly, his horse falters. Hannibal falls, a javelin in his thigh. The men waver. Some drop their weapons and flee headlong down the hill. Others desert the movable shelters that shield the battering rams. While Hannibal's personal physician, an Egyptian trained in Alexandria, treats the wound, the general marks each man. "I have watched and witnessed your valor . . . and your acts of courage I know by heart," he will tell them later. He also knows the acts of the cowards.

When Hannibal recovers, new waves of attackers besiege and hammer at the walls. Defenders fill every breach and hold like stone—for awhile. Then foot by foot, house by house, Saguntum yields. After eight months its towered citadel stands amid ruin. As the invaders hack toward this last redoubt, families fight to the death or set their homes ablaze and plunge into the flames.

Laden with scorched and bloodstained booty, the victors return to New Carthage, where they winter. When spring awakens the Iberian plains, they march past the blackened grave of Saguntum. Rome now knows that the treaty with

HANNIBAL'S RUBICON, *the Ebro divided Iberia. Crossing it, the Carthaginian invaded Rome's domain and began a 17-year war of attrition. Iberians of the Ebro* (Iberus) *Valley followed his rising star; ancients called them "men under a vow," for they pledged to kill themselves if their leader fell. Northward they trekked, past the port named for the Barcas who founded it— Barcelona, today the giant of Spanish commerce.*

Los Gigantes, *giants evolved from medieval morality plays, tower over Barcelona's Feast of Our Lady of Mercy. Some identify them with King Ferdinand and Queen Isabella, who welcomed Columbus home here in 1493. King's helmet plainly recalls Rome's reign in Spain. Effacing 30 years of Carthaginian rule, Rome would hold Hispania 600 years.*

Carthage is not worth the bronze tablets it was written on, for Hannibal defies the key phrase, "The Carthaginians are not to cross the Ebro in arms." The Second Punic War—Rome will call it Hannibal's War—has begun.

Aᴛ ᴛʜᴇ ᴇʙʀᴏ, some 275 miles' march from New Carthage, Hannibal arrays his army for that war. He orders 11,000 men to remain with the forces holding Iberia. Perhaps recalling the cowardice at Saguntum, he cashiers 10,000 others. He strips the army of heavy baggage and siege machines. He must travel swift and light, for no longer does he parade through an Iberia pacified by the Barcas.

His white-robed Numidian cavalrymen probe ahead. These Africans ride bareback, often without a bridle, lion skins flung over their shoulders. Some may have tamed the dappled mustangs that roamed the mountains of Iberia.

Horses, hating the scent of elephants, rear and whinny when the great beasts lumber near. Atop these sit grandly garbed mahouts, called *Indoi* by the ancients, who associated elephants with India. But the drivers, like their charges, come from Africa.

Fierce Lusitanians from western Iberia march eagerly with Hannibal, for their gods cherish the severed right hands of vanquished foes. Swarthy Libyans, veterans brought over by Hamilcar, tramp alongside Iberians who fought, then joined Hannibal. Their ranks bristle with motley weapons, each shaped by the hard lessons of battle.

An elite unit, a band of long-haired men, keeps close to Hannibal, fanatically faithful to him as they were to his father. Often they gaze seaward toward their homeland, the Balearic Islands. The name aptly suggests the Greek word *ballein*, to hurl. These wild islanders sling missiles with deadly accuracy. Coiled about their heads, waists, and arms are their slings of woven rush, hair, or sinew. In pouches they carry stones, almond-shaped baked-clay pellets, and lead balls that can smash a skull or shield.

I followed the army's probable route along hilly, winding roads that rimmed the coast. Ancient chronicles are vague about Hannibal's trail between the Ebro and the Pyrenees. So I sought signs of him in Tarragona and Barcelona, cities

LADY OF SPAIN *basks on the Costa Brava, surf-scalloped coast north of Barcelona that lures tourists with timeless Iberian delights: sun and song. Medieval tower guards bathers at Tossa de Mar; by night a bistro throbs to the rhythm of a Spanish guitar, descended from the Greek cithara. In a hilltop villa, now in ruins, Romans once reveled. "Country living . . . is the finest!" wrote Martial, Spanish-born poet of Rome.*

he would have known. Vibrant Tarragona, jutting like a balcony on the Mediterranean, stood in his day as the Carthaginian citadel of Tarchon. But soon after he marched by, the Romans came to campaign in his rear. Tarragona's great walls, rising from huge, crude stones to the dressed blocks of triumphant Rome, eloquently tell the story of the city's submission to the invaders.

Barcelona holds a clue to Hannibal within its very name; Hamilcar Barca, traditional founder of the city around 230 B.C., called it Barcino. In this teeming city where traffic jams clog medieval streets, I tried to peel away the centuries and find Hannibal's day.

I could imagine him pausing in Barcino, encamping his men near the shore, and climbing the hill where Hamilcar's city had been born. On this Hill of Taber the Romans would build a temple and Christians a humble church from which would rise the magnificent cathedral of St. Eulalia, patron saint of Barcelona. Like a root deep into the past, one of its massive foundation pillars pierces a Roman mosaic.

GLITTER HIDES Hannibal's trail along the Costa Brava. High-rise hotels and *escuelas de esqui*—schools for water-skiing—have tamed the Wild Coast, today the Spanish Riviera. Hoping for a detour into the past, I turned down a dirt road. It ended abruptly at an old deserted church, set in a deep cork-oak forest overlooking a broad valley—the kind of valley that would lure Hannibal's foragers. Here slingers and spearmen might bring down game. Raiding parties would seize cattle and grain. Some natives, anxious to see the marauders move on, would surrender their crops and livestock.

But not all yielded without a fight. In the 200 miles between the Ebro and the Pyrenees, Hannibal lost thousands of men in unchronicled skirmishes and desertions.

Near the Pyrenees lay another tempting source of supply —a great market where his army could stock up on lamps and lamp oil, tent cloth, sandals, rope, hide pouches, amphoras, cooking pots, and woolen cloaks for the Alps. In Ampurias I walked in Hannibal's time. He would have known it as Emporion, a Greek port and international trade center established centuries earlier. Its stone jetty still stands at the water's edge. Its streets run straight, meeting at sharp corners. The stumps of stone walls outline the rooms of houses where potters, weavers, and traders lived. The goods of this bustling emporium—graceful pottery adorned with Grecian gods, delicate glass bottles, sturdy bronze lamps— have emerged from the dust.

GREEK EMPORIUM *on Iberia's shore, Ampurias funneled Aegean art and the alphabet to western tribes. Founded around 575 B.C., it may have provisioned Hannibal's army. In this deserted mart diggers turned up Greek temples, the god of medicine Asclepius (at right), Roman villas, early churches. Its skilled weavers worked flax into cloth. Ancient mariners prized Iberian sails and nets, and rope woven of esparto grass.*

As I walked beyond the Grecian grid of streets to the site of a later Roman town, an encampment caught my eye. Where Hannibal's polyglot army once may have tented I found an international work camp. "We've volunteered to help at the dig here," explained Terry Green, a student from Michigan. Working beside him were young men from England, Ireland, the Netherlands, France, Germany, and Spain. He climbed out of a newly excavated Roman house and held up a roof tile.

"When you get down to these," he said, "you know you've reached the floor, not the roof. It caves in, you see, and the rest falls on top of it. The good stuff is usually near a wall. My favorite find was a chicken egg—unbroken!"

He told me he'd keep an eye out for elephant bones. By all reports, though, Hannibal had all his elephants with him as he headed toward the Pyrenees.

A natural border, the sea-to-sea mountain chain walled off Iberia in Hannibal's day and, since 1659, has separated the Spanish and French heirs of Iberians and Celts. Following Hannibal's traditional route through a 950-foot pass, I crossed into France at Le Perthus. Though officially French, the border village welcomes visitors with bewilderingly bilingual hospitality.

When Hannibal descended from the Pyrenees, the fiercely independent Celtic tribes "flew to arms." But, by parley and bribe, by threat and show of strength, he convinced their leaders that he aimed to war on the enemy of all, Rome. His diplomacy cleared his way to the marshy mouth of the Rhone River.

Along the French coast, from the Pyrenees to the Rhone, the tang of the sea and the waft of the vine summoned the past. Late at night, when the lights of seaside villages were few, when the rake of wave on pebbly beach was the only sound, I thought of Hannibal at the Rhone. Scion of Phoenician mariners, lifelong dweller by the sea, he now must venture into a rocky realm masted by mountain peaks.

Over the vast alluvial flatland the French call the Camargue, a soft blue sky rose from the horizon like a dome soaring into eternity. The sun glowed as Van Gogh had seen it here, "gloriously gold." Wild stallions flew across the Rhone-fed marshes, its glinting waters patched by wavering greens. Flamingos strutted in reed-fringed ponds, then suddenly skimmed into the sky. *Gardians*, the cowboys of the Camargue, galloped and splashed astride white-maned mounts. The gardians prodded cattle with long-shafted tridents that recall ancient fishing spears. They rode unshod horses, as did Hannibal's cavalry.

The medieval city of Aigues Mortes—Dead Waters—marks the probable spot where Hannibal turned northward, following the river's course in search of firm ground for a crossing. I walked the city's stone ramparts and, looking at the statue of its founder, King Louis IX, mused upon the ways of history. Here passed the Carthaginian on his crusade against Rome. And from here St. Louis the Crusader set forth, destined to die in the sands that shrouded Carthage.

Trumpeting in terror, Hannibal's elephants raft the Rhone

Lured onto sod-topped rafts that look like solid ground, Hannibal's elephants panic as their ferry moves out into the swift-moving stream; here one flings off his mahout. Trained to terrorize the foe, an elephant might run amok in battle and crush his own men; the mahout then had to kill the beast by hammering an iron wedge into an eyeball. Carthage, which stabled 300 and gave them prisoners to trample, portrayed the big-eared African species on coins. One coin, linked to Hannibal's time and place—217 B.C. in Italy—shows an Indian species. Scholars suggest that his herd of 37 included one Indian elephant, probably his pet Syrus (the Syrian).

Hannibal crossed the Rhone near Arles (above), which would flourish as a Roman city and center of Provençal culture.

Four days' march from the sea, somewhere near today's Arles, Hannibal paces the river's western shore. Diplomacy ends here. To cross, he must draw his sword against the Volcae, a Celtic tribe too wild for blandishment. He has commandeered every craft he can find — hollowed-out log canoes, timber rafts, hide-hulled boats. Infantrymen begin boarding. Cavalrymen lead horses into the swift waters.

Across the river, howling Volcae warriors brandish their shields and spears. Hannibal looks beyond, upstream, for a column of black smoke. Some of his men, sent miles up the river the day before, have already crossed. As their smoke signal curls up in the morning air, he leaps into a boat and orders the others launched.

The larger boats, some towing strings of horses, plunge in upriver of the frailer craft. Men, horses, and boats churn toward the Volcae, who line the bank screaming their war cry. Then, out of the woods behind them charge Hannibal's hidden men. Some of the Celts sprint toward their camp — but find it overrun and afire. At the river, war cries drown in the reddening shallows. The few Volcae survivors flee.

Mahouts on the western bank drive two lead elephants — females — onto a sod-covered train of rafts staked to the shore. Other elephants eagerly follow, unaware they are afloat until the rafts are cast off. Most freeze in terror as boats tow them out. Some plunge into the river, drowning their mahouts. But all the elephants make it across.

Meanwhile, Roman horsemen, riding hard from the Greek colony of Massalia (modern Marseilles), are nearing Hannibal. Numidian scouts intercept them and, in a savage skirmish, turn them back. By the time the Roman forces reach the crossing, Hannibal has vanished. Three days behind him, they break off pursuit. Whatever remnant survives the Alps the Romans will confront on the plains of the Po.

THE TOWERING, jagged crescent of the Alps caps the Italian peninsula. Behind these "vast fortresses raised by nature" the Romans felt secure, though they had little knowledge of the protecting peaks. Sixty years after Hannibal's crossing, the Greek historian Polybius "made the passage of the Alps to learn for myself." But his account is geographically vague. Scholars and alpinists still debate the route of Hannibal — and of Polybius.

For my guide I chose Sir Gavin de Beer, former director of the British Museum of Natural History. In his *Alps and Elephants*, he sheds new light on obscure passages in Polybius. So, following not only Hannibal and Polybius but also Sir Gavin, I drove along the broad, busy Rhone, a waterway to the Mediterranean since Roman times. At the juncture of the Rhone and the Drome River, I turned eastward into the tranquil vale of the Drome. Orchards edged the lazing river. Vineyards lay dappled in the shadows of the deep valley. Far to the southeast thrust a high ridge that bore on its prow the crude profile of a man.

"Hannibal's Rock," my host Albert Gueymard told me later. He was pointing up to it from the main street of Saillans, his small village on the Drome. Flat, red Roman tiles fleck the stone walls of Saillans' oldest houses. A Roman milestone, its top scooped out, holds holy water in the town church. And through this village so graced by antiquity runs a trail that since some dim time has been called Hannibal's.

309

"This valley could feed an army," said Georges Terrail, pharmacist and Hannibal enthusiast. "We are high. But we harvest even on our slopes. And our vines! The sun loves this valley."

In a chill, stone-walled cellar I saw the processing of the region's famed Clairette de Die. Paul Perminjat, a white-haired winemaker, led me from grape press to bottler, where the bubbly, crystalline wine, filtered 16 times, surged into bottles. A complex rig then gulped the last bit of air and pressed in corks, each selected by M. Perminjat. "All must be perfect," he said, "the grape, the bottle, the cork."

In another room, where fermenting wine rested in racked old bottles, the faint aroma of vinegar hung in the

GORGE *of the Guil, "overhung by a precipitous wall of rock," echoes Livy's word picture of the path Hannibal took into the Alps—and ambush by mountaineers "stiff with frost." They lived in "rude huts clinging to the rocks"; today's mountain folk thrive in snug hamlets, grazing sheep on mile-high pastures.*

damp air. "Bad wine," sniffed M. Perminjat. Small wire cages protected the light bulbs from shards when faulty fermentation burst a bottle. Ancient army wine was notoriously sour, almost vinegar. The French would call it *vin aigre*. Did a shattered amphora, I wondered, inspire Hannibal's wine assault on the Alpine rock?

Beyond Saillans, darkening clouds grayed distant peaks. Below me, streams roiled through a narrow, misty pass. Above glowered the sheer walls of the Gorges des Gas. Tall spruces guarded the canyon's rim. Rain blurred the world of today, and the past shimmered into view. . . .

As Hannibal's men file along a ledge in a narrow defile—the Gorges des Gas, by Sir Gavin's reckoning—Celtic mountaineers swarm down the precipitous slopes. The "sure-footed" raiders, in Livy's account, drive soldiers and pack animals "tumbling over the edge . . . like falling masonry." But, rallied by Hannibal, the army fights through, seizes a Celtic settlement on the heights, and pushes eastward. Natives soon reappear, proffering olive branches and wreaths, tokens of peace. They offer to guide Hannibal to the higher Alps.

Three days later, the column, strung out in a long line "on a narrowing track," threads another gorge. Suddenly, boulders rain down from the heights. Natives spill out of crevices and clefts in the walls of the defile. Half the army, led by Hannibal and the elephants, slashes out of the trap and makes a stand at a towering outcrop that commands the wide valley beyond. Soon after dawn, the survivors of the nightlong battle stagger out to join their comrades at the rock.

Sheets of rain veiled the road ahead. I slowed the car to an elephant's plodding pace. Rain-sluiced rocks tumbled from the cliffs above. Golfball-size hailstones sheared small branches off trembling trees. The muddy Guil River frothed hundreds of feet below my cliff-hanging road. I wound through a high-walled cut in the valley called Queyras—local dialect for "Huge Crag." When I emerged from

"On, on, you madman... over your savage Alps"

Juvenal

the gorge, the rain stopped. Athwart the valley ahead glistened the craggy rock that guards the hamlet of Chateau-Queyras. A medieval fortress roosts on the natural redoubt that may have sheltered Hannibal's army.

I twisted some 20 miles farther up the Guil Valley to a narrow, rutted road that switchbacked up a slope determined to become vertical. The remnant of the road ended

on a shelf hanging hundreds of feet over the river. Hiking up a dim path that clutched the slope, I reached a broad, tilted ridge gouged by brooks. A line of snow-streaked peaks—Hannibal's final barrier—now towered before me. Upon that vast and lofty stage, 9,600 feet above the sea where Hannibal and I had begun our journey, I saw what he once saw—a wall, a wall that touched the sky.

WINDS WHIP *sky-piercing peaks, flinging snow across the pass. Beasts flounder in drifts. Ranks thinned by ambush stumble on: Numidian horsemen, leather-hooded African and Iberian spearmen— a hungry, bone-weary army of nations driven by a single iron will.*

PAINTING BY PETER V. BIANCHI, NATIONAL GEOGRAPHIC STAFF

Monte Viso
Col de la Traversette

Guil Valley

Durance Valley

NORTH

THESE CRUEL RAMPARTS *Hannibal breached. Scholars reason that he turned eastward from the Durance up France's Guil Valley; treacherous guides (Livy writes of "deliberate deception") shunned easier passes and led him to the snow-clogged Col de la Traversette, guarded by Italy's 12,602-foot landmark aptly named Viso—Seen.*

Somewhere in that wall was a notch—the Col de la Traversette, Sir Gavin's choice for Hannibal's pass through the Alps. Following a trail marked by cairns, I forded a stream and clambered over piles of scree until I stood at the edge of the ridge. It sloped off steeply toward cloud-crowned Monte Viso and the jagged tiers of peaks that line the French-Italian frontier.

"The Col de la Traversette," said my guide, pointing to a narrow gap directly ahead. "Here is France—and there is Italy." I sat on a weathered rock, enraptured by the harsh beauty of the col, which pierced the Alps like a corridor, floored by rock, roofed by sky. Swifts sailed on cold, thin winds. Marmots darted through rippling patches of tiny, stubborn flowers. In this domain of hardy breeds, I could conjure up an army of survivors, led to the summit of their lives by a man whose will alone compelled them to climb.

They camped at the pass and waited two days for stragglers. Then, Livy wrote, on a snowy October dawn "the army struggled slowly forward ... the hopelessness of utter exhaustion on every face. Seeing their despair, Hannibal ... gave the order to halt, pointing to Italy far below and the Po Valley beyond the foothills of the Alps. 'My men,' he said, 'you are ... walking over the very walls of Rome.' "

Rallied, they pushed on, stumbling down steep, ice-paved ledges until the massive rock blocked their path.

How the troops must have marveled when their general applied crude science to break up the boulder! (I marveled too, back home in Maryland snows when, after building a fire around a 70-pound chunk of dolomitic limestone like that in the Alps, I poured vinegar over it and saw it crack. The acetic acid weakened the limestone by releasing carbon dioxide from it. Cold water worked as well; sudden cooling contracted the rock, triggering internal stresses. Hannibal probably could have used snowmelt and saved the wine to toast his triumph over the Alps.)

But the triumph had been costly. In 15 deadly days through gorge and col, Polybius tells us, 20,000 men perished—nearly half the force that crossed the Rhone. While modern scholars challenge Polybius' figures, none doubts the Alps punished Hannibal. Only 26,000 men survived to descend upon the city of the Taurini. The tribe's name lives on in Turin, capital of Italy's Piedmont.

Harvesting strength from the rich Cisalpine farmlands they ravaged, the invaders swept toward the Po. On its plains the Roman consul Publius Cornelius Scipio and

SUNNY HILLS and valleys and woods with streams" revived Hannibal's army as it limped out of the Alps not far from this quiet fold in Italy's Piedmont. Here in Cisalpine Gaul the Carthaginians rested and feasted. Starving animals fattened on slopes still fertile today.

Farm family reaps and stacks wheat in the Susa Valley, cut by the Dora Riparia. Language and heritage link them with France, just beyond the mountains—the Transalpine Gaul where Caesar, who passed here, would win fame.

his army finally met the ghosts he had scorned. In a cavalry clash at the Ticino River near Pavia, Scipio was outflanked and severely wounded. His young son saved his life, according to Livy. Years later the lad would again meet Hannibal and earn the name Scipio Africanus.

The elder Scipio regrouped near Placentia (Piacenza today), where the Romans were raising a stronghold against rebellious Celts even as this new nemesis crossed the Alps. Rome's other consul, Sempronius Longus, rushed to Scipio's aid. "The whole military strength of Rome and both consuls," Livy wrote, "were now facing Hannibal." The armies —some 40,000 Carthaginians and new Celtic recruits against a slightly larger force of Romans and their allies—drew up on either side of the Trebbia River.

Hannibal, scouting the battlefield, finds on his side of the river a steep-banked, bramble-lined stream. He orders his young brother Mago to take 2,000 handpicked men, half of them on horseback, and hide there during the night.

Early next morning, raw winds pelt the field with snow; the river, swollen by recent rain, crests breast-high. Hannibal checks to see that his men anoint their bodies with protective oil around warming campfires. Then, before the Romans can prepare for this frigid day, he sends Numidian horsemen whooping across the river into the Roman camp.

The feint provokes a flight of precious javelins and, as Hannibal had expected, goads Sempronius. The consul rashly orders all the troops into the freezing river to pursue the Numidians. Hannibal's horsemen draw the Romans across the Trebbia and past the stream where Mago's men are hiding. Hungry, cold, and exhausted, the Romans advance like robots—"marching in order at a slow step."

First-rank light infantrymen of both sides collide. As the Romans' heavier rear ranks move in, Sempronius scents victory. But trumpeting elephants and fierce horsemen crash upon his flanks. Then, behind the Romans, as if springing from the earth itself, rise Mago's bushwhackers.

Some 10,000 Romans, slashing through the thin middle of Hannibal's line, struggle to the walls of Placentia, a few miles away. The rest fall under spear, sword, and elephant's foot. Few of Hannibal's veterans die, for the brunt of battle hits where he has pitilessly placed his new allies.

THOUGH HANNIBAL was now master of the north, he ruled a restive realm. The Celts hated Rome, but they wanted neither war on their land nor occupation by Hannibal. Celtic chieftains plotted assassination. Warned by informers, Hannibal went about in disguise—donning a variety of wigs and a humble cloak. Grumblings about rapacious Carthaginians persuaded him to move on.

In the spring of 217, bearing wine in pitch-sealed barrels, driving herds of cattle and succulent acorn-fed pigs, the invaders headed south. Only one elephant now marched with Hannibal; Polybius says the others had perished in the rigors of that first winter in Italy. Avoiding "long and obvious" routes, the army traversed the Apennines on paths today unknown and descended into the immense marshes of the Arno. Swamp fever felled man and beast. To faint was to drown, so men slept on grisly islands— piles of bloated mule corpses. Delirious, half-blind from an infection, Hannibal clung to the last elephant—his brave pet Syrus, according to legend—and led his men to high ground. Near Faesulae (Fiesole) he halted and gazed upon the rich valley of the Arno with one eye.

Huge, crudely hewn stones from the Etruscan citadel are embedded in the medieval face of Fiesole. The once-bustling hilltop city has mellowed to a drowsy town. But the riverside settlement it founded grew into Florence and fills the broad valley below. From Fiesole I looked out over the Renaissance splendor of Florence, risen from the 1966 flood. The same river that spawned the flood had fed the baleful swamp of Hannibal's day.

Burning and pillaging, the invaders hacked southward through Etruria. Hesitant Rome took no step to protect its Etruscan allies. Then Hannibal passed so close to the Roman army at Arretium (Arezzo) that Consul Gaius Flaminius could no longer ignore him. "Swelled with fury and resentment," Flaminius led 30,000 men in pursuit. The Romans had chosen to fight. But Hannibal, luring them on, chose the site of battle—Lake Trasimeno near Cortona.

At Cortona I stood on ramparts rooted in Etruscan stone and looked down on the lush midsummer greenery of the broad Chiana Valley, whose plump grapes make Chianti wine. "Hannibal burned those fields," observed Giuseppe Favilli, the city's one-man chamber of commerce.

I had spiraled up to Cortona at a fine time to sample the bounty of land that had sustained Hannibal's army, for the "Beefsteak Festival" sizzled around me. Hundreds of steaks, basted with an olive-oil sauce, broiled over charcoal. Local Chianti flowed ceaselessly from barrel to pitcher to cup to wine-reddened lips. Luscious pears—a fruit Hannibal might have eaten in Italy—tasted as though they had fallen from tree to hand. Through the light-festooned piazza rose the aroma of fresh-baked bread and the swirling laughter of children on a carrousel.

ROGER-VIOLLET

"KING OF THE RIVERS" to Virgil, the Po rises at Monte Viso, waters the rich plain of Lombardy (above, near Milan), and silts a vast delta on the Adriatic. Disputes over irrigation rights to a rivus, or stream, led to our word "rival."

In days of Roman-Carthaginian rivalry Po Valley hams fed Rome; its sheep yielded fine wool for rugs and towels, coarse wool for slave garments. Hannibal and his brothers fleeced the north but couldn't tame it. Hasdrubal fell near Fano; Mago, wounded north of Genoa in 203 B.C., took sail for Carthage and died.

TUNISIA

Zama ✖
202 B.C.

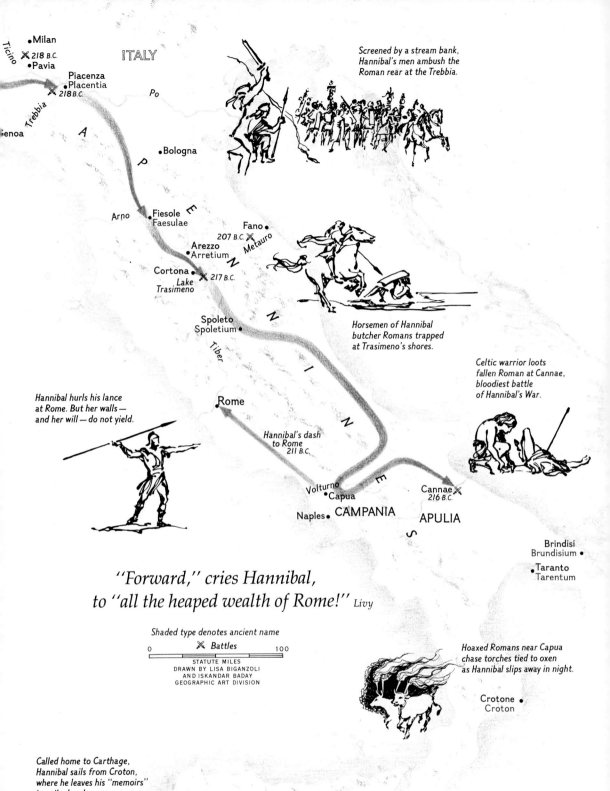

•Milan
✗ 218 B.C.
•Pavia

ITALY

Ticino

Piacenza
•Placentia
✗ 218 B.C.

Genoa

Trebbia

Po

A

P

•Bologna

Arno

Fiesole
•Faesulae

E

Arezzo
•Arretium

Fano •
207 B.C. ✗
Metauro

N

Cortona •
✗ 217 B.C.
Lake
Trasimeno

Spoleto
Spoletium •

Tiber

N

Screened by a stream bank,
Hannibal's men ambush the
Roman rear at the Trebbia.

Horsemen of Hannibal
butcher Romans trapped
at Trasimeno's shores.

Celtic warrior loots
fallen Roman at Cannae,
bloodiest battle
of Hannibal's War.

Hannibal hurls his lance
at Rome. But her walls —
and her will — do not yield.

Rome •

Hannibal's dash
to Rome
211 B.C.

I

N

E

Volturno
•Capua

Naples • CAMPANIA

Cannae ✗
216 B.C.

APULIA

S

Brindisi
Brundisium •

•Taranto
Tarentum

"Forward," cries Hannibal,
to *"all the heaped wealth of Rome!"* Livy

Shaded type denotes ancient name

0   ✗ Battles   100
STATUTE MILES
DRAWN BY LISA BIGANZOLI
AND ISKANDAR BADAY
GEOGRAPHIC ART DIVISION

Hoaxed Romans near Capua
chase torches tied to oxen
as Hannibal slips away in night.

Crotone •
Croton

Called home to Carthage,
Hannibal sails from Croton,
where he leaves his "memoirs"
inscribed on bronze.
Polybius reads them to give
his history of the war
"first-rate authority."

S I C I L Y

•ica

• Carthage

Syracuse •

"Hannibal spared Cortona," Giuseppe observed. I knew Hannibal bypassed the towering cities of Etruria, probably because he lacked the manpower and equipment to besiege them. But Giuseppe had another reason: "Cortona seems to be a blessed place." In World War II, he told me, Cortona prayed to its patroness, St. Margherita. German bombs shattered nearby towns but none fell here. "Whenever the bombers flew over," Giuseppe said, "clouds covered the city. One of the fliers heard of the miracle. Each year he comes here to pray at the shrine of our saint."

I asked about another time when mists veiled nearby Lake Trasimeno. "Ah!" exclaimed Giuseppe. "The *nebbione* that hid Hannibal! A *nebbia* is only a fog. Our nebbione is a *big* fog." It had to be big to shroud an army.

Soft winds off Lake Trasimeno trickled through the silvery leaves of the olive trees that shaded Don Bruno Frescucci and me. We had driven here from his ninth-century church in Sant'Angiolo, a village of mulberry trees, silkworms, and 300 people, in the lee of Cortona's hill. We stood near *Malpasso*, the Bad Pass —a lakeside trail hemmed by steep hills that had funneled a Roman army into

TRANQUIL TRASIMENO, *where fishermen glide today, devoured a Roman army in 217 B.C. Hannibal's Celtiberians cut and thrust with double-edged sword (sheathed at left), whose design Romans copied. An Italian fashioned this cuirass, chest and back plates decorated with Minerva, goddess of war; a Carthaginian bore it to Africa, where it adorned his grave.*

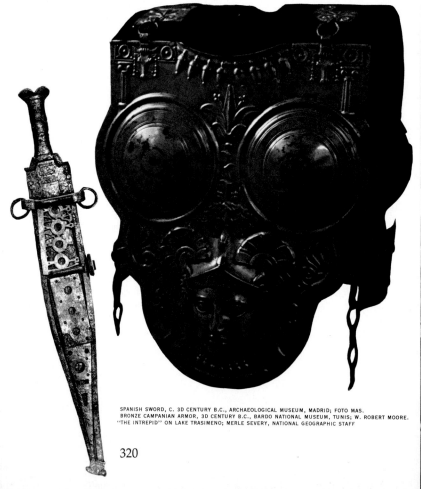

SPANISH SWORD, C. 3D CENTURY B.C., ARCHAEOLOGICAL MUSEUM, MADRID; FOTO MAS.
BRONZE CAMPANIAN ARMOR, 3D CENTURY B.C., BARDO NATIONAL MUSEUM, TUNIS; W. ROBERT MOORE.
"THE INTREPID" ON LAKE TRASIMENO; MERLE SEVERY, NATIONAL GEOGRAPHIC STAFF

a deadly trap. Trasimeno, shrunken by irrigation taps, now lies half a mile away.

Hannibal, aware that Flaminius was closing on him, left a decoy detachment at the mouth of the pass. The rest of his men he posted on the hills that curved around the lake, blocking the farther end of the trail.

Seeing only the decoys, Flaminius led the entire Roman army after them, past the hills where Hannibal's men hid. "By the battle-cry which arose on every side of them," Livy wrote, "the Romans knew they were surrounded.... In that enveloping mist... it was sounds, not sights, they turned to face—the groans of wounded men, the thud or ring of blows on body or shield... the cry of fear."

A horseman shouted, "There is the consul!" He galloped through guardsmen, slew the consul's armor-bearer, and skewered Flaminius on a lance. Romans plunged into the lake and drowned or were cut down by cavalry who waded in after them. Others scrambled up the hills but were felled by arrows and slingstones.

Don Bruno, who has long studied the battle, pointed to a faint trace of vanished shoreline on an aerial photograph. "Here in the Malpasso Hannibal killed 15,000

Romans," he said. Some 10,000 survived. According to Polybius, most of them were captured, including those in the van who managed to struggle out of the trap.

"Now," said Don Bruno, "we shall go to Hannibal's camp." He squeezed into my car and directed me to a 15th-century villa half hidden on a slope near a hamlet called Ossaia. "It was called that because so many *ossi*—bones—were found there long after the battle. Over there is Sanguineto, named for the blood shed here."

The villa serves as a home and a personal museum for Prof. Teodorico Moretti Costanzi of the University of Bologna. The professor led me through his garden, where a bust of Hannibal (page 274) gazes out on the lake, and into a man-made cavern under the villa. "Decades after the battle," he told me, "Romans carved out this shrine to Flaminius, I believe, and cremated the bones they found." He showed me relics he had sifted from the ashes: a Celtic spearhead, a Roman lance tip. He handed me a heavy iron arrowhead. "This," he said, "killed a Roman."

Triumphantly, Hannibal marched southward. Tradition says he besieged Spoletium (Spoleto), a Latin colony in the heart of Umbria. He may have wanted a base to prepare for an assault on Rome, 60 miles to the southwest. Whatever his plans, Spoletium thwarted them, according to Livy. "Repulsed with heavy loss," Hannibal veered toward the Adriatic coast.

In Apulia, a fertile realm between the Apennines and the Adriatic, Hannibal's men killed every Roman man old enough to bear arms. They carried off slaves, cattle, grain, oil, and so much wine that they bathed their horses in it. Burdened by their plunder, they spread slowly through Apulia, then crossed westward over the mountains and fell upon the rich orchards and vineyards of Campania.

Now the patchwork of Roman colonies and their allies that formed the map of Italy became a chessboard for a grim game that would last 14 years. Hannibal's first opponent was Quintus Fabius Maximus, dubbed "the Delayer" because he

"The vineyard is of first importance"

Cato the Elder

Wine of Apulia rolls along the Appian Way past vines whose "little yellowish grapes" would delight Cato. Tips in his second-century B.C. handbook on farming—how to test for watered wine, make imitation Greek wine, scrimp on slave upkeep—profited absentee owners. Chain gangs toiled under a foreman, "first to rise . . . last to go to bed," who auctioned off feeble slaves. His wife must not gossip with neighbors or "go out anywhere to dinner." A model vintner squeezed 23,000 gallons a year from 62 acres, doctoring batches with resin, marble powder, and seawater.

You could trade an amphora (5-7 gallons) of wine for a slave among the Greeks in Marseilles. Rome's exports were so profitable she would restrict planting the vine beyond the Alps. Only later did France's viticulture burgeon.

Cato, who had fought Hannibal, urged war again. In the Senate he brandished fresh figs from Carthage—proof that the foe stood but "three days' sail from Rome."

avoided a direct fight and aimed to wear out his foe by harassment. Slipping away from the Romans, Hannibal recrossed the Apennines and spent the winter of 217 in Apulia. There he plotted a move to sweep two Roman armies off the board.

The sky rumbled and flashed the name of the Barcas as I drove down the narrow road to the epic battlefield of Cannae. Twilight darkened into night, and the mood of battle seemed to prowl the ranks of gnarled olive trees. As darkness hid the field from my eyes, I was left with the specters of my mind. Now I could see the battle,

PENNED FOR SLAUGHTER, *more than 50,000 Romans fall in the bloody dust of Cannae. Slashing from the saddle, Hannibal holds the center of his line with Iberians and bare-chested Celts as he caps a brilliantly waged battle. He had arched his center toward the enemy, then bent it back under pressure (right). Libyans at the ends swung in, pocketing the Romans. His cavalry hit flanking enemy horse and swept round to complete a classic double envelopment.*

PAINTING BY PETER V. BIANCHI, NATIONAL GEOGRAPHIC STAFF ARTIST

*"The Romans charged
straight into. . . . the trap"*

Livy

ROMAN TROOPS

HANNIBAL'S TROOPS

DAN McCOY, BLACK STAR

as once I had seen another when I walked at night the bloodied ground of Gettysburg.

Hannibal pounced on Cannae, a Roman grain and arms depot in Apulia, in the spring of 216. Determined now to wipe out Hannibal's 50,000-man force, Rome ordered to Cannae the largest force the Romans had ever fielded—two consular armies totaling about 86,000 men. Leading them were two feuding consuls, cautious Lucius Aemilius Paullus and rash Gaius Terentius Varro. By custom, each consul assumed supreme command of both armies on alternate days.

On one of Paullus' days, Hannibal sends a troop of Numidian cavalry out to cut off the Romans' water supply. The enemy thirsts through the hot summer night. Next morning, Varro's red ensign of battle flutters over what men will call the Plain of Blood.

The Romans advance in battle array. The legionaries hunch behind tall shields, helmets gleaming in the sun, red and black plumes whipped by the dusty wind. A thicket of javelins ripples in the front ranks of Roman and allied foot soldiers. On the flanks of the infantry prance the elite cavalry, drawn from the best families of Rome. Golden rings glitter on the hands that grip the reins.

On both ends of the thin Carthaginian line stand Libyans wielding Roman arms, the spoils of Trasimeno. Iberians in purple-bordered white tunics and Celts stripped to the waist muster in the center, which arches toward the massive Roman line. Here Hannibal places himself and his brother Mago. Numidians gallop out on the right wing, hard-riding Iberians and Celts out on the left. Balearic slingers range the front of the line, their long, coiled hair their only helmets. Whirling long-range slings, they hurl their first volley at the advancing Romans. A stone strikes Paullus. Though mortally wounded, the consul rides on.

The heavy Roman line drives like a wedge toward the arched center of the Carthaginians. The arch buckles as Hannibal's Iberians and Celts fall back. The Romans press into the pocket. Now Hannibal signals for the Libyans to swing inward and hack the Roman line on left and right. Crushed by a vise of sword and spear on three sides, the Roman ranks collapse into a churning, crimsoned mass.

Hannibal's cavalry, meanwhile, has killed or routed all the Roman horse. Now the cavalry charges down upon the rear of the Roman line. So compressed they can barely swing their swords, the Romans fight and die, rank by rank. One, arms dangling uselessly, falls upon a Numidian and, dying, gnaws him. Maddened Romans try to smother themselves by burrowing their heads into the earth. Leg tendons

"**GOLDEN PLENTY** *from a full horn is pouring forth her fruits upon Italy,"* exulted Horace. Hannibal savored such bounty in Apulia. Pigs went to market live or as sausage: pork, nuts, and* piper *(pepper) stuffed in gut casings and hung as now; the word* salami *stems from* sal *(salt). Sheep cheese flavored pizza-type pastry. Romans raised chickens but gourmets preferred peacock, parrot—and flamingo tongue.*

severed, hamstrung men bare their throats and beg for death. Hannibal's wearying men clamber over the dead and dying to cut down Romans who still stand.

On the field at daybreak lie 50,000 to 70,000 dead. Some 10,000 Romans surrender at nearby camps. Hannibal later sends to Carthage a macabre offering: three pecks of golden rings stripped from noble hands. Hungering for more booty, Carthage's Senate agrees to give him more troops.

Maharbal, Hannibal's brash cavalry commander, exults: "Within five days you will take your dinner, in triumph, on the Capitol!" But Hannibal will not march on Rome. Stunned, Maharbal blurts what historians shall ever echo: "You know, Hannibal, how to win a fight. You do not know how to use your victory."

LIKE HANNIBAL, I turned westward from the horrors of Cannae to the charms of Campania, where farmers still delight in recalling how their bountiful land enchanted the conqueror's army. High living in Capua, capital of Campania, "weakened the fibers of both body and mind," Livy dourly reported.

Near Capua I wandered along the banks of the Volturno River. A vast irrigation system has tamed it, but the Volturno still flows through history, as it had in the third century B.C. Here the Romans drew their post-Cannae line that held Hannibal in the south, and here the German defense line cracked in 1943.

Terrorizing allies of Rome, winning over turncoats, Hannibal ravaged the south. He razed hundreds of villages, destroyed the peasant-farm culture, and set the

DAN McCOY, BLACK STAR

329

desolate stage for a slave-plantation economy that enriched absentee owners but would retard the development of the region until modern times.

For months a trembling Rome awaited him. The Senate closed the city's gates, not only to bar him but also to keep citizens from fleeing. To placate the gods, the Senate buried alive in the Forum a Celtic man and woman and two Greeks. "A most un-Roman rite," Livy commented.

As the months drew on without a blow, the Roman backbone stiffened. In his slash from the Trebbia to Cannae, Hannibal had slaughtered 100,000 Romans and their allies. Teen-agers, slaves, and convicts refilled the ranks. Yet each year, from the despairing summer of 216 to the turning of the tide in 207, Rome's determination grew, dimming Hannibal's hope of a climactic victory. He had but a lifetime. Rome, confident of her destiny, had shaped a society to span centuries.

Too weak to attack Hannibal directly, Rome opened new fronts in Sicily and

Spain, where no genius of war confronted them. Their navy gained control of the sea and all but cut Hannibal off from Carthage. Then, in 212, the Romans moved on traitorous Capua, which had gone over to Hannibal. He was on the other side of Italy, trying to seize the vital port of Brundisium, modern Brindisi, and the harbor citadel of Tarentum (Taranto). By the time his army reappeared at Capua in 211, Roman besiegers had dug in. Unable to crack the double ring of ramparts and trenches that encircled the city, he spun suddenly northward—toward Rome itself.

As Hannibal approached, Livy wrote, women "poured out into the streets and ran aimlessly amongst the shrines of the gods, sweeping the altars with their loosened hair, or . . . raising their palms to the gods in heaven with prayers that they might save the City . . . and keep inviolate Roman mothers and their little children."

Rome's leaders did not panic. When Hannibal encamped near the walls, he happened to occupy land up for sale. A Roman audaciously bought the parcel—at the asking price! Hannibal impulsively threw a spear at the Colline Gate, an

TARANTO'S WATERS *lure youths to frolic, elders to fish with conical traps (right). When traitors opened Tarentum's gates, Hannibal made it a thorn in Italy's heel. In 209 B.C. new treason restored it to the Romans, who sold 30,000 Tarentines as slaves.*

Taranto named the tarantula, whose venom, men said, caused a fatal hysteria. The antidote: a wild dance set to special music. Science today makes light of this spider's bite, but the rhythmic tarantella still charms.

act that embedded itself in Roman folklore. For centuries, Roman mothers would frighten naughty children with "Hannibal ad portas!—Hannibal is at the gates!"

Historians assess Hannibal's dash to Rome as a feint to draw off the besiegers of Capua. Perhaps the general in him knew he could not take Rome. But I see a man, not a general, hurling that lance in rage and frustration. And, as he sets a flaming, wrathful path to the south, I see a man who knows he shall never tread the Forum in triumph.

Capua fell in 211. A year later a brilliant young general from the famed Scipio family took New Carthage. By 207 Scipio had nearly conquered Iberia. But Hannibal's brother

ON AN AFRICAN PLAIN *near ancient Zama a camel plows land that trembled when Hannibal sent 80 elephants toward Scipio's army. Legions opened formation and the beasts charged in; stampeded by lances, they turned on their masters. The Romans cut through Hannibal's line but reeled before his last-rank veterans. Regrouped, the legions outflanked Hannibal and hit his rear with cavalry—a lesson Scipio had learned from Cannae.*

Years later, the old soldiers met again, in peace. Asked by Scipio how he ranked history's generals, Hannibal named Alexander and Pyrrhus—but added he'd have put himself first had he beaten Scipio.

"The conqueror's heart... was itself vanquished and led captive by love"

Livy

As Roman troops invade Hannibal's African homeland, Masinissa, their Numidian ally, takes Cirta (now Constantine, Algeria) and its Carthaginian queen, Sophonisba (right). They wed. But the Roman general Scipio, fearing treason, moved against the bride. To forestall him, she took poison from Masinissa. "I accept this bridal gift," she said. "But ... I should have died a better death if I had not married on the day of my funeral."

In 202 B.C. Masinissa, still faithful to Rome, led his hard-riding horsemen—precursors of Tunisia's presidential guard (below)—to help Scipio defeat Hannibal at Zama. Scipio's mercy and Hannibal's plea for peace saved Carthage—for a time. Embittered by intrigues, Hannibal fled. A general for hire, "a bird ... grown too old to fly," he faded away, pecking at Rome's allies.

PAINTING BY PETER V. BIANCHI, NATIONAL GEOGRAPHIC STAFF ARTIST. OPPOSITE: JOHN J. PUTMAN AND (UPPER) MERLE SEVERY, BOTH NATIONAL GEOGRAPHIC STAFF

Hasdrubal fought his way out. He followed Hannibal's trail across the Alps, then cut diagonally across Italy, pausing at the Metauro River, near Fanum Fortunae (Fano) on the Adriatic. From his camp sped riders with a dispatch to Hannibal: March north for a victorious linkup of our armies in Umbria.

Near Tarentum a Roman foraging party, happening upon the riders, captured them with the dispatch still sealed. In a race to intercept history, 7,000 crack Roman troops marched day and night up the peninsula to rendezvous secretly with another Roman army. The reinforcements slipped into the camp opposite Hasdrubal. Next morning, two trumpets sounded in the camp and Hasdrubal knew that he faced two armies and doom.

A few days later, horsemen galloped through Hannibal's camp in Apulia and hurled at him a message from his brother—the head of Hasdrubal. Weeping over it, Hannibal said, "At last I see the destiny of Carthage."

He fled southward to Bruttium, the very toe of Italy, to await that destiny. It came in 205 when Scipio, at 30 the conqueror of Iberia and a consul of Rome, stunned the Senate with his plan to carry the war to Carthage itself.

With the disgraced, vengeful survivors of Cannae forming the core of his army,

Scipio struck at Utica in the Gulf of Tunis. In little more than a year Carthage sued for peace. Cursing the gods who had deserted him and the Senate of Carthage which had denied him help, Hannibal sailed home, where the war erupted again.

I HELD a small clay box in my hands. "They put the children's ashes in these after they burned them alive for sacrifice," the guide told me. Similar boxes lay piled in the palm-shaded garden of the National Museum of Carthage. Seeking here some sign of Hannibal, I found only these hideous relics of the civilization he served. Surely, I thought, there must be somewhere a monument to the greatest man Carthage ever produced.

He left no monument on the plain of Zama, 75 miles southwest of Carthage. Here, in 202, Scipio Africanus earned his name by defeating Hannibal. Outflanked in a maneuver ironically like his own at Cannae, Hannibal lost 80 elephants and thousands of men, many of them veterans of the march over the Alps 16 years before. Carthage and Hannibal both began to die that day. A pathetic exile hounded

"Carthage must be destroyed!"

Cato the Elder

Dreading a resurgent Carthage, Cato ended every Senate speech with his cry of hate, finally goaded Rome into the third and final Punic War in 149 B.C.

The Carthaginians meekly surrendered, giving up 2,000 catapults and all other weapons forged since Hannibal's defeat half a century earlier. But, told to leave their doomed city, they chose to die with her. Temples became arsenals, turning out 300 swords a day. Slaves and masters manned walls; 100,000 died in the three-year siege.

Now the walls crumble. But each house is a fortress, each roof a battlefield (right). For six flaming days the Romans fight to take the hilltop citadel. Its general deserts. Cursing him, his wife slays their sons and plunges with them from a burning temple. A Scipio— adopted grandson of Hannibal's nemesis—weeps over his triumph. At his side stands Polybius, history's witness: "All cities . . . must, like men, meet their doom."

PAINTING BY PETER V. BIANCHI,
NATIONAL GEOGRAPHIC STAFF ARTIST

334

by agents of Rome, he was not destined to die as once he had urged his men—"in the heat of the fight, struggling till your last breath." In 183, in the kingdom of Bithynia near present-day Istanbul, he chose poison rather than capture.

Carthage, which challenged Rome one last time in the Third Punic War, flickered out in 146 when the adopted grandson of Scipio burned it, plowed its ashes under, and symbolically sowed the furrows with salt.

Only the memory of Hannibal would endure, brilliant as a general, baffling as a man. The Roman satirist Juvenal would mock him as a madman destined only to "thrill young schoolboys." The historian Arnold Toynbee would say his searing course of conquest left an imprint still discernible in Italy—the north, singed by war, could quickly heal; the south, devastated, still shows the scars of poverty.

Lingering in the seaside ruins of the Roman bath at Carthage, I gazed northward. Beyond the blue seam of sea and sky lay Rome. There, I realized, stood Hannibal's monument: the city that had learned survival in the shadow of his sword. For he had made of her a crucible where Romans tempered the iron will of empire.

By Pierre Grimal

The World of Caesar

*J*KNOW of no better place to awaken the splendor of
imperial Rome than the small esplanade on the Capitoline Hill
behind the Palazzo dei Conservatori. Before me spread
the broken monuments, the sacred Forum, the Palatine Hill
with its trees still haunted by the shadows of the emperors.
From every direction, from all corners of the world it seems,
roads converge at this spot. The rush and swirl of the great
city fade, and I can hear the tread of victorious legions,
the exultant cries, *"Io triumphe!"*
It is late summer in the year 46 B.C. Julius Caesar,
after bloody years in the field, has subdued an empire
and captured its heart; now he reaps the glory. With four
triumphal processions, prescribed by custom already ancient,
he celebrates his victories in Gaul, Asia, Egypt, and Africa.
Screaming throngs jam every vantage point as magistrates
and senators stride out of the Field of Mars amid a fanfare
of trumpets. Next comes booty almost beyond reckoning—
wagons heaped with gold and silver, ivory, jewelry, objects of art.
Posters on gilded poles portray the fall of Caesar's enemies.
One adversary leaps into the sea; another tears at his own wounds.
Gasps turn to roars of laughter when the crowd glimpses
the comical picture of the king of Pontus in Asia Minor
fleeing from the legionaries. Caesar's inscription reads:
"Veni, Vidi, Vici—I came, I saw, I conquered."

*Julius Caesar, cool as first-century marble, keeps a calculating eye on seats of power
in Rome's City Council chamber on Capitoline Hill; Adam Woolfitt*

HAIL CAESAR! *Romans roar as white steeds draw him toward the Forum in triumph in 46 B.C. Spoils of Africa*

parade ahead, legions behind. Doles of money and grain, shows, revels, a 22,000-table feast follow.

Priests lead white sacrificial bulls, accompanied by children who will catch the warm blood in bowls as it spills. Prisoners, blinking in the sunlight, drag their chains. Soon they will return to the dungeons, some never to see the light of day again. Behind them in a four-horse chariot rides Caesar, clad in purple tunic and gold-adorned toga, his face rouged like Jupiter's; a slave holds a laurel crown over his head. At this moment he is not a man but the very image of the god who governs Rome's destiny.

Clowns dance around his chariot, taunting him with jests, lest the gods grow jealous at his glory. Legionaries marching behind call out, "Romans, lock your wives away—home we bring our bald rake!" These veterans well know their leader's conquests, on the field and off.

Through the Circus Maximus the procession moves, then around the Palatine, onto the Sacred Way, through the Forum, and up the Capitoline—I can see the gray stepping-stones of the ascent—to the Temple of Jupiter, where Caesar offers the god the spoils of the universe.

In less than two years daggers would cut Caesar down. The empire that rose in his footsteps would embrace the civilized world; beyond it lay only desert, lands spiked by mountains and peopled by barbarians,

WRAITHS OF MIST *haunt the Forum, once-marshy vale below the pine-clad Palatine. Here Romans shopped, gladiators fought, emperors raised monuments to pride. Shrine of law and rite, focus of ambition and might, it witnessed dark deeds and days of glory. Here Caesar refused the crown, and here his pyre flamed. Cicero addressed the people from the Rostra; his head and hands were nailed to it after his murder ordered by Mark Antony.*

ERICH LESSING, MAGNUM

and the vast ocean in which the day died. Yet two centuries earlier Rome scarcely controlled the Italian peninsula. Then, countering Carthaginian moves, she seized Sicily and Spain. Next came Macedonia, Hannibal's ally. As war followed war, the empire took shape like a huge cloth being woven — the Greek city-states, Syria, North Africa, Asia Minor, Gaul, Egypt. The Mediterranean became a Roman lake.

The ancient institutions of the Republic strained at the task of governing so vast a realm. Magistrates sent out as governors often looted their provinces and returned with fortunes, leaving smoldering resentment. Generals swelled with victory and booty threatened the capital. The Republic reeled until Caesar grasped power. Henceforth, though the noble senators might meet to legislate and consuls might be elected in the old way, Romans understood that the gods had invested power in a "divine" man. For had not Caesar revealed his divinity with superhuman deeds?

His successor and adopted son, Octavian, shrewdly encouraged that belief in the provinces. But in Rome he lived simply and sat in the Senate merely as *princeps* (first citizen). He took the name Augustus, connoting increase, innovation, and reverence. His family name, Caesar, evolved into a title that would echo in "kaiser" and "czar." "Imperator," which had signified a leader entrusted by the Senate with military power, now was applied to the man who ruled Rome — an emperor. Despite the pretense of republican forms, the Republic was dead.

During his 41-year reign Augustus did not press for new conquests; he pacified the vast realm already won. For centuries afterward a line of emperors — some good, some brutal, some mad — governed an empire embracing tens of millions,

laced by fine roads and safe sea lanes, administered
with ability, joined by a common culture.
Rome's remarkable achievement is our heritage.

Augustus could boast he had found Rome
a city of brick and left it a city of marble.
His massive urban renewal, carrying forward
the work begun by Julius Caesar, clothed the heart
of empire with grandeur. It badly needed it.

Neglected for centuries, Rome had grown ugly,
its flaking shrines hardly a match for those of the
humblest Greek town. Hovels cluttered the hillsides,
mobs choked the Forum, squatters invaded
the sacred woods. In spring and fall the Tiber
in spate flooded the valleys.

Caesar built a second forum. Augustus raised
a third and expanded the city's lungs. Clearing
slum areas, he gave Rome shaded groves, porticoes,
statues, cooling fountains. Gardens transformed
the Esquiline Hill, a foul dumping ground where

"TO HOLD *by your eloquence
the minds of men . . . to move them
to and fro in whatever direction
you please"* — this, to Cicero,
*was life's noblest ambition
in a republic ruled by rhetoric.
Undisputed master of the art,
he fires accusations at Catiline
(above) in* 63 B.C.; *senators shun
their guilty colleague, who plotted
revolt when he failed at the polls.*

*A citizen of Republican Rome
drops his ballot in a voting urn
(below). Under the empire, votes
and golden voices counted little.
"A hush has come upon eloquence,"
mourned the historian Tacitus in the
first century as emperors eroded
the Senate's power, made elections
a formality, and ruled the state
religion as divinely favored
beings. Toga over
his head, Marcus
Aurelius (right)
presides as priest
during a sacrifice
to Jupiter on the
Capitoline.*

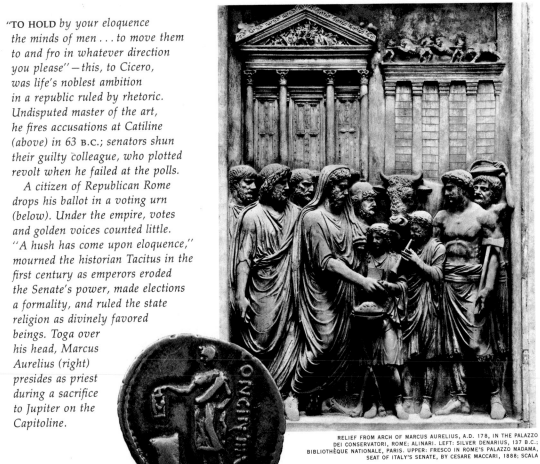

RELIEF FROM ARCH OF MARCUS AURELIUS, A.D. 178, IN THE PALAZZO
DEI CONSERVATORI, ROME; ALINARI. LEFT: SILVER DENARIUS, 137 B.C.;
BIBLIOTHÈQUE NATIONALE, PARIS. UPPER: FRESCO IN ROME'S PALAZZO MADAMA,
SEAT OF ITALY'S SENATE, BY CESARE MACCARI, 1888; SCALA

dogs and birds tore at human refuse—corpses of slaves, paupers, criminals. Here wealthy Maecenas built a luxurious villa where poets gathered to sing the glories of Augustan Rome. Horace saw the enduring virtues of the Roman people embodied in the emperor. Virgil, fired with faith in the destiny of Rome, created the *Aeneid*, which traced the city's founding to the Trojan hero Aeneas. The poet died in 19 B.C. with the epic unpublished. He willed its destruction, but Augustus would not hear of it. Rome at last had found its *Iliad*.

While the early emperors gave Rome an appearance worthy of its world role, they did little to enhance the comfort of the poor. Flimsy *insulae*—"high-rise" apartments built by profit-hungry speculators—often collapsed. Fire was a constant danger; an overturned lamp or a gust of wind might touch off acres of buildings. Companies of *vigiles* patrolled the streets, forming bucket brigades to fight fires.

The conflagration of A.D. 64 gave Nero an opportunity to rebuild half the city. Romans knew the emperor was avid to do this, and they also knew the old saying: *Is fecit cui prodest*—He who profits by crime is guilty of it. There was even talk that Nero strummed a lyre and recited his own verses while Rome burned. In fact, however, Nero was at the sea resort of Antium (Anzio) and hastened back to fight the fire. He blamed it on the Christians, who had begun to appear in Rome some 20 years earlier; their strange beliefs made them suitable scapegoats.

On razed land Nero built his fabulous Golden House with immense gardens and an artificial lake, drained 15 years later for the site of the Colosseum. He also laid out broad streets which served as firebreaks and let sunlight in. Though some grumbled about losing the shade, this made Rome somewhat safer for the masses.

LIFE OF ROME *still pulses in her streets. Policemen, peddlers, parents, and playful children chat, dicker, and relax under the amused eyes of window-watchers in tenements that echo* insulae—*"islands" of walk-up flats where ancients roomed.*

Further progress came with the Antonines. Between A.D. 96 and 180 these enlightened monarchs—Nerva, Trajan, Hadrian, Antoninus Pius, and Marcus Aurelius—not only sought comfort for the city but also insisted on scrupulous administration and speedier justice in both Rome and the provinces. It was, wrote 18th-century historian Edward Gibbon, "the period in the history of the world during which the condition of the human race was most happy and prosperous." It was the Golden Age of Rome.

*L*ET US SPEND a day in the Rome of the Antonines. At cockcrow the sun's rays strike gilded statues atop the Temple of Jupiter. Along the old Forum's southern edge the Vestal Virgins are already at work tidying up their shrine, tending the fire sacred to Vesta, goddess of the hearth. Chosen in childhood, the priestesses observe chastity for 30 years. For breaching this rule they may be buried alive. Rome honors them, allowing them to save from execution any condemned criminal they meet.

345

Nearby, men gather before the benches of the tribunal. Every citizen of importance has at least one suit pending, and expects friends to appear as witnesses or stand bond. Trials often become shouting matches, and the praetor, or chief magistrate, calls in six burly lictors to restore order with their rods.

Senators arrive, each with a small army of friends, slaves, and secretaries. One attendant, the *nomenclator*, whispers in his master's ear the names of all who greet him. Although the city swells with a million people, politicians still follow customs begun when Rome was a small town. From earliest times politics has rested on a personal basis; a Roman votes not for a party or a policy but for a man—a friend, a relative, or a benefactor. And a public man's importance is judged by the size of his clientele. As the senator vanishes into the Curia— the Senate chamber—his *clientes* lounge outside.

Free men, the clients choose flattery of a patron as a way of life. Before dawn they rush to his *domus* and jostle for position in the atrium, the spacious central room open to the sky. Still yawning, the great man settles into his curule chair, greets his followers, and offers sage advice, perhaps to such a thorny question as "Should the child of a slave girl be considered income or a property increase?" At times an enemy may slip into the house and try to dispatch the noble with a quick dagger thrust. But for the most part the crowd consists of humble supporters who eagerly await the gifts of food and money which servants distribute, and which liberate the recipients from the daily cares of survival.

In Republican days Senate meetings touched off great debates, even battles. Rioters ripped apart benches, awnings, and documents to feed bonfires, while politicians fled for their lives. Now things go more smoothly. Senators rise as the emperor enters the Curia. He announces plans for dealing with the latest financial crisis or barbarian uprising—and they approve.

Outside, on scribed paving stones (the stones still bear the marks), idlers play knucklebones, dice, and checkerlike *latrunculi*. Though the Forum has lost much of its commercial activity to the new imperial forums, especially the gigantic semicircle of Trajan's Forum which cuts deep into the Quirinal Hill, slave sellers still hawk their human wares by the Temple of Castor and Pollux. Continuing prosperity draws more and more bankers to the city's center; their stalls crowd even the Curia's walls.

By noon, the emperor departs and the Senate adjourns. Life in the Forum begins

PAINTING FOR NATIONAL GEOGRAPHIC BY H. M. HERGET. OPPOSITE: RELIEF, 2D CENTURY A.D.; OSTIA MUSEUM. MOSAIC FROM POMPEII, 1ST CENTURY A.D., NATIONAL MUSEUM, NAPLES

ALBERT MOLDVAY, NATIONAL GEOGRAPHIC STAFF. MAP DRAWN BY
SNEJINKA STEFANOFF AND COMPILED BY RUTH B. LANE, GEOGRAPHIC ART DIVISION

"The City, the City....
Residence elsewhere ...
is mere eclipse" *Cicero*

*Like a hitchhiker from the past, Caesar in
bronze stands beside his forum as modern Rome
whizzes by. S.P.Q.R.—Senatus Populusque
Romanus—symbolizes the Senate and people
who voted him dictator for life, thus yielding
the ancient authority of the Republic.
Temple of Saturn rises behind the conqueror.*

*By his day the hamlet that once nestled
between the Palatine and the Capitoline had
spread to all seven hills. Augustus clothed
the capital in marble to match its majesty.
Shrines and monuments multiplied, to gods who
smiled on Rome and emperors who glorified it.*

*Aurelian (A.D. 270-75) walled the city
against barbarian invaders. When Constantine*

*shifted the capital to Constantinople in 330,
Rome's decline began. Sacked by Vandals and
Visigoths, stormed by Saracens and Normans,
wracked by fire, flood, and earthquake,
it shrank to 17,000 souls in the Middle Ages.
Refuse filled valleys, cows grazed in the Forum.*

*Over the city of Caesars rose the splendors
of papal Rome. Michelangelo, Bramante, and
Bernini raised Renaissance and Baroque palaces
and churches, among them St. Peter's, near
Nero's gardens, where Christians first burned.
Today, vital and hospitable as ever, its grandeur
and glamor undimmed, Rome renews its claim
to the ancient paean—"first among cities,
the home of gods is golden Rome."*

PYRAMID OF

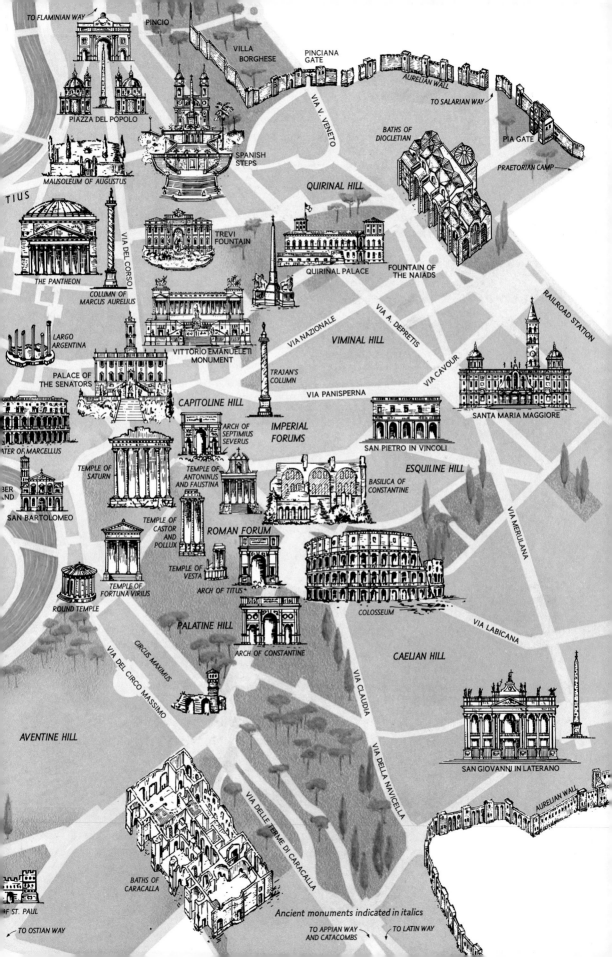

TO FLAMINIAN WAY

PINCIO

VILLA
BORGHESE

PINCIANA
GATE

AURELIAN WALL

TO SALARIAN WAY

PIAZZA DEL POPOLO

MAUSOLEUM OF AUGUSTUS

SPANISH
STEPS

VIA V. VENETO

*BATHS OF
DIOCLETIAN*

PIA GATE

PRAETORIAN CAMP

TIUS

QUIRINAL HILL

THE PANTHEON

*COLUMN OF
MARCUS AURELIUS*

VIA DEL CORSO

TREVI
FOUNTAIN

QUIRINAL PALACE

FOUNTAIN OF
THE NAIADS

RAILROAD STATION

*LARGO
ARGENTINA*

VITTORIO EMANUELE II
MONUMENT

VIA NAZIONALE

VIMINAL HILL

VIA A. DEPRETIS

*TRAJAN'S
COLUMN*

VIA CAVOUR

SANTA MARIA MAGGIORE

*PALACE OF
THE SENATORS*

VIA PANISPERNA

CAPITOLINE HILL

*ARCH OF
SEPTIMIUS
SEVERUS*

*IMPERIAL
FORUMS*

SAN PIETRO IN VINCOLI

ATER OF MARCELLUS

*TEMPLE OF
SATURN*

*TEMPLE OF
ANTONINUS
AND FAUSTINA*

*BASILICA OF
CONSTANTINE*

ESQUILINE HILL

VIA MERULANA

SAN BARTOLOMEO

*TEMPLE OF
CASTOR
AND
POLLUX*

ROMAN FORUM

*TEMPLE OF
VESTA*

ARCH OF TITUS

COLOSSEUM

VIA LABICANA

*TEMPLE OF
FORTUNA VIRILIS*

ROUND TEMPLE

PALATINE HILL

ARCH OF CONSTANTINE

CAELIAN HILL

AVENTINE HILL

VIA DEL CIRCO MASSIMO

CIRCUS MAXIMUS

VIA CLAUDIA

VIA DELLA NAVICELLA

SAN GIOVANNI IN LATERANO

AURELIAN WALL

VIA DELLE TERME DI CARACALLA

*BATHS OF
CARACALLA*

F ST. PAUL

TO OSTIAN WAY

Ancient monuments indicated in italics

TO APPIAN WAY
AND CATACOMBS

TO LATIN WAY

to ebb and the heat of day sends everyone to the baths. We will follow them, but first let us meet Romans whose business seldom leads them into lawcourt or Senate.

THE LURE OF MONEY, abundant stores of grain, and the pleasures of the city brought thousands upon thousands flocking into Rome from the countryside and the provinces. Often they found themselves packed into tiny rooms on the upper floors of the insulae. (Shops and well-heeled tenants filled the lower floors.) Charcoal stoves smoked up the flats; narrow shafts never let in enough light or fresh air. Pigeons often shared the drab quarters. With no plumbing, housewives tossed slops along with garbage into the streets, hoping the next rain would wash it into the sewers. Roman engineers worked marvels bringing water from the hills through aqueducts into the city, but they never piped it to the top floors of the tenements. People had to fill their jugs at the corner fountain.

Small wonder menfolk spent little time at home. They returned in the evening for the main meal, the *cena* — usually wheat porridge with chickpeas or other vegetables. Everyone went to bed early, though not always to sleep, for darkness did not quiet the racket in this pulsing capital.

"How dearly one must pay for sleeping in the city," complained Juvenal, an impoverished rhetorician whose *Satires,* published in the early years of the Antonine dynasty, mercilessly exposed the sordidness he saw in Roman life. At night delivery wagons clattered through the streets. (Caesar had banned them during the day to ease congestion.) The cries of street toughs and their victims, of a pedestrian deluged with slops from an upstairs window, filled the night.

"You will be a fool to go out without making a will," Juvenal warned.

Dawn ends the fitful sleep of the poor; their daily tasks begin early.
At the Tiber wharves, lines of stevedores shoulder sacks of grain into warehouses while clerks record each load. Priced low, even given away at times, grain guarantees the peace of the city, the popularity of the emperor.

Eastward, toward the Forum, streets swarm with peddlers of second-hand clothing. Cobblers and cutlers add their din. Butchers hack up lamb and kid (beef is mainly for sacrifice). The street of the fabric merchants delights the eye with cotton veils from Cyprus and Syria, and silks woven in Damascus from raw goods brought by caravan from China. The street of the jewelers offers the world's most beautiful pearls.

Along the Argiletum, the street running north through the vice-ridden Suburra, stand booksellers' stalls. Posters announce public readings to introduce new books, inscribed by skilled slaves on rolls of papyrus called *volumina*. Stonecutters hack away on the Field of Mars. Barbers, notorious for their sharp-edged gossip and cruelly dull razors, set up here and there beneath little awnings. Rustics congregate at the Forum Boarium, the cattle market between the Forum and the Tiber; to the nearby Forum Holitorium donkeys haul baskets of vegetables from gardens outside the city. A squealing pig darts across a street, bumping cursing pedestrians. It belongs to the neighborhood miller, who fattens it on his leftovers.

Fortune tellers in weird garb tug at passersby and swear they come from Babylon, home of Chaldean astrology; but their voices bespeak the Tiber. Women of the streets beckon; drawn here from every province in the empire, they dress in native attire. Taverns offer bread and wine; frequent customers are cutthroats and secret police.

"WHILE STANDS THE COLOSSEUM, *Rome shall stand," quoth the poets of the marvel that has endured 1,900 years. Jarred by quakes and traffic, scarred as a medieval fortress, flayed of its marble skin by Renaissance builders, the brick and concrete skeleton shows cells for beasts and gladiators under the 287-foot-long* arena, *Latin for "sandy place." Floored with timbers, it was sand-strewn to soak up blood. On hot days giant awnings shaded combatants and 50,000 spectators.*

WALTER MEAYERS EDWARDS, NATIONAL GEOGRAPHIC STAFF

Still, times are better than when Nero sent a flunky around the taverns singing songs the emperor had composed. Those who failed to tip the singer faced treason charges!

A world capital, Rome welcomes *peregrini*, or foreigners, though satirists rail at the "hungry Greeklings" and the Syrians, "scum of the Orontes." Most frequently met on the streets, however, are the slaves. Rome's shops, mills, and grand households depend on slave labor. Once war provided an endless supply; now most slaves are offspring of slave parents. The more fortunate serve in the household hierarchy of masters like Seneca, who care for their servants' well-being. At the other end are the wretches who must trot for miles as escorts for their master's carriage, or those sent to toil on far-off cattle ranches.

Many a slave is freed as a reward for service. Some rise to become surgeons, architects, trusted officials of the emperor. A few duplicate the feat of Trimalchio, fictional hero of the *Satyricon*, Petronius' novel written in Nero's time. Brought to

Rome from Syria, this slave boy won the heart of his owner with gentle ways and shrewdness. He gained freedom and his master's wealth, and went on to build another fortune. Trimalchio never tired of telling his rags-to-riches story.

"*T*HE PEOPLE that once bestowed commands, consulships, legions, and all else, now meddles no more and longs eagerly for just two things—bread and circuses." *Panem et circenses!* Juvenal's harangue leads moderns to think of the Roman games merely as distractions offered to an idle and cruel people, thirsty for blood. They held deeper meaning, however. Since Rome's early days they had been regarded as sacred rites, especially required at crucial periods to ensure the benevolence of the city's gods.

Each crisis in Republican days, and later the accession of each emperor, led to more and more games. By the reign of Claudius (A.D. 41-54) the calendar held 159 holidays, 93 devoted to games at public expense, usually chariot races.

Dignified magistrates, followed by figures of the gods

ROMAN HOLIDAY *splinters ship against ship in the flooded Colosseum. "Here just a while ago was dry land," marveled Martial.*

Caesar dug a lake for the first naval spectacular; the last feted Rome's millennium, A.D. 248; *the biggest was Claudius' gala of* A.D. 52 *in which two fleets and 10,000 men turned a lake red.*

The 100 days of games dedicating the Colosseum drenched it in blood. Prisoners who helped build it faced lions or, armed, slew naked comrades, then died in turn. Men hunted beasts amid rocks and trees; beast fought beast; 5,000 animals were killed in a day. Later totals topped 10,000.

In the afternoon spectators found best sport. Then gladiators— trained, pampered, adored by fans— dueled to the death in various styles. Myrmillo with sword and helmet (left) might meet retiarius with net and trident or sagittarius with bow and arrows. Caesar matched charioteers blinded by eyeless helmets. Victors got gold; losers often read the crowd's death signal—thumbs down.

carried on litters, and dancing clowns and satyrs lead the *pompa circensis* to the racecourse at the Circus Maximus. Seats full, an official signals—they're off! Round and round in a cloud of dust race the chariots, urged on by 250,000 throats (they say one can hear the roar at Ostia 12 miles away). Fans identify their own fortunes with the teams, distinguished by colors—Reds, Blues, Whites, and Greens. Darlings of Rome, the drivers stare down from countless posters, women seek them out, police wink at their escapades; when they die in spectacular collisions, poets lament them. Horses also have their followers. "Winner or not, we love you, Polydoxus," reads a mosaic on the floor of a villa.

Romans also crowd the "scenic games"—legends performed to music by mimes, and comedies of love and avarice, deception and ignorance. But the great playwrights of the Republic, such as Plautus and Terence, find no counterpart in imperial days. (Seneca, tutor to Nero, wrote tragedies that later inspired Shakespeare, but they were intended to be recited, not acted.) Realistic staging now overshadows all else. The blazing walls of Troy become a real conflagration. If a play calls for a character to be slain by a mob, a condemned criminal takes the part and the audience watches the players tear him to pieces.

"HAIL CAESAR, we who are about to die salute you!" The emperor nods at the two men before him. A slave hands them weapons. A trumpet sounds. Slowly, like boxers, they circle and feint. Suddenly, weapons clash and the Colosseum echoes with 50,000 voices howling for blood. In minutes one man lies on his back, one finger raised for mercy, his opponent over him with dagger poised. The loser's performance smacked of cowardice; the spectators murmur, turn thumbs down. Agreeing, the emperor turns a thumb down. *"Jugula! Jugula!"* the mob cries. The blade sinks into the victim's throat. The victor collects palm and prizes.

Gladiatorial combats emerged from Etruscan funeral sacrifices. Mourners staged them in the belief that the precious libation of blood momentarily animated the deceased. The contests became a badge of family prestige, eventually a path to popular favor. Generals, senators, and emperors put on ever more elaborate shows. When the emperor Titus opened the Colosseum A.D. 80, the spectacles lasted 100 days.

A typical day might begin with hunters stalking wild beasts (5,000 animals died on

LAVING IN LUXURY *at the Baths of Caracalla, Romans frolic in the* frigidarium. *They took to the cold pool after a hot soak in the* caldarium *and a warm dip in the* tepidarium. *For a pittance this "Palace of Roman Water" also offered gymnasiums, shops, gardens, libraries, sculpture galleries. Masseurs, anointers, and perfumers groomed patricians; poor plebeians scraped themselves. Hypocaust (left) with underground fires stoked by slaves carried furnace air through floor and wall ducts. Central heating was a Roman invention.*

In 33 B.C. *Rome had 170* thermae *(baths), later a thousand. In the second century Emperor Hadrian banned mixed bathing; separate hours were set for the sexes.*

PRIDE *of Caesars and panoply*
of Pharaohs make opera grand in
summertime Rome. Under a celestial
roof, piers of Caracalla's baths
frame a scene from Verdi's Aida.

Completed A.D. *235, the baths*
sprawled over 33 acres, surpassed
in size only by Diocletian's baths,
which could hold 3,000 bathers.
Here Caracalla offered Rome the
"attractions of civilization";
yet this fear-crazed emperor,
known for the Gallic hooded cloak
(caracalla) *he preferred to the toga,*
drenched the city in rivals' blood.

WALTER MEAYERS EDWARDS, NATIONAL GEOGRAPHIC STAFF

one of Titus's hundred days). Then buffalo are pitted against bears
or elephants. Criminals, dragged into the arena, face lions. When
the last poor wretch lies still, out come attendants clad as demons
to dig hooks into the torn flesh and drag the men off. A furrow
traced in the sand is the only memorial to a hapless victim.
Now and then clowns and musicians perform. Not until the sun
drives the day's heat to its peak, stretching spectators' nerves taut
and blunting their pity, do the gladiators appear.

Desperate circumstances drive men into the arena. Usually they
are slaves, captives of war, criminals, sometimes wastrel sons
of good family lured by promises of glory and wealth. They pledge
to endure without complaint the cruel discipline of training.

In return their master supplies food, weapons, medical care. They also enjoy the favors of some of Rome's highest-born women. On the eve of combat the fighters may feast in public while people stroll among them, noting those who appear carefree and those who sit without eating, throats closed tight with fear of the morrow.

ROMANS BORROWED the idea of the baths from the Greeks, who bathed after exercising in the palaestra. Rome's earliest baths were merely washhouses. But in the first century A.D. the emperors began to build lavish *thermae* with libraries, gardens, and porticoes for study, strolling, and gossiping, with balconies for sunbathing, and with courts for exercising. Unlike the Greeks, Romans did not delight in exercise for its own sake. Many a noble took exercise only under

SCENES FROM A SHORT LIFE *on a boy's sarcophagus tell of Roman childhood. Suckled by his mother, he was held by his father in token of support, harking to days when Romans slew unwanted infants. At nine days a lad got a charm and three names: his own* praenomen, *the* nomen *of his* gens, *or clan, and the* cognomen *of his family. Thus the boy Gaius was born to a family in the Julian clan, the Caesars. Girls got a feminized clan name like Julia. Toys and pets lightened lessons, sometimes with father as tutor. Dropouts by 13, girls prepared for wedlock; boys graduated to loftier learning and soldiering.*

Imps with pens, third-graders of modern Italy (above) cannot erase, thus think before they write. They wear uniforms through fifth grade; dark colors hide ink stains.

2D-3D CENTURY RELIEF FROM TRIER, IN THE LOUVRE; GIRAUDON. ABOVE: LEE E. BATTAGLIA

doctor's orders—perhaps tossing a little leather ball around or trundling a hoop. And if the ball was missed, one did not bother to chase it. A slave brought another.

Seneca complained of the noise—the splash of bathers, the cries of brawlers and of vendors offering grilled sausages and honey cakes. But for most Romans a visit to the baths was the highlight of their day. The bather enjoyed hot, cold, and lukewarm pools. As he sweated in the steam room, he doused himself with cold water and drank glass after glass of watered wine. Afterward an attendant oiled his body and scraped it with a strigil to remove sweat and dirt. Use the strigil, Martial advised, and "the fuller will not so often wear out your towels." A masseur smoothed muscles with perfumed hands; a depilator plucked unwanted hairs from face and body. The citizen departed, refreshed in body and spirit.

Martial, whose *Epigrams* detail the spectacle of first-century Rome, had harsh words for the educators of his day. "You cursed schoolmaster, what right have you to disturb us before the cock crows with your savage threats and beatings?" Others shared his view of the miserably paid teacher who set up his chair and benches under an awning amid the street clatter. From dawn to noon he drove his pupils—boys and girls—at reading, writing, and reciting maxims. Because of the awkwardness of Roman numerals (88 = LXXXVIII), they pushed beads *(calculi)* on an abacus to add, subtract, multiply, and divide. Wealthier students advanced to the *grammaticus* for instruction in composition and in Greek and Roman literature.

In the second century B.C., Cato the Elder advised his sons: "Stick to the point and the words will come." Later, would-be orators studied with rhetoricians, sharpening their wits and delivery by extemporizing on themes such as "Aristotle, the tutor of Alexander, tries to dissuade his pupil from his plan to conquer Asia."

Young men learned law at the feet of senators. Except for the Twelve Tables, compiled, according to tradition, in the fifth century B.C., and Justinian's famed code in the sixth century A.D., there were few codifications of Roman law. Thus lawyers had to develop a prodigious memory for precedents. They also developed legal principles which formed the basis for the Napoleonic Code and modern international law, and which still guide much of the Western World. The Apostle Paul knew that as a Roman citizen he had the right to face his accusers and could

appeal the acts of provincial magistrates to the highest authorities in Rome.
Our concepts of justice today owe much to those senators of old who, amid cruelty,
corruption, and self-indulgence, pursued the ideal that each case must be judged
in the light of reason, to balance the scales between spirit and letter of the law.

By the end of the Republic the ancient custom which gave the *pater familias* the
power of life or death over his family had fallen into disuse. Yet fathers retained
much influence over their children's lives, and those with daughters haunted
the rhetoricians' schools to seek out young men of promise. Often girls were
betrothed at seven, wed at puberty. Since Romans believed nothing more vital
than beginnings, the wedding was wrapped in ritual. It began at dawn with a
sacrifice and the reading of entrails—the signs had to be propitious. The couple
exchanged vows: *"Ubi tu Gaius, ego Gaia,"* the girl would say. "Where you are Gaius,
I shall be Gaia." When the evening star appeared, the bride pretended to flee her

"I CANNOT KEEP TRACK OF FASHION," *sighed Ovid as Roman ladies primped
for hours: first the coiffure—"tiers and stories piled one upon another,"
scoffed Juvenal; then rouge, eye shadow, chalk for arms and forehead.
Laden with jewels (below), milady wore her dowry on her body, as Seneca
sneered. And exotic perfumes stirred only a growl from Plautus: "The right
scent for a woman is none at all."*

Gourmands scorned Cicero's counsel: "Eat to live, not live to eat"

Rome's rich clustered at banquets to flaunt fortunes and swap gossip, "discuss whatever is afoot and turn grumbling into guffaws." Though plebs gulped gruel and many patricians favored simple fare, spendthrifts built a legend of lavish dining. Quitting baths at midafternoon, they took to couches; to recline was comfortable and let one eat more. Slaves, children, barbarians ate seated. So did women until Caesar's day, when they might join the guests on couches.

Out marched well-drilled slaves with dishes that kept guests guessing. Bragged Trimalchio of one chef, "he will make you a fish out of a sow's belly . . . a chicken out of a knuckle of pork." Live thrushes might burst from a roast boar, or cooked ones from eggs under a wooden hen. Romans relished venison, lark, peacock, flamingo tongue, fine fish such as mullet or sole. Cicero's favorite was salt fish mixed with brains, poultry liver, eggs, and cheese, cooked in oil and sauced with pepper, lovage, marjoram, rue berries, honey, and oil; "bind it with raw eggs." One slave, the *scissor*, carved the food bite-size.

Diners dug in with spoons and fingers, rinsing hands in perfumed water between courses. Some came with napkins, took home leftovers in them. Wine, cooled by snow, soothed spice-seared throats—ideally the "immortal Falernian" vintages, certainly not the "black poison of a Corsican jar." Overfull banqueters returned from the *vomitorium* for more. Menus might offer:

Gustus
(Appetizers)
TREE FUNGI IN FISH-FAT SAUCE
JELLYFISH AND EGGS
SOW'S UDDERS STUFFED WITH
SALTED SEA URCHINS

Cena
(Main Course)
DORMOUSE WITH PINE KERNELS
BOILED OSTRICH

Secunda Mensa
(Dessert)
FRICASSEE OF ROSES WITH PASTRY

Table talk might be lofty or ludicrous. A guest shares his stomach remedy: "Wash your feet and drink the water." As they belch politely, we observe: *De gustibus non est disputandum*—there is no accounting for tastes.

PAINTINGS FOR NATIONAL GEOGRAPHIC BY H. M. HERGET. MOSAIC FROM MUSEUM OF ANTIQUITIES, TRIPOLI. GOLD JEWELRY FROM POMPEII; LEE E. BATTAGLIA

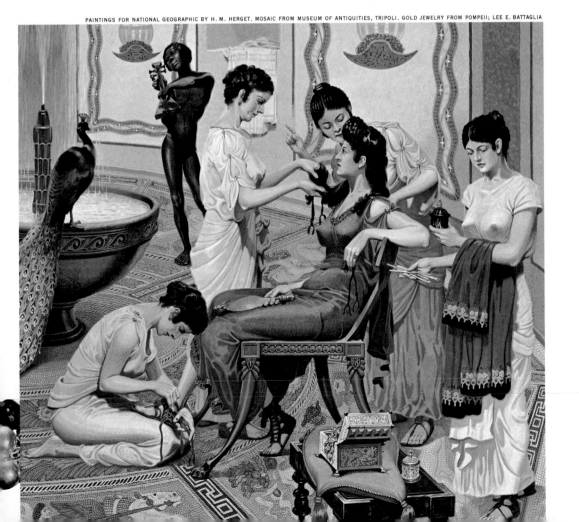

mother's arms and went to her new home. She was lifted through the doorway lest her foot touch the threshold— a bad omen. Some said the custom recalled how Rome's founders took brides by carrying off Sabine women.

By Caesar's time wives had won increasing freedom; they could own property and obtain divorces. While Cicero struggled from one crisis to another, his wife Terentia increased her own fortune. And the beautiful Clodia— "Juno of the big eyes," Cicero called her—surrounded herself with admirers, gave swimming parties in the Tiber, and summered in Campania. Among those smitten was Catullus, fresh from the provinces, burning with poetry: "Let us live my dear, let us love and never fear."

Wives now graced banquets, though usually they sat on chairs instead of reclining on couches. Trimalchio, the self-made man in Petronius' the *Satyricon*, asked his Fortunata to chat with guests and keep an eye on the silver. She had, he said, the eyes and claws of a hawk. Yet he spared no expense to delight his company. Servants clad as hunters carried in a roasted wild boar while hounds yelped at their heels. Roman cuisine abounded in spices and herbs, and few recipes omitted *garum*, a sauce made by steeping the intestines of fish in salt.

"*T*HAT CORNER of the land beyond all others for me smiles, where heaven sends warm mists and a slow spring." Thus Horace hymned the beauties of the countryside. Despite the attractions of the city, Romans never lost their love of the land. All who could fled from Rome's stifling summers to airy villas in the mountains or at lakeside or seashore. High society favored Campania (Baiae and especially Pompeii and Stabiae before Vesuvius buried them A.D. 79). Many chose Antium, down the coast, or the hills south of Rome we call the Castelli Romani.

From a simple farm owner's dwelling, the villa evolved into an elegant retreat with a magnificent vista. Campaigns in Asia had opened Romans' eyes to the beauty of gardens. Soon villas boasted climbing roses, vine-covered paths, grottoes, fountains, pavilions. Gardeners shaped boxwood into hunters and hounds, into ships with sails set.

Wealth and ease led many Romans into gay, dissolute lives. Some, however, used their leisure to explore the great questions of life, even kept resident philosophers to guide them. The Epicurean, Philodemus of Gadara, instructed

ADAM WOOLFITT

HADRIAN *brought the world to Tivoli, fashioned it into a villa, and here found respite from worldly Rome.*

He filled 750 sylvan acres with temples, palaces, theaters, a canal evoking the Nile, an academy like Plato's—all that delighted him on tours of empire. Here sisters of Athens' caryatids face Mars across a pool.

Power-thirsty Romans drank deeply at wells of rural solace. Cicero had at least seven villas. Grandest of all was Hadrian's, still abuilding when he asked, mortally ill: "fleeing little soul . . . where do you go now, pale, cold, and naked . . . ?"

Caesar's father-in-law. Augustus had the Stoic Athenodorus in his house for years. Epicureans taught that the chief end of human existence is pleasure, the pleasure found in temperate living. Stoics valued a life of reason, restraint, and self-mastery. Athenodorus once tried to teach Augustus the virtue of restraint. Knowing the emperor's weakness for women, the philosopher disguised himself as one. Augustus paid court until Athenodorus finally revealed that the emperor's ardor was in vain. Augustus was not angered, but neither did he change his ways.

On an ordinary day the Roman devoted little time to the gods; religion was largely an affair of state. Priests performed prescribed rituals; in return Jupiter would produce rain and guide rulers, Ceres would provide grain, Mars would protect armies. Before important actions officials turned to augurs, who sought divine revelation in the flight of birds, the crash of thunder, the birth of a malformed infant. Skeptics questioned such rites and wondered how diviners could pass each other on the street without laughing. "It is useful that there should be gods," wrote the poet Ovid in Augustus' time, "so let us believe there are." Countryfolk held that spirits lurked everywhere. On certain nights the family clustered around the hearth while the father tossed cooked beans into the darkness to propitiate the dead who roamed the streets. From of old, every home had its altar to the Lares, protective household gods. In time Romans added symbols of Mercury, god of profit; Venus, goddess of fortune; and Bacchus, god of the vine who promised a haven after death. Imported cults grew popular. Soldiers favored Mithras, Persian sun god who slew a bull in cosmic battle; in grottoes believers were baptized with the blood of sacrificial bulls. The Egyptian goddess Isis proffered immortality.

Many Romans looked on Christians as heretic Jews who sacrificed children and longed for the end of the world when their god—an agitator executed in Jerusalem during Tiberius' reign—would return. Their secretiveness and refusal to pay lip service to Rome's gods angered usually tolerant Romans. So crowds gleefully watched when Christians, tarred and staked, were set ablaze to light one of Nero's lawn parties. Yet when Pliny the Younger, as governor of Bithynia in Asia Minor,

SEA GATE *to imperial Rome, Ostia on the Tiber welcomed vessels heavy with grain and other imports. Cargoes packed warehouses to await the 16-mile trip upstream to the capital by mule- or slave-drawn barge. Craftsmen filled arcades with their din. Traders crowded the Square of the Corporations (lower right), where mottoes in mosaic include this mark of a Narbonne merchant.*

Excavators at Ostia revealed what had all but vanished in Rome: insulae, apartment blocks with jutting balconies (upper right). Here throbbed the life of the common folk.

consulted Trajan about punishing Christians, the emperor decreed punishment only after legal process and added, "they are not to be hunted out." And it was over the Roman network of communications that the new faith spread.

A major terminus of that network was Rome's port of Ostia, developed by Claudius and Trajan near the mouth of the Tiber. Here one could feel with Petronius that Rome possessed "the earth and the seas and the . . . field of stars." To Ostia came stubby roundships with grain from Egypt and the Crimea, copper and tin from Britain, salt and fish sauce from Spain, glass and leather from the Levant, parchment and horses from Asia Minor, wine and honey from Greece, iron and timber from the Balkans, gems and spices from Ceylon.

Under the Republic freewheeling traders reaped fortunes in a single venture, and lost them as quickly. Experts

WILD-EYED HORSES LUNGE *under the lash as a quarter of a million howling Romans pack the Circus Maximus for a day at the races. Bookies keep busy; "the young," says Juvenal, "shout and make bold wagers with a smart damsel by their side." Hairpin turns tax chariot teams at ends of the spina, backbone of the oval track. Officials flip over a bronze dolphin and remove a white egg to tick off the seven laps—two and a half miles. Colors mark* factiones, *clubs whose drivers gamble lives for fortunes.*

PAINTING FOR NATIONAL GEOGRAPHIC BY BIRNEY LETTICK

called *numerarii* were required to fix values for dozens of currencies. The emperors built roads and harbors, simplified currency, set controls on trade. The great cities of the East—Alexandria, Antioch, Miletus, Ephesus—glowed with new splendor. In Europe and Africa cities rose in the image of Rome. Each boasted its baths, theater, amphitheater, triumphal arches, covered markets, and forum. Their ruins grace Europe's modern cities and the coast and mountains of Africa.

THE EMPERORS who ruled this world came from many lands—Syria, Spain, Illyria, and Germany, as well as the Italian homeland. We often remember them for their eccentricities: Tiberius, who deserted his capital and ruled from a villa on Capri, consulting the stars with an astrologer; Caligula (a nickname meaning "little boots," bestowed in childhood when he went about shod like a soldier), who in his madness proposed his horse for consul; the miser Vespasian, skeptical of his future divinity, who on his deathbed quipped, "I think I'm becoming a god."

When the Praetorian Guard, elite protectors of the imperial city, assassinated Caligula, they pulled his uncle from behind a curtain and named him emperor. Claudius proved a good ruler but an unlucky lover. His third wife plotted against him with her paramour; probably it was his fourth, Agrippina, who poisoned him. She enthroned her son Nero, then fought him for power. Nero had her thrown into the sea; when she swam ashore, his troops caught and killed her. Henceforth, as if to drown his guilt, he pursued pleasure above all else. He competed as a chariot racer, harpist, and actor; not surprisingly, he won every event he entered, even some he did not. At last, when everyone turned against him, he ordered a retainer to kill him, crying: "What an artist the world is losing!"

But Rome survived its eccentrics, survived and benefited millions until, in the fifth century, it could no longer resist the relentless pressure of the barbarians. It had well performed the noble mission set down by Virgil:

> Others, no doubt, will better mould the bronze
> To the semblance of soft breathing, draw, from marble,
> The living countenance; and others plead
> With greater eloquence, or learn to measure,
> Better than we, the pathways of the heaven,
> The risings of the stars: remember, Roman,
> To rule the people under law, to establish
> The way of peace, to battle down the haughty,
> To spare the meek. Our fine arts, these, forever.

Ancient Rome's great buildings lie now in ruin, but some things in the city have not changed: the light of her sky, heat of her summers, life in her squares, the swarming of children in the markets. As I walk her streets I think of Terence's line, "I am a man, and nothing human is alien to me." This too is Rome's legacy. I think also of that remarkable man who tore Rome from her ancient ruts and demonstrated the full potential of her might and majesty. When Julius Caesar faced his Rubicon, so too did Rome herself.

THE STONES OF ROME, *from humble paving to triumphal marble, glowed in the glory of empire, when legions bound "scattered nations into one." Titus's victory over Jerusalem rebels,* A.D. 70, *raised this arch on the Sacred Way. Rome's sun set over ravaged grandeur, but her legacy would enrich "regions Caesar never knew."*

In the Footsteps of Caesar

From Britain to the Black Sea, National Geographic's John J. Putman follows the battling legions and their relentless leader on the

Conqueror's Path to Mighty Empire

A PARTY of Roman officers hastens from Ravenna at dusk in a mule-drawn carriage. In the night their lamps sputter out and they lose their way. At dawn they find a peasant who will guide them, but on foot. As they climb down, he notices the leader: tall, middle-aged, with quick, dark-brown eyes in a cadaverous face. The peasant leads the officers along country paths until they reach a river, where legionaries wait. Centurions rise, approach the commander, salute, and await orders.

But Julius Caesar is silent. In nine years he has conquered the whole of Gaul, bridged the Rhine to punish German tribes, and penetrated Britain, a "hitherto unknown land." All Rome has hailed his victories. Yet the Senate now demands he lay down his command and return as a citizen. To do so, he is sure, means a rigged trial and possible death; political

Men of pride and power, Roman soldiers stand firm in a 2d-century A.D. *relief in the Louvre, Paris; Jonathan S. Blair*

enemies have accused him of misconduct in Gaul. Yet to cross this river—the Rubicon, the border between his province and the territory of Rome itself—is to plunge his nation into civil war. Suddenly, he strides forward: "The die is cast." His legionaries cheer as he leads them across toward Rome. It is 49 B.C.

I was across the narrow stream before I knew it, swept along by holiday traffic bound for Rimini and other resorts along Italy's Adriatic coast. Only a small, rusty plaque marked it as the storied river of decision. Half a mile downstream, where it meets the sea, fishermen cast butterfly-shaped nets. But upstream the river vanished among reeds, and I found on its banks only a shepherd and his flock.

I had come in quest of Caesar—genius, enigma, one of history's most remarkable men. In a little less than 15 years he set Rome on the path to empire, shaped the future of western Europe and indeed our world, triumphed on battlefields from the Atlantic to the Black Sea, reformed our calendar, fathered a son by Cleopatra, and at his death became a god by decree of Rome's Senate. Caesar—the man and the legend—has fascinated the ages. Scholars have labeled him both "the complete and perfect man" and "a crook," agreeing only with Shakespeare that he bestrode the narrow world like a colossus.

To follow his footsteps I would travel 20,000 miles through a dozen nations. I would search the pages of Suetonius, Plutarch, and other ancient writers. But my principal guide would be Caesar's own *Commentaries*—the *Gallic War* and the *Civil War*. Packed with detail, they tell much about the conqueror but little of the man. Perhaps my journey would give me a sharper picture. I tossed a pebble into the reeds of the silent river and headed south toward Rome.

A TEEN-AGED LAD, wracked by fever, hides out in the Sabine hills northeast of Rome, the quarry of bounty hunters. Gaius Julius Caesar has seen his world shattered. He had known the privileges of a noble Roman family. His mother, the worthy Aurelia, had instilled in him the traditional virtues of *disciplina* and *severitas;* his tutor, a Gaul, had taught him Greek as well as Latin, literature and philosophy. He had sat in the Senate to watch his relatives debate.

He had watched, too, as his uncle Marius rose to power by championing the masses, winning glory in war, finally bending the Senate to his will with the help of a band of cutthroats. Marius had made young Caesar a priest of Jupiter.

But now Marius is dead. Sulla, leader of the aristocrats, has returned from his Asian campaign, seized Rome, and convulsed it in a carnival of blood. He has posted the names of his enemies and awards their property to their killers.

The hunted Caesar hears footsteps, prepares to flee, but recognizes a friend. He learns that at the request of the Vestal Virgins (Caesar charmed, even then), Sulla will grant him a hearing. The ordeal ends. But the harsh lesson—the power of the sword and the strength of men's greed—will burn in his memory.

In the years that followed, Caesar fought in Asia Minor as a junior officer and

CILICIAN PIRATES GUFFAW *as young Caesar vows to crucify them. They had seized him en route to Rhodes and hold him on rocky Pharmacusa, off Asia Minor, where they loll in stolen finery. Potbellied chief guards the cooling wine. The bandits also scorned verses Caesar composed. "Barbarous!" he fumed. Ransomed, he returned with a fleet and—having "mercifully cut their throats" to shorten the agony—crucified them.*

PAINTING FOR NATIONAL GEOGRAPHIC BY BIRNEY LETTICK

won a decoration for bravery in combat. Voyaging to Rhodes to study rhetoric, he was captured by pirates and ransomed. He tracked down the brigands and crucified them. Bold, direct, his reaction revealed the thrust of his will.

Returning to Rome at 26, he began to climb the political ladder. He won a seat in the Senate and held the administrative posts of quaestor, aedile, and praetor. He even gained—and manipulated—power as pontifex maximus, or chief priest.

As I walked among the Forum's ruins, dusk softened the shattered columns. I could picture Caesar here amid a swirl of togas, haranguing senators with his high-pitched voice and impassioned gestures. Even Cicero, by common consent the greatest of Rome's orators, marveled at Caesar's force and wit. The crowds, Cicero's "wretched starveling mob," adored their new Marius. To woo them, Caesar plunged deeply into debt to stage wild-beast exhibitions, theatrical presentations, gladiatorial combats—some on these very stones.

During this time he lost his first wife, his beloved Cornelia. When scandal touched the second, he divorced her—"Caesar's wife must be above suspicion."

GREENER PASTURES *still lure Swiss farmers as they did the Helvetii, forebears of these sturdy mountain folk of Reidenbach. When the Helvetii set out with their herds to find a new life in Gaul, Caesar marched across the Alps to bar them from his provincial domain. In 58 B.C. he caught them near the stronghold of Bibracte in eastern France (below), slaughtered their warriors, and sent survivors back to their homeland—chalking up a solid victory in the first great battle of the Gallic Wars.*

His remark brought snickers. He was Rome's most notorious rake, and a fop who added fringed sleeves to his senatorial toga and combed his thinning hair forward to conceal his increasing baldness.

In 60 B.C., having gained a year's experience in military command in Spain, he joined with a general and a millionaire to control the politics of Rome. The gruff Pompey measured Caesar with a soldier's eye. Pompey's conquests in Syria and Asia Minor had almost doubled Rome's revenues. Yet the Senate refused to vote bonuses for his soldiers. Caesar vowed to push the bonus bill through. He also married his daughter Julia to Pompey. She grew to love her husband and, as long as she lived, would keep the two ambitious men from each other's throats.

Crassus, third member of the Triumvirate, was Rome's richest man, a speculator whose "many virtues," says Plutarch, "were darkened by the one vice of avarice." Courage he had. When the gladiator Spartacus revolted at Capua in 73 B.C. and terrorized the land with his slave army, Crassus crushed the rebels and hung them on crosses along the Appian Way. Yet the power he sought escaped him. The Senate refused to vote a rebate for his tax collector friends. Caesar promised aid.

For Caesar, the payoff was a consulship, Rome's highest office, and later the governorship of two provinces—Cisalpine Gaul (northern Italy) and Transalpine Gaul (stretching from the Alps along the coast of France to Spain). To him they seemed "likeliest to supply . . . wealth and triumphs," for north of them lay free

"All Gaul is divided into three parts"

Opening words of Caesar's **Gallic War** *sketch the sundered realm of the Aquitani, Celtae, and Belgae; by the close, all Gaul is won to Rome. Caesar first crosses the Alps to help Gauls rout invaders from the east. Time and again he returns to crush feuding tribes, put down coastal uprisings, stem German encroachment, sally into Britannia. As savior turns oppressor, proud tribes unite, only to lose all at Alesia.*

Caesar's campaigns (58-51 B.C.) won him undying military glory and brought Rome a fertile land now comprising France, parts of Switzerland, Germany, and the Low Countries. Into Gallia Comata—Long-haired Gaul— poured Rome's language, laws, architects, merchants to spur civilization. The conquerors banned human sacrifice but let other Druid rites persist. Sanctuary of Sequana at the Seine's source has yielded cowled statues in wood (left). Romans built in stone: temples, aqueducts, amphitheaters such as that at Arles (lower), where bloodless bullfights now fill the arena. "Let the Alps sink," exulted Cicero. "The gods raised them to shelter Italy from the barbarians ... now they are no longer needed."

STATUTE MILES
DRAWN BY LISA BIGANZOLI
GEOGRAPHIC ART DIVISION

TORRENTS *of tourists course the famed Pont du Gard, triple-tiered aqueduct that watered Nîmes from sources 25 miles away. No mortar binds its stone arches that leap 900 feet across the Gard River. Yet for 2,000 years it has attested to Rome's sway in Provence,* its provincia *in southern Gaul. Block and tackle raised six-ton slabs 160 feet to roof the sluice (right). Jutting stones (opposite) held workers' scaffolds.*

Sixty-eight aqueducts (page 443) slaked the empire's thirst; 11 poured millions of gallons daily into Rome, its Tiber fouled by mud. Rules limited private taps, but scofflaws piped water to farms, shops, even brothels.

Gaul, vast, bountiful, untouched by any civilized conqueror. Soon after he received the governorship of the provinces, Caesar found the opportunity to march.

I DROVE NORTH from Rome, along misty Apennine ridges, up the broad Po Valley, and across the Alps to Geneva. Here Caesar hastened in 58 B.C. when he learned that the Helvetii, "a stalwart race," planned to cut across Transalpine Gaul in a westward migration. For two years they had stored grain; then they put the torch to their farms and villages in the land we know as Switzerland and gathered along the east bank of the Rhone. Caesar, deeming them "a hostile people," burned the bridge at Geneva and built a rampart that stretched about 18 miles downstream. The Helvetii seemed penned between the Alps, the Jura Mountains, and Caesar's wall. But at the southern end of the wall they slipped through the Pas d'Ecluse, a gorge Caesar found "scarcely wide enough for the passage of wagons in single file." I found French road crews toiling to straighten and widen the highway that overlooks the Helvetii's path.

Caesar pursued them into the heart of free Gaul. As I drove west I envisioned his legionaries swinging along. "Marius' mules," they called themselves, honoring the memory of Caesar's uncle, who had transformed Rome's citizen soldiers into a professional army. Over their shoulders they carried sword, shield, helmet, javelins, a spade or ax for entrenching, as well as cooking pot and a ration of grain; behind came the mule train with catapults, supplies, camp followers, slaves. Surely the soldiers wondered about their new commander. Would he lead them to loot and glory, or through some blunder to a shallow grave?

At the Saone, Caesar caught the Helvetii's rear guard, and the river ran red. The chase continued into the hills of Burgundy—today gentle, lavender, mantled with vineyards; in his day, dark with primeval forest and marsh.

Near Autun the Helvetii turned to fight. They fashioned a stockade of their carts and placed women and children behind it. Caesar formed his legions in three lines up a hillside, then ordered his mount and those of his staff to the rear, so his men

"If won over . . . they willingly devote their energies to useful pursuits"

Strabo

As a village of Gaul holds its breath, the headman proffers drink and welcome to a Roman centurion. An awed lad's donkey-powered mill grinds to a halt; fields beyond the open gate provide its grist. Wary matrons—two may share a husband—peer

at legionaries from huts of stone, log, and thatch.
Heads of slain enemies hang in some. Hammer poised,
a smith glowers at masters his weapons once slew.
Helmets, shields, shovel heads line his forge.
Iron rims wheels for the wagons and chariots prized

by ancients; the words "chariot" and "car" stem from
a Celtic root. First with the harrow, spiral drill,
perhaps the wheeled plow, Gauls bartered with Rome's
soldiers and traders and learned their rough Latin.
Altered by Gallic brogue, it lives in modern French.

PAINTING FOR NATIONAL GEOGRAPHIC BY BIRNEY LETTICK

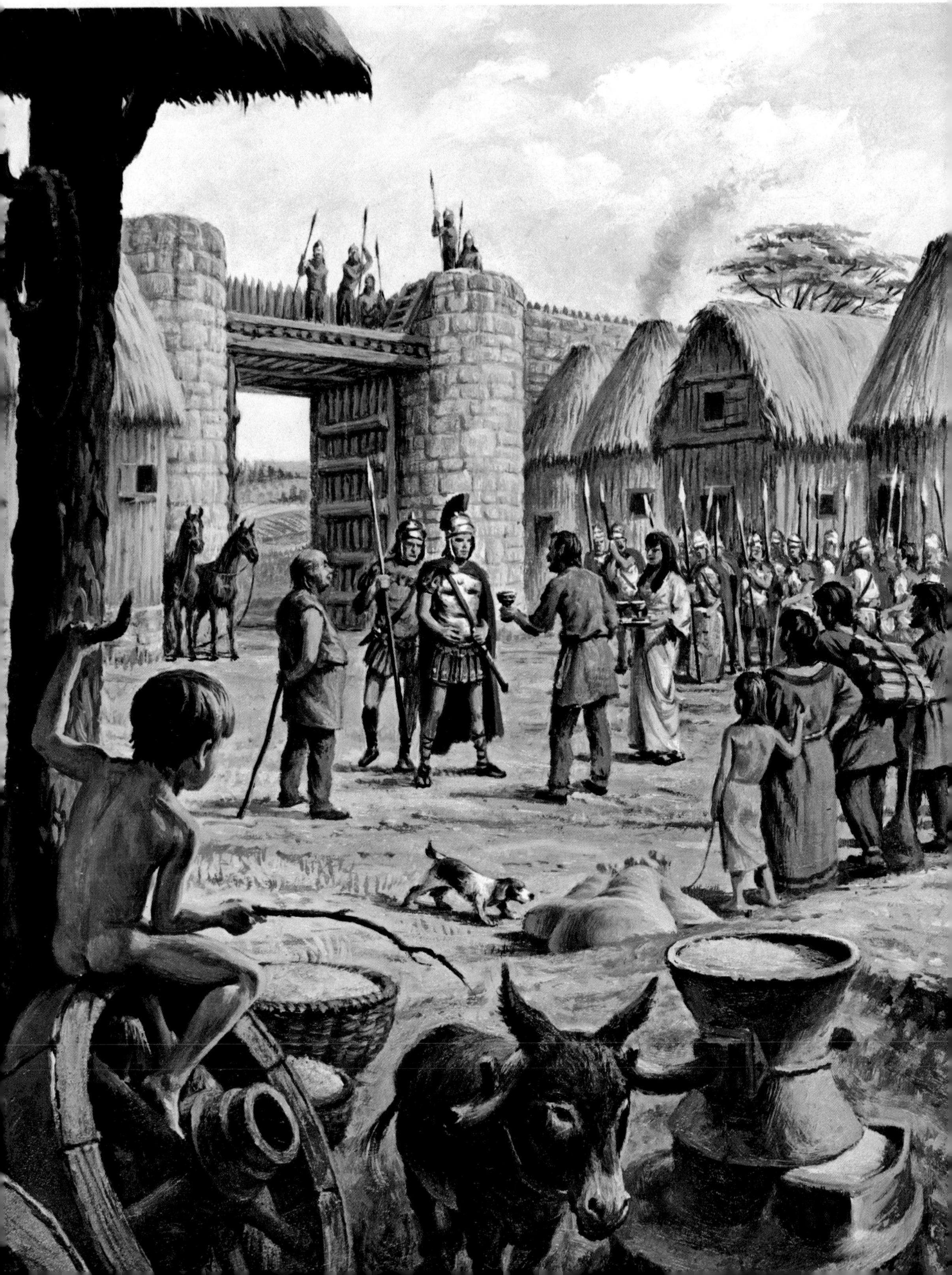

would know their leaders would not desert. With a shout, the Helvetii charged —into a shower of javelins that pinned many of their shields together and slowed their drive. Then the Romans drew short swords and swept downhill, pushing the tribesmen back on their camp. The fighting raged on into the night, with the defenders pouring missiles out from behind their carts. At last they broke and fled. When Caesar overtook them, they "groveled and begged for peace." Records found in their camp revealed that 368,000 Helvetii had begun the journey. "Those who returned home," Caesar noted, "showed a total of 110,000."

Cows graze the battle site today. The bark of a dog, the voices of farmers in their fields echo across haunted hillocks. At nearby Bibracte, mountaintop citadel of free Gaul, only wind and strolling tourists disturb the dark copses where Gallic chieftains gathered. They knew the victorious Roman would want a parley.

From "well nigh the whole of Gaul" they came—big, broad-shouldered men with blonde locks and moustaches, clad in wool trousers and tunics, some with golden torques around their necks. They thanked Caesar for ridding their land of the invaders and proposed an assembly to discuss future relations. He agreed.

The land Romans called Gaul was peopled by tribes of Celtic stock—the Belgae, the Aquitani, and the Celtae, or Galli. They dwelt in villages and hilltop citadels, cleared land for grain, worked iron mines, and coursed rivers and trekked forest

AT HOME *underground, a family dines in a Loire Valley cavern near Le Thoureil. Hundreds of cave dwellings, some with water and electricity, pock the area. Many date from Roman times; Gauls holed up in them, seeking refuge from Caesar's legions.*

A farmer of Châteauneuf (left) pitches hay near Dijon, Roman Dibio. Caesar fought invaders lured by these fertile farmlands. In the fifth century a Germanic tribe, the Burgundians, settled here and gave the region its name.

Wine of Burgundy flowed first from Roman vines. Gauls had quaffed mead, barley beer, and a brew of honey-laced wheat. "Wits dulled by continual drunkenness," the Gauls "rush about in aimless revels," wrote one Roman critic.

DEAN CONGER AND (LEFT) JOSEPH J. SCHERSCHEL, BOTH NATIONAL GEOGRAPHIC STAFF

paths to trade for luxuries such as wine from Marseilles.

Caesar called them "slaves of superstition." Their priests, the Druids, memorized endless verses, decided criminal cases, regulated sacrifices, and met each year on the plain of Chartres, reckoned the center of Gaul. They held spectacular funerals: "Everything, including even animals, that the dead man is supposed to have treasured is added to the pyre." They believed in the immortality of the soul and, Caesar observed, regarded this belief "as the finest incentive to courage since it inspires contempt of death."

I asked Prof. Joël Le Gall, a distinguished archeologist at the University of Dijon, how Caesar's descriptions stand the test of modern science. "He's usually right," the professor replied. "But now and then he errs—for instance, when he gives Gallic gods Roman names and describes their functions in Roman terms. The Gallic mentality was entirely different. Gauls believed lightning to be a fragment of the sun sent down by a god, and where it struck they

385

A "nation . . . war mad . . .

Face of a valiant breed outlasts the
centuries in a wrought-iron portrait
(left) of a fallen warrior of Gaul.
At ancient Alesia, where Gauls made
their last stand against Caesar in
52 B.C., scholars and schoolchildren
(below) strain for glimpses of the
world Gauls built—and lost.

Bronze cavalryman (opposite)
harks to hard-riding Gallic
horsemen, peers of Caesar's own.
Gauls prized horses and may have
bred them first for meat and milk,
later as mounts and burden bearers.
In the earthy faiths of the Gauls
they stood for power; many graves
have yielded horse bones.
Idols often show a mounted deity—
possibly Taranis, the thunder god—
whose steed tramples a giant,
symbol of the underworld.

Brandishing a bolt, Taranis in
bronze (below, left) holds a sun
wheel, probably a divine symbol.

ADAM WOOLFITT. FUNERAL MASK FROM CHASSENARD AND THUNDER GOD FROM
LE CHATELET, 1ST CENTURY A.D., MOTHER GODDESS FROM TOULON SUR ALLIER
AND BRONZE HORSEMAN, C. 2D CENTURY A.D.; ALL ST. GERMAIN-EN-LAYE MUSEUM.
BOWMAN ON GLAZED VASE FROM ALESIA; ARCHEOLOGICAL MUSEUM, DIJON

...therwise simple and not uncouth" Strabo

To earn his favor, Druid priests burned human victims in sheaths of wicker; other deities demanded drownings or hangings. Some were gentler: Mother goddess statue (with babes emerged from mold above) to gladden Gallic matrons.

Wanderers from central Europe, Gauls lived by hunting before settling on farms. On a vase a hooded hunter draws a bead; backward bow proves the artist was no archer. Chain mail, or perhaps iron-studded leather, served as armor.

Tamed after eight years of war, Gauls gave Caesar's Romans lessons in crafting leather and metals—and joined their ranks to patrol the edge of empire.

thought they would find water. They built shrines at springs to which pilgrims came with offerings to seek a cure or protection from danger. We find images of their gods—one grasps a wheel, another is shown between two birds. Gallic literature and traditions were transmitted in the chanting of poets, and so are lost."

Caesar's Gauls came alive for me in Burgundy's hills, where farmers with reddish moustaches seemed to step from ancient carvings. They take deep pride in their horses, as did their Gallic forebears. So bountiful was this land, Caesar wrote, that Germans and Romans gazing on it desired it for themselves. As I drank the fine wines of the Mâconnais and the Côte d'Or, as I feasted on rabbit stew and wrist-thick tripe sausage in farmhouse and Dijon restaurant, as I joined in festival and harvest, I found his observation still valid.

The Gallic chieftains who met Caesar near Bibracte asked him to drive another enemy from their land—Germans who had seized choice territory and taken hostages. The troubled area lay outside his province, but Caesar saw the aggression as a "reflection on the majesty of Rome." He would march against the Germans.

I FOLLOWED the legionaries east into Alsace, the French border province whose cuisine and architecture reflect the flow and ebb of German influence here over the centuries. When the Romans marched in, villagers filled their ears with tales of German prowess, their enormous stature, their incredible fighting skill, their piercing eyes that stared people down. The locals' fears infected the legions. "All over the camp there was much signing and sealing of wills," Caesar wrote. Some even whispered of mutiny. Caesar summoned his officers and tongue-lashed them for their lack of faith in him. He himself was not worried in the least. He told them he would strike camp before dawn and note carefully those who answered the call of duty and those who yielded to cowardice. He knew he could count on the Tenth Legion, his favorite, "a fine body of troops." But the others? When dawn broke, the entire army marched.

Near the site of today's Mulhouse, an industrial city on the Rhine River plain, the two forces collided, so swiftly that the legionaries had no time to hurl javelins. Some leaped atop the close-packed German masses, wrenched away their shields, and hacked from above. The Germans broke, racing for the Rhine 15 miles away. There the German chieftain Ariovistus and a handful of followers boated or swam across to find safety in the thickly wooded slopes of the Schwarzwald, or Black Forest. Caesar's cavalry cut up the rest.

As he stood at the Rhine, Caesar could look back on a year of triumph. He settled the legions in winter camps and crossed over the Alps to hold court in Cisalpine Gaul. Such would be the pattern during most of those years in Gaul: summer in the field north of the Alps, winter in Italy.

In 57 B.C., Caesar struck boldly into the land of the Belgae—northern France, Belgium, the southern Netherlands. "There were frequent rumors," he explained, "that the Belgae were plotting against Rome." From tribes seeking peace, he demanded children of chieftains as hostages. Others (Continued on page 397)

GLOWING WITH GAIETY *and bright raiment, visiting dancers shine at Dijon's international wine and folk festival. Ancient Gauls loved "dyed garments besprinkled with gold" and feasts where heroes gorged on heroic helpings—at times, some said, an entire pig.*

JOHN J. PUTMAN, NATIONAL GEOGRAPHIC STAFF

Catapults, towers, battering rams seal the fate of a citadel in Gaul

NIGHT FILLS with the noise of war: whistling of missiles, splintering of houses, screaming of people smashed by stones or seared by fireballs, cursing of men locked in mortal struggle. Caesar's legionaries have invested a Gallic citadel. Now his dreaded siege engines begin to soften, pound, and crush it.

Troops wind down the arm of an onager, powered by twisted skeins of sinew or hair. Under tension, it flies up with the kick of the wild ass it was named for, to drive a flaming log (at left) or a rock missile (below) into the fortress.

For rapid fire the crossbowlike *catapulta* flung arrows, pebbles, or lead shot, and the *ballista* hurled stones up to 60 pounds. For breaching massive stone-and-timber walls the Romans' big weapon was the iron-headed ram, shown nearing the gate under a roof that deflects defenders' fire. One assault unit moves in under shields locked in a "tortoise shell." Other troops zigzag up steps of a hide-shielded assault tower rolled into position; its drawbridge slams down. Prizes reward the first men on the wall.

With siegecraft learned from the Greeks of Sicily and southern Italy, the Romans battered, burrowed, pulled down walls stone by stone with hooks. Gauls dreaded the scraping of spades as much as the thud of siege engines. Sappers tunneled under a wall, doused the shoring timbers with pitch, and set them afire. Down came the wall.

At Avaricum (Bourges), Romans labored 25 days raising a siege terrace 77 feet high, 319 feet long,

while defenders poured flaming tallow on them. Gauls caught Roman grappling hooks in nooses and reeled them in. With skills learned in the iron mines, they countermined Roman tunnels. "A most ingenious race," Caesar noted.

It availed them little. From the log terrace archers, slingers, javelin hurlers rained missiles on the defenders as towers trundled up great ramps and legionaries stormed into the city.

Not all Gallic towns were so stoutly defended. When Caesar's diggers diverted water feeding the spring at Uxellodunum, townspeople discovered their well running dry, decided the gods had turned on them — and surrendered.

In one uprising the Gauls reversed the roles, besieging a legion near Namur. Caesar sent a native rider to heave a spear with a message over the wall of the beleaguered garrison. But the spear stuck in a tower and two days went by before the message was spotted. It rallied the troops. As promised, relief came.

That time Caesar wrote in Greek, less likely to be understood if Gauls intercepted the message. In letters to Rome, he used a simple substitution code, replacing the intended letter with one three characters later in the alphabet — as though we wrote "Jdxo" for "Gaul." Cryptographers still call this system the "Caesar cipher."

Though each legion had its own service troops and the army's mule train numbered thousands of animals, food supplies often dwindled in long siege operations. Foragers risked ambush, so Caesar got nearby tribes, enlisted by self-interest or terror, to gather grain or drive in cattle.

Caesar's army in Gaul grew from four to eleven legions, each frequently well below its 6,000-man complement. A legion had ten cohorts. The cohort, basic tactical unit comparable to our battalion, was divided into three maniples, and the maniple into two centuries of 100 legionaries each. Legates of senatorial rank headed legions and independent commands; military tribunes handled the cohorts; centurions, veterans up from the ranks, led the centuries. And when the battle came to sword's length, these 60 seasoned centurions could spell the difference between defeat and victory.

Portfolio of sketches by William H. Bond, Geographic Art Division.
Above: Model of onager in the Museum of Roman Civilization, Rome

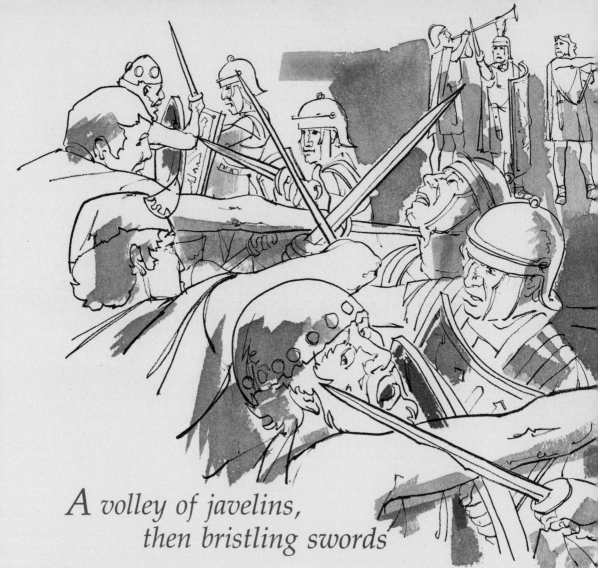

A volley of javelins,
then bristling swords

Facing a Gallic or a German army, Caesar had one supreme advantage—the Roman legions. No longer a citizen muster, they formed a force of professionals honed by his uncle Marius into a precision instrument for killing. "Their drills are bloodless battles, their battles bloody drills," wrote Josephus, historian of the Jewish War (A.D. 66-70) in which Rome razed Jerusalem.

Unlike the unwieldy phalanx, the legion could advance over broken ground and quickly shift units to threatened sectors. It was deep enough to provide constant support for the fighting front.

A Roman army went into action in three lines, each many ranks deep. Centurions in crested helms relayed the order to charge; trumpets blared, standards signaled. Legionaries showered the foe with barbed javelins; these stuck in shields, weighed them down. Closing in on the run, Romans drew short Spanish-style swords, handier than the Gallic broadswords. Now it was man-to-man, a line of single duels—thrust and slash and pray you survive the day. Romans fought behind curved wooden shields covered

with canvas and leather and rimmed in iron. They wore brass helmets with hinged face flaps, metal-studded leather jerkins, sometimes a greave on the unshielded right leg. If a man survived enemy blows, exhaustion took him out of the line after about 15 minutes. The legionary behind stepped up to fill the gap. Fighting in relays, Romans faced combat with a steadiness unknown to barbarians.

On the flanks cavalry—mainly Gallic, German, or Spanish recruits—waited to pursue a broken foe. They usually dismounted to fight. Caesar's rule was never to let routed troops rally. If his own lines wavered, he plunged in to hearten them.

On the march Caesar led his army, more often on foot than mounted. Reaching an unfordable river, he would promptly swim across or ride an inflated skin. Caesar brought to war not military innovation but an incisive mind and a motto, *celeritas*—swiftness. He might carefully lay the groundwork, but then he moved decisively. Suetonius wondered "which was the most remarkable . . . his caution or his daring." With his matchless legions, Caesar could play it both ways.

Legionaries lift a fallen comrade, bandage another's wounds. Medical care was spotty; some officers brought their own surgeons. *Relief on Trajan's Column, Rome; Alinari*

Victorious cohorts cross a pontoon bridge. Fate of the conquered: slavery for women, death to men. *Column of Marcus Aurelius; German Archeological Institute, Rome*

Legionaries wield spades more than swords, building camps and bridges as they conquer

THEY were calloused soldiers—the greatest entrenching army in history. In hostile land they halted each afternoon to build a fortified camp, an astounding labor that gave a night's safety and a base for the next day's operations.

A tribune and centurions rode ahead to pick a hill site with water and grazing at hand. When weary legionaries arrived, they dug a 13-foot-wide ditch, tossing dirt inward to form a wall. This they palisaded with stakes, toted as part of their 60-pound packs.

A square camp 2,000 yards on a side sheltered two legions. Tents rose along a grid of streets. At night no one entered without the password, changed daily and passed from maniple to maniple on a tablet. In the morning three trumpet blasts signaled breakup of camp. At the first, tents were struck; at the second, mules loaded; at the third, the army marched.

In Caesar's day engineers fought as part of combat units and put special skills to work on roads and bridges. They fitted out ships for his Brittany campaign in 56 B.C. To bridge the Rhine, they drove 18-inch piles into its bed, buttressing with diagonal ties and iron dogs. They built permanent forts of brick and stone.

The legionary did all this on a few handfuls of grain a day, occasional meat, and vinegary wine. Rations were deducted from his *salarium*. "Salary" comes from this army word meaning "money to buy salt" (*sal*)—hence the expression "not worth his salt." They also got plunder, bonuses, pensions in land (recalling the Roman soldier's origin as a farmer). Augustus studded the frontiers with watchdog colonies of veterans and their families; a 20-year hitch brought Roman citizenship to foreign recruits.

Caesar wooed his men by doubling their pay, sharing spoils generously, issuing handsome arms (men with gold- and silver-inlaid weapons were less likely to abandon them). He addressed them as "comrades" and winked at off-duty escapades: "My men fight just as well stinking of perfume."

But military misconduct drew swift punishment. Deserters, mutineers, sleeping sentries were stoned to death. A cowardly unit might be decimated— every tenth man slain. The rest slept outside camp until they redeemed themselves with gallantry.

Caesar himself needed little sleep and often appeared at night work parties to encourage his toiling men. To all this the legions responded with unbounded loyalty, and triumph piled on triumph. After the siege of Dyrrhachium, Pompey was shown bread Caesar's starving men had made from herbs. "I am fighting wild beasts!" Pompey cried. Caesar's soldiers knew no finer tribute.

Opposite: Legionaries shape a platform for siege engines. From Trajan's Column; German Archeological Institute, Rome

WALTER MEAYERS EDWARDS, NATIONAL GEOGRAPHIC STAFF

"ONE OF THE FAIREST TOWNS *in Gaul, the main bulwark and the glory of their state," wrote Caesar of defiant Avaricum. Today's Bourges, it mirrors Gothic glory. Worshippers stored offerings in the 13th-century tithe barn (opposite) for the cathedral towering behind. At nearby La Borne a potter (above) plies his ancient craft.*

While other tribes burned their towns and fled Caesar, men of marsh-girt Avaricum held their ground. But he pressed the siege so relentlessly that finally its warriors planned a breakout under cover of night. The women begged on their knees not to be left with the children; ignored, they alerted the Romans. So all stayed. The next day, when the legionaries swarmed over the walls, only 800 out of 40,000 escaped the massacre that drowned Avaricum in blood.

he fought. At the Aisne he scattered one Belgic host. But at the Sambre the "fierce, extremely hardy" Nervii burst from ambush as the legionaries began to entrench for the night. Caesar rallied his men and the arrival of his rear guard turned the tide. The Nervii fought on until their dead lay in mounds. "The enemy's courage," Caesar marveled, "was sublime." When they begged for peace, Caesar, "wishing to demonstrate my traditional clemency," granted it and even confirmed their territorial rights. But when the Atua-tuci attacked the Romans after peace talks, Caesar stormed their hilltop bastion on the Meuse near Huy and had the entire tribe sold at auction in one lot—53,000 souls.

Now the Belgae were humbled, but they would not remain so. And their land would know the agony of conquest again and again through the centuries.

In the railway station at Namur, fortress city of southern Belgium, an elderly woman asked me what had brought me there. "The ancient battle sites nearby," I replied. She shook her head. This part of Europe, she said, is nothing but a battlefield. Each generation sees loved ones perish. "In 1914 my uncles were killed; in 1940 my brother." When she left, her seat in the waiting room was taken by a cadet from military school, fresh-faced, quite proud of his uniform.

In 56 B.C., Veneti tribes along the coast of Britanny

397

"On reaching the confluence of the Moselle
and the Rhine they realized that . . . escape was barred" Caesar

*Between walls of water at far right Caesar trapped two German tribes that had invaded Gaul.
Legionaries slaughtered tribesmen, cavalry cut down fleeing women and children; survivors
"flung themselves into the water and perished." Bridging the broad Rhine downstream,
Caesar terrorized the countryside until "the Germans were overawed." In 9 B.C. Romans founded
Confluentes here (today bustling Coblenz), then pushed eastward to the Elbe; 18 years later,
amid rain and lightning in Teutoburg Forest, the Roman-trained chieftain Arminius ambushed
and massacred three legions under Varus, who took his own life. "Quinctilius Varus, give me back
my legions," moaned Augustus. He pulled the frontier back to the Rhine, where it stayed*

"**IMPORTS OF WINE** *are absolutely forbidden . . .*
it makes men soft and unequal to hard work."
This tribal prohibition, reported by Caesar,
kept Roman wine out of Germanic drinking horns.
But repeal came with the conquerors' vines, which
spread green ramparts along the Rhine and the
Moselle, where this cask-jammed galley
adorned a Roman wine merchant's tomb.

Today harvest time empties schools and
homes in 2,000 communities on these rivers.
Near Burg Katz, "Cat Castle" (right), a young
Rhinelander picks grapes for Liebfraumilch—
white, like most Rhine wines.

Rome's Rhine region filled fleets with grain,
wool, timber, pottery, and gave rise to cities
we know as Trier, Mainz, and Strasbourg.
Veterans of legions manning the limes, *a*
tower-studded barrier on the Rhine-Danube
frontier, founded Augsburg and Cologne—
Colonia Agrippina, a colony named for Nero's
mother. Roman and German ways mingled,
like the language of a cafe sign in Cologne
today: In Vino Veritas; in Bier ist
auch etwas. *In wine there is truth;*
there is also something in beer.

BRUCE DALE, NATIONAL GEOGRAPHIC PHOTOGRAPHER.
ROMAN FUNERARY SCULPTURE, 2D-3D CENTURIES A.D.,
LANDESMUSEUM, TRIER; ADAM WOOLFITT

challenged Caesar. He built a fleet and destroyed their ships and homes. His lieu-tenants led other sweeps through Gaul. Then, in 55 B.C., German tribes again crossed the Rhine, this time near its mouth. Caesar rushed to meet them.

I drove now through darkly wooded ridges of the Ardennes, by towns which felt the shock of mechanized armies in World War II—St. Vith, Malmedy, Bastogne. Somewhere along here ancient Germans struck Caesar's cavalry, racing in on their small horses, leaping down to slash the bellies of the Roman mounts, routing survivors. From then on Caesar took no chances with the tough warriors from be-yond the Rhine. When their leaders came to negotiate, he seized them and sped to attack their camp. The tribesmen fled in panic, only to be trapped and slaughtered by pursuing legionaries at the juncture of the Rhine and the Moselle.

So long as the Germans felt safe across the Rhine, Caesar reasoned, they would be tempted to invade Gaul. He decided to teach them otherwise. The valley rang with the crash of timber. Within two weeks he had bridged the river and the legionaries were across, burning villages, destroying crops. The Germans fell back on forest citadels and awaited further blows. But Caesar recognized the limits of his power and the vastness of the land stretching eastward. After 18 days he felt that "the demands of honor and interest had been satisfied." He recrossed the Rhine, destroying the bridge behind him.

From the fortress of Ehrenbreitstein I looked down on the confluence of Rhine and Moselle, where Romans founded Confluentes 46 years after Caesar fought there. Bridges span both rivers, and trains bring commuters from half-timbered villages to the city of Coblenz, which grew from Confluentes. Upstream, medieval castles keep their watch on the Rhine. In time the Rhineland flourished as a Roman province, its glory reflected today in monuments at Trier, Mainz, and Bad Homburg. The grapevines that march in rows up its hillsides and the bustling barge traffic that links this heartland to the sea at Antwerp were introduced by Rome. The legions drove eastward but did not stay. Thus in the north the Rhine became the divide between Roman and Germanic culture. The river remained a military barrier. Not far from the site of Caesar's bridge, American soldiers rolling east in World War II seized the Rhine's last undestroyed span at Remagen.

Only a few weeks of summer remained when Caesar finished with the Germans —enough time, he decided, for an invasion of Britain. "I thought," he wrote, "it would be a great advantage merely to have visited the island, to have seen what

kind of people the inhabitants were, and to have learned something about the country with its harbors and landing places." It was also an opportunity to even scores with Belgic tribes which had settled in Britain decades before and had helped their mainland cousins resist him.

Crossing the English Channel on a car ferry, I clung to the rail in a bitter wind and watched a ribbon of white grow larger—the chalk cliffs of Dover. When Caesar saw these cliffs, they were lined with warriors and chariots. He swung his invasion fleet north to the beach at Deal, ran shoreward—and quickly found out what the Britons were like. As his legionaries, hampered by heavy armor, struggled through the surf, the British horsemen raced out to cut them down. Caesar rushed men in boats to threatened units and sent light galleys in close to fire catapults. Reaching solid footing, the legionaries sent the Britons reeling. Caesar probed inland, engaging in a few minor clashes, but as winter approached he broke off and departed.

He returned the next year with an armada of more than 800 ships and landed unopposed. I followed his route across Kent to Bigbury Woods near Canterbury, where tribesmen gathered to bar his crossing of the Great Stour. He drove them from his path and proceeded toward the Thames. There he found only one place where the river could be forded— and that with difficulty. Stakes had been driven into

"I reached Britain . . . and saw the enemy"

Caesar

The white cliffs of Dover bristled with men under arms. "Clearly no place to attempt a landing," Caesar concluded, and veered the invasion force up the English Channel toward "an open and evenly shelving beach." But native horsemen and charioteers sped to the strand to confront him there.

Caesar came to reconnoiter and to chastise tribes aiding his enemies in Gaul. He mistakenly called them Britanni; they had been known as the Pretani ever since Pytheas of Marseilles (page 101) explored the island in the 4th century B.C. But history favored Caesar and spoke of the Britanni and their home as Britannia instead of Pretania. Men in its hinterland still tinted their bodies; hostile tribes of the north came to be called Picts—Painted People.

ALBERT MOLDVAY, NATIONAL GEOGRAPHIC STAFF

"They had to jump from the ships, stand firm in the surf, and fight"

Caesar

Weighed down by armor, Romans struggle against waves and wild-eyed Britons as Caesar launches his first invasion of Britannia in 55 B.C. Deep-draft transports grounded well offshore; out of their element, troops froze on deck. Then the Tenth Legion's standard-bearer leaped overboard, shouting: "Come on, men! Jump!" They plunged in after him. Wise to the shallows, the Britons galloped out.

PAINTING FOR NATIONAL GEOGRAPHIC BY BIRNEY LETTICK

Caesar countered with slingers, bowmen, and catapults
on swift small craft. His men seized a beachhead.
  In land clashes Caesar saw enemy charioteers,
"quick as lightning," hop on and off their cars,
"run along the pole, stand on the yoke." They fought
in pairs; one leaped out to battle while the driver
hovered nearby, ready to pluck his comrade from peril.
  Caesar's bold amphibious raid swelled his repute in

Rome. He returned to the island the next year
with 30,000 men. But the Britons, "cruel to strangers,"
as Horace noted, eluded Rome's yoke another century.
  Emperor Claudius, embarking at Boulogne,
had to quell a mutiny; troops balked at being led into
"another world." But his invasion of A.D. *43 gave him*
a triumph and his infant son the name "Britannicus."
Agricola, governor in 78-84, completed the conquest.

ROME'S IMPRINT, *from 400 years
of rule, endures in England.
Cavalryman's tombstone stood in
Corinium (Cirencester). In the
theater of Verulamium (opposite)
Romans watched bearbaiting and
cockfights. This town grew into
St. Albans (right), named for
the Roman soldier who became
England's first Christian martyr.
Britons tip glasses in Colchester,
once Camulodunum, Britain's first
Roman colony and oldest recorded
town. Roman camps,* castra, *
live on in place names ending
in* caster, cester, *and* chester.

WINFIELD PARKS, NATIONAL GEOGRAPHIC PHOTOGRAPHER. ABOVE AND OPPOSITE: ADAM WOOLFITT. RELIEF IN THE CORINIUM MUSEUM, CIRENCESTER

the banks and riverbed, and defenders lined the opposite shore. The legionaries plunged into neck-deep water, mastered the obstacles, and scattered the Britons.

Scholars have long debated the site of that crossing. Amid legions of bowler-hatted Britons with tightly furled "brollies" I marched through London's financial district to call on Ralph Merrifield, Assistant Director of London's Guildhall Museum and an expert on Thames archeology. His eyes sparkled at my question. With an ancient Roman trident he jabbed at a map:

"Brentford, nine miles upstream, is the traditional site, marked by a monument. They have found evidence of battles, settlements, and stakes — but the stakes could be of any date. Dash it, I don't believe it was Brentford. It would have been out of character. Caesar was decisive; everything he did had a direct way about it. He would not have gone poking about upstream when there were crossings closer down, possibly at Westminster, more likely at Chelsea. Southeast England has sunk some 18 feet since then. He would have found the Thames much shallower."

I asked about Caesar's description of long-haired Britons with faces dyed with the blue of woad. "Bronze Age people like that may have existed in Yorkshire or the back counties, but not here," Mr. Merrifield replied. "The Belgae had invaded southeast Britain and brought their culture. You would have seen men in wool trousers and tartan cloaks, gold and silver coins minted by local kings, and a few imported Roman luxuries. They were stock raisers and traders, mainly."

Caesar marched north into Hertfordshire, realm of Cassivellaunus, first hero of British history. Despairing of besting Caesar in head-on battle, this chieftain hid his people and hounded the invaders with 4,000 chariots, picking off raiding parties. Finally, Cassivellaunus gathered men and animals into his *oppidum*, a woodland base fortified by a ditch and timbers. Caesar found it and stormed it.

Many scholars believe a giant ditch at Wheathampstead, near St. Albans, to be the remains of that oppidum. Twelve feet wide, fringed by trees, it transports the visitor to Cassivellaunus' day. Walking beside it, I envisioned the "vigorous assault on two sides," the clash of swords, the pellmell flight of the Britons.

This was the last of Caesar's victories in Britain. He had come to explore the land and impress its people with Rome's might, not to conquer. Fixing tribute and taking hostages, he left before summer's end, never to return.

Few solid objects remain in Britain that can be traced to Caesar. He left no forts, built no cities. Yet the memory of his achievement spurred the second invasion a century later by the emperor Claudius that subdued all but the northern regions. Cities grew and Roman culture took root. Then early in the fifth century a declining Rome withdrew her legions, and *Britannia* became the battleground of native Celts and invading Angles, Saxons, and Jutes.

Today Britain wears its Roman heritage proudly, in the well-preserved thermae at Bath, the fortress at Richborough, the remains of the once-flourishing city of Verulamium at St. Albans, in villas, legionary posts, Hadrian's Wall, above all in living cities like Colchester, York, London.

As my jet lifted above London's sprawl and thrust eastward, I thought of something Mr. Merrifield had said: "Romans gave shape to our country. Their roads became our roads; their towns became our towns. Before the Romans, you could not really say we were civilized."

The Channel slipped under the jet's wing, and I saw once again the orange tile roofs and the green fields of France. After Caesar returned, war erupted across these lush fields

ROMAN LONDON, *Londinium, in the third century* A.D. *spreads from the Thames to a three-mile wall buttressed by a fort. Thatched huts flank mansions, baths, and temples along paved streets. Drawbridge, near site of today's London Bridge, leads to huge basilica and forum. Where smoke rises from kilns and workshops at left, St. Paul's Cathedral now stands; Billingsgate Market spreads where ships load at right. Merchantmen filled holds with slaves, cattle, silver, iron, lead, and "clever hunting dogs."*

PAINTING, BASED ON ARCHEOLOGICAL AND HISTORICAL STUDIES, BY ROBERT W. NICHOLSON, GEOGRAPHIC ART DIVISION

as the Gauls reacted fiercely to the realization that their Roman ally had become their master. The resistance began with brushfire clashes, escalated to an assault on a legionary camp and a massacre of Roman traders at Cenabum (Orleans). Finally, in 52 B.C., the tribes joined in a general uprising under Vercingetorix, a young noble of Auvergne. It was better, the Gauls decided, "to die in battle than to forego . . . ancient military renown and . . . liberty."

Vercingetorix fell back before Caesar, burning towns and fields, stretching the Roman supply lines. But when the people of Avaricum (Bourges) begged their leader on their knees to let them defend their town, he agreed. Legionaries laid siege to it, scaled its walls, and spared "neither the aged nor women nor children." Caesar then moved on the citadel of Gergovia, perched on a volcanic peak. When it held, he withdrew, and the two armies maneuvered northeast into Burgundy, clashing near Dijon.

Vercingetorix encamped in the nearby oppidum of Alesia. A new battle loomed; on its outcome hung the fate of Gaul.

With Professor Le Gall I stood on the brow of a hill where Caesar stood at the head of some 70,000 men. "Here Caesar placed his command post," he told me. "From it he could see everything and shift his troops as necessary." As I scanned Alesia's height and the plain of Les Laumes to the west, I felt that I was looking through the conqueror's eyes. Caesar judged the citadel "clearly impregnable . . . except by blockade."

Thereupon he blockaded it with an incredible siegework 9½ miles in circumference, strengthened by 8 camps and 23 redoubts. One night, before the ring had been completed, Vercingetorix sent his cavalry to summon a relief force. Caesar guessed their mission, and the weary legionaries, hands raw, backs aching, started digging again. When the Gallic cavalry returned with a force of 250,000, they found a second rampart facing outward—this one 13 miles around!

From within and without, the Gallic armies struggled to crack the double ring—to no avail. In the climactic battle Caesar personally led reinforcements to plug breaches in the outer wall. His shrewdly placed cavalry fell on the attackers from behind, panicked them, destroyed them.

The next day Caesar watched Vercingetorix lead his forlorn tribesmen down from Alesia in surrender. They were "distributed as loot among the whole army, one to every man." Their chieftain went to Rome to prison and death.

Professor Le Gall led me across the battlefield where digging has yielded arrowheads, swords, and little mortars in which legionaries ground their (Continued on page 418)

Noble Vercingetorix defies Caesar's might in Gaul's last stand

Fierce gaze frozen in bronze, Vercingetorix still guards his ramparts at Alesia. To rid their land of Caesar, Gallic chieftains forgot rivalries and rallied under this young Auvergnian, famed for boldness and savage punishments. He sliced off ears and gouged the eyes of petty offenders.

Wintering in Italy when the Gauls rose, Caesar cut through Alpine drifts and dodged enemy patrols to rejoin his legions. Avoiding a showdown, Vercingetorix nibbled away at the Romans with Fabian tactics—named for Hannibal's foe, Fabius the Delayer. Finally, Vercingetorix chose to make his stand at Alesia's hilltop fortress in Burgundy. With him went grain, cattle, and 80,000 men led by the flower of Gallic nobility in gleaming helmets. Thousands more roamed the land, awaiting his call.

Around the citadel Caesar strung his legions, with their axes and spades, their javelins, short swords, and siege engines. Then he drew the noose tight.

GALLIC NOBLE'S HELMET, 4TH CENTURY B.C.; THE LOUVRE, PARIS. ROMAN SWORDS, 1ST CENTURY B.C.; MUSEUM OF ROMAN CIVILIZATION, ROME. OPPOSITE: JOHN J. PUTMAN, NATIONAL GEOGRAPHIC STAFF

"The Gauls beheld our . . . squadrons in their rear. . . . They broke and fled" *Caesar*

Gaul's flickering freedom dies under the hoofs of Roman cavalry. The mounted force strikes the rear of a Gallic relief army at Alesia, pinning it between bristling spears and the Roman siege walls. From within the citadel Gauls stream down in a futile attempt to crack Caesar's stranglehold.

Judging Alesia invulnerable to direct assault, Caesar ringed it with two walls—his greatest feat of siegework. The inner ring of contravallation, 9½ miles in circumference, blockaded the fortress. The outer ring of circumvallation, 13 miles around, faced outward to shield the besiegers against a relief army. Caesar braced the earth-and-log ramparts with 8 camps, 23 redoubts, and towers every 130 yards. He sowed the approaches with man-traps: a forest of logs implanted in earth, topped with iron hooks the legionaries dubbed "goads"; concealed pits spiked with fire-hardened stakes ("lilies"); rows of trenches studded with pointed tree limbs ("tombstones"). Rapid-firing catapults and ballistas spewed a rain of death.

As the siege wore on, Alesia's grain dwindled; women, children, and other noncombatants poured out of the gates with piteous appeals for food. Caesar posted guards to turn them away. Starvation stalked the besiegers too.

The arrival of the relief army, 250,000 strong, filled the defenders with joy. Gallic warriors darkened the nearby plain of Les Laumes, crowded the hills beyond. In the decisive battle pictured here the two Gallic armies in a coordinated attack drove against both of Caesar's encircling rings with grappling hooks, scaling ladders, and piles of brush. From his command post, Caesar watched the play of battle, shifting his outnumbered forces back and forth like a master chess player. When Gauls breached the outer wall, he led five cohorts to the scene. "The enemy recognized my scarlet cloak," he noted. "Both sides raised a cheer."

Now Caesar's cavalry, auxiliary troops, swept down out of a concealing wood on Mount Rea to rout the relieving troops. Vercingetorix watched helplessly, then bowed "to the decree of fate." Astride a proud stallion, clad in his finest armor, the young chieftain led his army down from Alesia in surrender. Borne in chains to Rome, he lived to enhance Caesar's triumphal processions in 46 B.C. After his degrading march through the Forum, he was led back to prison and executed.

IN THIS PAINTING FOR NATIONAL GEOGRAPHIC BY BIRNEY LETTICK
DISTANCES HAVE BEEN TELESCOPED TO CLARIFY THE ACTION

to heel, though untamed nature frightened Rome's mariners rounding the isle; they told of water thickening under their oars off the dark northern shores. That wild north never yielded; Hadrian cordoned off its irrepressible Picts and Celts with a mighty wall of stone, begun A.D. 122, that snaked from sea to sea (far left). Trajan already had subdued Dacia, pushed to the Caspian Sea and down the Tigris and Euphrates valleys.

In the wake of conquerors came builders to adorn the provinces with enduring symbols of Rome's sway. Massive gateway, Porta Nigra (left), still guards Trier, "Rome beyond the Alps," on the Moselle in Germany; six of the world's largest columns dwarf Lebanese dancers in the Temple of Jupiter at Baalbek (lower).

Iron legions ringed the realm to enforce the Pax Romana, "Roman Peace"; galleys (bottom) made the Mediterranean Rome's mare nostrum, "our sea."

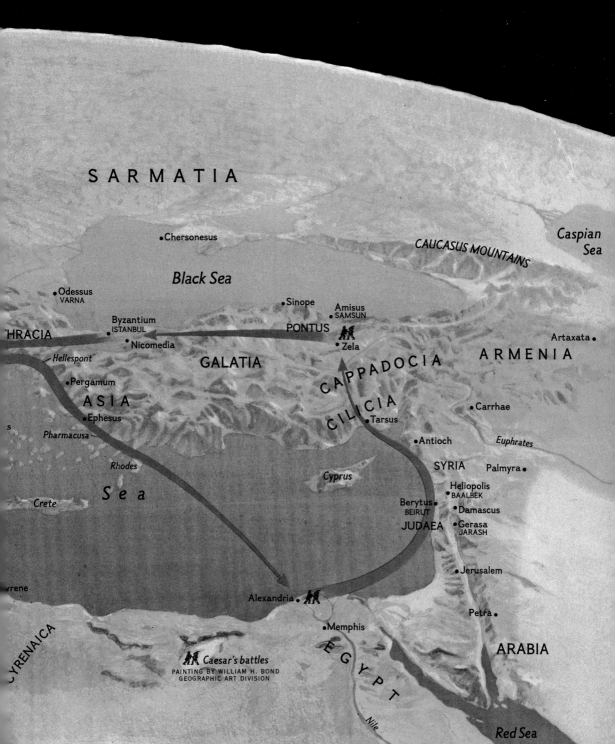

SARMATIA

Chersonesus

Black Sea

CAUCASUS MOUNTAINS

Caspian Sea

Odessus
VARNA

Sinope

Amisus
SAMSUN

Artaxata

HRACIA

Byzantium
ISTANBUL

PONTUS

Zela

ARMENIA

Nicomedia

Hellespont

GALATIA

CAPPADOCIA

Pergamum

ASIA

CILICIA

Carrhae

Ephesus

Tarsus

Antioch

Euphrates

Pharmacusa

SYRIA

Palmyra

Rhodes

Cyprus

Heliopolis
BAALBEK

Crete

Sea

Berytus
BEIRUT

Damascus

Gerasa
JARASH

JUDAEA

Jerusalem

rene

Alexandria

Petra

yrene

Memphis

ARABIA

CYRENAICA

EGYPT

Caesar's battles
PAINTING BY WILLIAM H. BOND
GEOGRAPHIC ART DIVISION

Nile

Red Sea

grain. We walked the walls of Vercingetorix's Alesia and, nearby, streets of the town that rose in Caesar's wake. Ruins of a theater, temples, and smelters proclaim the fusion of the two cultures—the distinctive Gallo-Roman civilization that flourished for 500 years. "The measure of Caesar's influence on France?" mused my guide. "Our language, our law, our art, our borders, even the logical, precise cast of our thinking bear his mark and that of Rome. Gaul was ready for Rome's gifts."

After Alesia, Caesar's struggle in Gaul drew to a close. The next year saw only scattered encounters, ending with the siege of Uxellodunum. He had come to Gaul to defend it and had remained to conquer it. The campaign brought death to thousands of Gauls, glory to Caesar, and a vast new territory to Rome. For Caesar, even greater glory lay ahead.

CAESAR HAD ARRANGED with his fellow triumvirs, Pompey and Crassus, that he would return to Rome as consul, protected by the majesty of that office against political prosecutions. But the Triumvirate had disintegrated and so had its plan. Crassus and his legions, hunting glory on the plains of Parthia, found only death at Carrhae. Julia, Pompey's wife and Caesar's daughter, died, breaking a strong link between the two men. Caesar now faced a circuitous path to supreme power, a

"Caesar was first captivated by . . . Cleopatra's bold wit" Plutarch

At Alexandria a boatman unrolls a rug—and out steps Cleopatra, royal outcast scheming to regain Egypt's throne. His defenses down to such a siege, Caesar makes her cause his own. They warred together, then dallied on the Nile, seeing wonders of a civilization grown old before Rome's founding. Her charms adorned the stage of history—and dram In Shakespeare, "Age cannot wither her, nor custom stale her infinite variety." He has her say she loved Caesar "in my salad days, when I was green in judgment, cold in blood." Riper passion quickened her love of Mark Antony; it consumed them both.

PAINTING FOR NATIONAL GEOGRAPHIC BY BIRNEY LETTICK. OPPOSITE: NAGGAR SAILING THE NILE; HELEN AND FRANK SCHREIDER, NATIONAL GEOGRAPHIC STAFF

path that would lead him around the vast rim of the Mediterranean, to many battles, and into the arms of Cleopatra.

Fearful of his ambition, aristocratic senators backed by Pompey demanded that he disband his army and return from Gaul as a citizen or be considered a traitor. Thus Caesar faced his Rubicon. (Strangely, Caesar himself never mentions the river.)

When he decided to move on Rome, he had only one legion south of the Alps. But he relied on his famed *celeritas* and the loyalty of his men, who cheered when he called on them to defend the honor of their commander. As they moved south, city after city threw open its gates. "The country towns are treating him as a god," mourned Cicero, watching his Republic die. Pompey abandoned Rome and from Brundisium (Brindisi) sailed eastward with a fleet across the Adriatic. Caesar detoured to Spain to defeat a Senate army, besieged Marseilles, and paused in Rome long enough to empty the treasury and be named dictator and elected consul.

419

"What was but now a path has become a high road" *Martial*

From Britain to the Persian Gulf, Rome tied her world in a net of roads—50,000 miles of military highways crosshatched with some 200,000 miles of secondary roads.

Laid out by legions (page 443) to move men, packtrains, and siege engines, arteries of empire bore trade too. Silk and spice caravans scarred huge blocks (opposite) that linked Aleppo to Antioch, capital of Syria. Caesar visited the province en route to Zela.

Appius Claudius began the web with the Via Appia from Rome to Capua in 312 B.C. In time "all roads led to Rome" and to Augustus' golden milestone in the Forum. Mansiones *(lodging places) offered beds, food, smiths, horses to travelers who rumbled in by chariot, wagon, or covered sleeping coach. Caesar did 800 miles in 10 days, and one courier sped 360 miles in 36 hours. Horse carts could average 5 or 6 miles an hour—a rate unsurpassed until the 19th century.*

Then he swept on to Brundisium and risked winter storms to sail a fleet in pursuit of Pompey. Caesar besieged his foe at Dyrrhachium, modern Durrës in Albania. But while Caesar's men starved in their hill forts, Pompey drew supplies from the sea at his back. Greatly outnumbered, Caesar abandoned the siege, and both armies marched eastward across the mountains of Greece, encamping near Pharsalus.

I followed, across the Adriatic from Brindisi on a car ferry, then over mountain roads whose hairpin turns brought squeals from tortured brakes. Finally the mountain walls vanished; below me, like a green sea, lay the plain of Thessaly. I was welcomed to the farming town of Farsala by Panayotis Mihopoulos, English teacher at the school and a former Greek airman. As we sat beneath his arbor, his wife brought melon and *ouzo*, the famed grape brandy of Greece. Alekos Fasoulas, a farmer of immense dignity whose father owned much of the battlefield of Pharsalus, offered to guide us over the site. We bumped across grainfields and past shepherds' grassy sheds until we came to a rise overlooking a plain cut by the Enipeus River.

Pompey sought to avoid this battle. Day after day he had ignored Caesar's troops parading in challenge. But the young aristocrats on his staff, eager for glory, disdainful of Caesar, persuaded him at last to engage. Looking down on the plain I could envision the armies closing, Caesar with 22,000 men, Pompey with more than twice as many.

At 150 paces Caesar orders the charge. His men rush forward, hurl javelins in a volley. Shields scrape, swords clash, wounded men scream. Pompey orders his massed cavalry

WHEN IN ROME'S ORBIT, *distant cities did as the Romans did. Palmyra (right), Syrian oasis that watered caravans to Babylon, burgeoned as Biblical Tadmor; both names mean "city of palms." Under Rome it raised triumphal arches, colonnaded streets—and beautiful Zenobia, whose passion for power matched Rome's.*

At her husband's death—some whispered murder—she seized the eastern provinces and Egypt, crowned herself Empress of Rome. Emperor Aurelian sacked her city A.D. 273 and marched her in chains at his triumph in Rome. Now diners at the Zenobia Hotel gaze on Palmyra's ruined grandeur.

MERLE SEVERY, NATIONAL GEOGRAPHIC STAFF. OPPOSITE: BRIAN BRAKE, RAPHO GUILLUMETTE

421

to swing round and smash Caesar's right flank and rear. Everything, he knows, depends on this sweep. But Caesar shifts six cohorts to his flank with orders to mass their javelins into a bristling wall and jab at the faces of the horsemen. Pompey's cavalry thunders into disaster; his legions, demoralized, retreat. Caesar hounds them to their camp, drives them out, and pins them against a hill by the Enipeus. There some 24,000 surrender, 15,000 lie dead. "They would have it so," Caesar notes bitterly. Pompey escapes, flees to Turkey, then to Cyprus and on to Egypt, desperately seeking men, money, aid. Caesar follows, the hunter after his quarry.

W HEN CAESAR ARRIVED in Alexandria, he learned that his rival had eluded him once again—but would trouble him no more. The Egyptians, seeing little future in backing a loser, had assassinated Pompey. One story has it that Caesar wept when he was presented with Pompey's head. Caesar found Egypt wracked by civil conflict between the boy king Ptolemy and his sister Cleopatra, who had been driven from the city. The quarrel, Caesar concluded, "fell within the jurisdiction of Rome, and therefore of myself." He moved into Ptolemy's palace.

In the family dispute Ptolemy held all the troops. Cleopatra's strength was not so obvious, but she deployed it skillfully. One night, Plutarch says, a man carried a carpet from a skiff into the palace and unrolled it before Caesar. From the carpet stepped Cleopatra. She was 21 years old, attractive rather than beautiful, dark but not Egyptian—she came from the Macedonian house that had ruled here since Alexander's day. Strong-willed, well educated, raised in a corrupt court, she saw in Caesar the means to regain the throne. Witty, bold, sensual, she enchanted Caesar.

While passion possessed the palace, Ptolemy besieged it. Once his men ran seawater into the drinking-water conduits. Caesar got his small, desperate force to dig wells and found sweet water in abundance. He fought through Alexandria's streets to seize the island on which stood the Pharos, a lighthouse nearly 400 feet high, one of the Seven Wonders of the World. He had little opportunity to marvel at this "miracle of size and engineering." Once, fighting along the island causeway, he was trapped and had to swim for his life.

When reinforcements from Syria marched into the Nile Delta to aid Caesar, Ptolemy turned to head them off. In a sharp clash a few miles north of Cairo, the young king drowned in the Nile. Now Cleopatra ruled Egypt, and Caesar ruled Cleopatra. They had shared perils; now they could take their pleasure.

Off they went, the conqueror and the queen, gliding up the river of the Pharaohs in a barge of cedar and cypress, propelled by oars, to gaze on the matchless panorama of grain-rich delta and red desert, pyramids and temples more than 2,000 years old, herds of cattle, the endless rise and fall of *shadoofs* lifting water from Africa's heart, and clear night skies ablaze with stars.

"He often feasted with her to dawn; and they would have sailed together . . . to

Triumph in Pontus: "I came, I saw, I conquered"

Turkish farmers thresh wheat where scythe-wheeled chariots raced uphill against Caesar's dug-in legions. The brevity of his immortal words echoes the speed of his victory:
Veni, *he came to Zela;* Vidi, *he saw Pharnaces, King of Pontus and enemy of Rome;*
Vici, *he vanquished him four hours after getting sight of him. Pharnaces' father,*
Mithridates the Great, had fared better; 20 years earlier he crushed a Roman army here.

JONATHAN S. BLAIR

"Africa always offers something new" Pliny the Elder

In the ruins of Thapsus, where Caesar defeated diehard allies of Pompey, a Tunisian girl draws water from land that throve under the Romans. They irrigated 2,000 miles of North African coastland and planted scores of miniature Romes: towns with baths, amphitheaters, temples, forums. They ran vast plantations from luxurious villas (below). Pliny claimed that six men once owned half of Roman Africa and told of one estate with 4,117 slaves, 3,600 yoke of oxen. Rome's exotic realm sent her grain, olives, gold, ivory, ebony, dyes, ostrich eggs and feathers—and so many wild animals that whole populations of elephants and hippopotamuses ("water horses") were wiped out. Crescent of shields (right) hides torch-bearing hunters corraling lions and leopards, destined for bloody sport in the arenas of Imperial Rome.

Ethiopia had his soldiers consented to follow," writes Suetonius. When Caesar left after eight months, Cleopatra was with child—the boy Caesarion, in whom Romans would see the gait of the conqueror.

Scholars have wondered at Caesar's Egyptian interlude. Did he succumb to Cleopatra's charms and ambitions? Was it, as one of Shakespeare's characters says, that this "Royal wench . . . made great Caesar lay his sword to bed"? Or did he use her to control Egypt? Prof. Pierre Grimal believes Caesar combined Rome's business with his own pleasure. "He had been at war for a decade," the professor told me. "I think he felt he had earned a vacation with her." Yet, Grimal added, when it ended, Egypt was firmly within Rome's orbit.

Caesar sailed to Syria to organize local administration, thence to Tarsus in Cilicia. There

OPPOSITE, LOWER: MOSAIC FROM TABARKA, 4TH CENTURY A.D.; BARDO NATIONAL MUSEUM, TUNIS. UPPER: JOHN J. PUTMAN, NATIONAL GEOGRAPHIC STAFF

he turned inland, marching across Asia Minor to punish Pharnaces, King of Pontus, for trying to expand his realm while Rome was locked in civil war.

I traced the route by air, looking down on harsh peaks, dry rivers, and vast plateaus, until green valleys and the Black Sea proclaimed the land of Pontus. The startling white domes of a radar complex, an American flag whipping in the breeze on this lonely edge of Turkey, and U. S. servicemen waiting to greet replacements at the Samsun airport reminded me that this still is strategic country, as it was in the days when legionaries patrolled it against Parthia.

My car headed up the misty valley of the Yesil Irmak and out of the 20th century. Carts creaked along on solid wooden wheels, girls came to village wells with buckets on yokes, women sickled grain in the fields. At Zela, where the armies clashed, streets echoed to the clatter of wainwrights.

When Pharnaces charged uphill against the legionaries, Caesar was amazed at the suicidal move. The rout was quick and neat. So was Caesar's report, which I read on a column of uncertain date atop the citadel of Zela: *Veni, Vidi, Vici.*

R ETURNING TO ROME, Caesar talked balky legionaries out of mutiny, then set sail for North Africa to face a new challenge. Pompey's allies, the famed family names of Scipio and Cato among them, had raised a new army with King

425

STAGE OF EMPIRE, rimmed by the Mediterranean, plays to a marble mother and child at Leptis Magna in Libya. For harboring Caesar's enemies this Punic port paid him three million pounds of olive oil in annual tribute. But Leptis prospered under Rome, gave birth to Emperor Septimius Severus, outshone neighboring Oea (Tripoli) and Sabratha. The trio of cities (poleis) named the region Tripolis and Tripolitania.

BRIAN BRAKE, RAPHO GUILLUMETTE

Juba of Numidia. Caesar put ashore at Hadrumetum, modern Sousse in Tunisia.

Near his landing place I found women washing newly shorn wool in the sea, pounding it against stones. One offered me something to eat: bread and oil. Once a breadbasket of Rome, Tunisia preserves the traditional food of the ancient world.

South of Sousse a dusty track led to a headland where once stood the flourishing city of Thapsus. Here the armies had met, and here I found a hardscrabble farm inhabited by a family with a camel, two goats, and chickens. Children led me across fields where every step crushed fragments of Roman mosaic and brick, seemingly the city's only remains. Then, atop a mound, they showed me their "secret." I squeezed down through a hole and found myself in a Roman building, cool and dark, with central hall and side rooms.

The battle here in 46 B.C. was brief. The legionaries attacked, the enemy broke, trampled by their own elephants, and Caesar's soldiers butchered everyone they caught. Scipio, Cato, and Juba escaped, only to commit suicide.

Caesar moved on to Utica, Zama, and Carthage. He added Numidia to the province of Africa, heralding a day when Rome's dominion would spread over the continent's entire northern rim. Roman cities would rise amid the mountains of Algeria and Morocco; legionaries would push south into the Sahara to conquer the Fezzan region of Libya.

Back in Rome, the populace welcomed Caesar with a 40-day thanksgiving and cheered themselves hoarse as he staged triumphal processions (page 338). Joyous crowds thronged to wild-beast hunts, gladiatorial combats, mock sea battles. Then came incredible news. Pompey's sons had assembled an army in Spain too tough for Caesar's generals to handle. Again Caesar took to the field, driving his foes across sere Andalusian hills until at Munda, a Roman bastion of which no trace has been found, he defeated them.

When he returned home in 45 B.C., no man or army remained to challenge his supreme power. Plunging into the task of reform, Caesar sent thousands of Romans to build colonies at Corinth and Carthage. To curb conspicuous luxury he limited the use of litters and the wearing of scarlet

ALBERT MOLDVAY, NATIONAL GEOGRAPHIC STAFF

Stark slopes of Andalusia saw Caesar's last great battle

Speeding to Spain to quell a rising led by Pompey's sons, Caesar ran into the toughest fight of the civil war. When he saw his legions give ground, he thought of suicide. But he "rushed . . . like a madman to the forefront of battle," wrote the historian Florus, and rallied his ranks. "He had often striven for victory," said Plutarch, "but now first for his life." Caesar's men drove the foe into Munda, walled the town with corpses, and left staked heads, eyes staring, to guard the grisly rampart.

Police of the Guardia Civil patrol beneath Sierra Nevada ramparts (opposite) in Andalusia, where Caesar campaigned. Speech of vaquero above recalls that of Roman colonists; Spanish, like all Romance tongues, evolved from Latin.

429

robes. He included in the Senate Gauls from northern Italy. His record of public business, posted daily in the Forum, became the world's first "newspaper."

Not even the calendar escaped his attention. To the old one of 355 days, priests added months or days to make it conform to the solar year. But it sometimes fell so far behind that harvest festivals came in the wrong season. Guided by an Alexandrian astronomer, Caesar decreed a 365-day year with an extra day every fourth February—basically our calendar today. To start the year 45 B.C. right, aligned with the seasons, he extended the year 46 to 445 days!

The Senate changed the name of Quintilis, originally the fifth month, to July in Caesar's honor. Augustus would convert Sextilis into August. Because the year began in March rather than January, the Roman numbers seven, eight, nine,

and ten remain embedded in our months of September, October, November, and December.

Caesar thrilled Rome with his reforms, with his plans to beautify the city, with his dreams of new conquest. Yet fear stalked the streets, for his dictatorial ways trampled traditions of the Republic. When tribunes opposed him, he deposed them. His statues began to appear among those honoring the gods. Then came the Lupercalia of 44 B.C., a February festival when half-naked youths ran through the Forum lashing women with thongs—an invocation of fertility. Mark Antony, Caesar's burly lieutenant, ran with

A ROMAN ARMY—*infantry, cavalry, artillery, and baggage train— marches over the Tagus. Caesar bridged Spain's rivers in war. Alcántara's span rose A.D. 105 in a pacified Hispania, source of metals, soldiers, statesmen, poets. Two hundred feet high, 617 feet long, it was built of enduring granite by Spanish-born emperor Trajan. He also raised Segovia's mighty aqueduct (page 9). Both serve today, living symbols of Rome's legacy.*

PAINTING FOR NATIONAL GEOGRAPHIC BY H. M. HERGET

"He was stabbed with three and twenty wounds" *Suetonius*

Ripped by daggers, Caesar falls beside a statue of his dead rival Pompey. Assassins slew him less than a year after his last battle, as he dreamed of new conquests.

Fearing he sought to be king, plotters scrawled "Would that you were alive now, Brutus" on placards by the statue of Lucius Junius Brutus, who had driven monarchy from Rome in the 6th century B.C. They drew his descendant, Marcus Brutus, into the plot. Most came to violent ends, Brutus by his own hand.

Caesar lived on in legend. Romans deified him, told how he had come into the world through an incision in his mother's body — the operation we call "Caesarean." They saw his soul in a comet. He has never ceased to dazzle.

them, a diadem in his hand. Shouldering his way onto the Rostra, the speaker's platform at the edge of the Forum, he sought to place the crown on Caesar's head. A roar of shock rose, reflecting the centuries-old Roman hatred of monarchy. Caesar pushed the diadem away. The crowd cheered.

Still, many were convinced the dictator would take the crown at the first politic moment. Conspirators met. Among the 60 enlisted, some claimed they loved Caesar but loved the Republic more. Envy rankled others. Shakespeare, who drew his characters in *Julius Caesar* from Plutarch, has the lean and hungry Cassius whisper to the respected Brutus: "Why man, he doth bestride the narrow world like a Colossus, and we petty men walk under his huge legs, and peep about to find ourselves dishonorable graves."

There were ominous signs. The diviner Spurinna warned Caesar of danger that would not pass until the Ides of March. The ides, nones, and calends (whence our word "calendar") were days that divided Roman months; in March the ides fell on the 15th. On that day the Senate met in Pompey's Theater, its own meeting place being under repair. Caesar felt ill, but he was persuaded to go by a conspirator. He spied Spurinna and derided him: "The Ides of March have come." The diviner replied, "Ay, Caesar, but not gone."

"ASSASSINATION OF CAESAR" BY GEORGES ROCHEGROSSE; GRENOBLE MUSEUM. OPPOSITE: RE-CREATION OF PLOTTERS' PLACARDS BY A BRONZE BELIEVED TO REPRESENT LUCIUS JUNIUS BRUTUS, C. 3D CENTURY B.C., IN THE PALAZZO DEI CONSERVATORI, ROME; ALBERT MOLDVAY, NATIONAL GEOGRAPHIC STAFF

433

As Caesar took his seat the plotters crowded round, as if to pay their respects. One caught his shoulders. "This is violence," Caesar snapped. Another, from behind, stabbed him below the throat. Caesar struggled to break free. Now, surrounded by daggers, he covered his face. Twenty-three times the blades plunged in. Caesar suffered in silence, though Suetonius records, "that when he saw Marcus Brutus about to deliver the second blow, he reproached him: 'You, too, my son?'" The Senate dispersed in terror, the killers waving bloody daggers.

I strolled the site, today the busy bus-transfer point of the Largo Argentina. At its center—a parklike excavation—a wizened woman scurried amid the ruins, setting out milk for dozens of cats. I turned from their squalling and walked southeast to the Forum. Shadows fell across the Via Sacra. Along this sacred way Caesar's body was borne on an ivory catafalque. From the Rostra Mark Antony eulogized his patron in a speech which, through the genius of Shakespeare, has inspired generations of thespians: "Friends, Romans, countrymen, lend me your ears. I come to bury Caesar, not to praise him. The evil that men do lives after them, the good is oft interred with their bones. So let it be with Caesar. . . ."

The mob went wild. Some threw torches onto the bier. Into the flames actors tossed their robes, soldiers their arms, women their jewelry. Romans thirsted for blood, but the slayers had vanished. All night long mourners watched the flaming bier. The dark stone altar of the ruined Temple of the Divine Julius marks the spot. On it I found a faded rose. *Sic transit gloria.*

T HE ASSASSINS could kill but could not rule. Fifteen years of chaos followed. Cicero was slain, his head and hands nailed to the Rostra. Mark Antony lost his heart to Cleopatra and his fleet to Octavian, Caesar's adopted son. After the defeat at Actium in 31 B.C., the lovers took their own lives in Egypt—Cleopatra with an asp, divine messenger of Egypt's sun god. Caesarion, Cleopatra's 17-year-old son by Caesar, was killed by Octavian as a political rival.

Under Octavian, known to history as Augustus, Rome consolidated its empire, drawing together lands of the Western World in a superstate which, with all its faults, brought peace and order and a better life for millions. Even when barbarian hordes rent that empire, the light of its civilization flickered down the centuries, bursting into flame in the Renaissance, whose radiance shines on us still.

Did Caesar envision Rome's creative role as he struggled to master his world? Or did he seek merely to aggrandize himself, pursuing the will-o'-the-wisp of military glory? I pondered this as my Alitalia jet lifted from Leonardo da Vinci airport into the skies of Rome, bound for a land Caesar never dreamed of but which is enriched by the inheritance he passed on. In months of following his footsteps I watched a ruthless character develop. He had stifled liberty, slaughtered men beyond count, mercilessly destroyed towns. Yet I also saw in him the strengths of the ancient world's giants—the wiliness of Odysseus, the creative leadership of Pericles, the burning ambition of Alexander, the tactical genius of Hannibal. Whether from pride or from vision, in towering over his age, he shaped ours.

ETERNAL ROME —*tumultuous city of Caesar, radiant heart of empire—rests in the soft shadow of twilight. Her day darkened, yet night never came. Her staunch spirit, quickened by the gifts of Athens, transformed by events in distant Judaea, shone forth to light the way of Western man.*

Index

Text references are indicated in roman *type;* illustrations and illustrated text in **boldface.**

*Designates map.

CAPTIVE DIONYSUS, *god of wine, sails a 6th-century* B.C. *cup in Munich's State Museum of Antiquities. When he made their mast sprout grapes, panicked pirates leaped overboard, whereupon he changed them into dolphins. Mycenaean herdsman ropes a bull by the leg on a gold cup (opposite) from a beehive tomb at Vaphio, near Sparta; National Museum, Athens.*

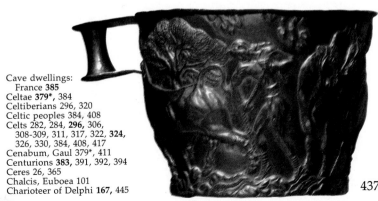

437

Highlights in the building of western culture

Years in this chronology reflect a consensus of scholars; many dates are approximations

GREEK

B.C.

Minoan Age in Crete 2500-1200
Height of Mycenaean civilization 1350

1000

Dorian invasion of Greece 1200

Lycurgus codifies Spartan law c. 800
First recorded Olympic Games 776
Homer composes *Iliad* and *Odyssey* c. 720
Zaleucus of Locri, Magna Graecia, earliest recorded Greek lawgiver, prohibits private vengeance; the state sets the penalty c. 650
Earliest officially coined money in Greece c. 650
Draco codifies the law for Athens 621
Aesop writes *Fables* c. 620-560
Sparta mobilizes permanently after putting down Messenian revolt 620
Solon reforms Athens' aristocratic government c. 593
Thespis introduces independent actor to song-and-dance dithyrambs (dramas) c. 534
Pythagoras, philosopher of Samos, formulates multiplication table c. 530
Athenians expel tyrant Hippias 510
Cleisthenes reorganizes Athens into democracy; institutes ostracism 508

500

Aristagoras leads Ionian Greeks in revolt against Persian rule; Sardis burned 498
Persians burn rebellious Ionian city of Miletus 494
Athenians repel Persians at Marathon 490
Spartans make heroic stand against Persians at Thermopylae; Athenian navy defeats Persian fleet at Salamis 480
Greeks defeat Persian army at Plataea 479
Athens becomes imperial power after taking over Delian League 478
Parmenides, western man's first rationalist, says that reason is only way to truth c. 475
Under Pericles, Athens' Golden Age flourishes 460-430
Athens builds Long Walls to Piraeus 457
Athens accumulates rich treasury, first in European history c. 454
Parthenon begun on Acropolis in Athens 447
Herodotus, "Father of History," writes of Persian wars c. 446
Peloponnesian War breaks out between Athens and Sparta 431
Euripides writes *Medea* 431
Pericles dies in plague that hits Athens 429
Sophocles writes *Oedipus Rex* c. 429
Syracusans wipe out Athenian forces in Sicily 415-413
Aristophanes pleads for peace in *Lysistrata* 411
Thucydides, first critical historian, writes *History of the Peloponnesian War* c. 404
Lysander of Sparta destroys Athenian navy, makes Athens subject city; tyranny replaces democracy during reign of terror 404
Democracy and peace restored in Athens 400
Hippocrates founds school of medicine at Cos c. 400
Antisthenes founds Cynic school of philosophy c. 400

400

ROMAN

Villanovans invade Etruria and Umbria; Latins settle Alban Hills and Palatine Hill, Rome 1000

Etruscans settle in Etruria 1000-80[...]
Tyre founds Carthage c. 814
Legendary founding of Rome by Romulus 753
Romans expel Etruscan king Tarquin the Proud and found the Republic 509

Office of Tribune created to protect rights of plebeians 494
Rome admitted to Latin League 493
Cincinnatus, dictator of Rome, defeats the Aequi 458
Twelve Tables guarantees Romans liberty, property, due process 451
Censors instituted in Rome to take census and assess taxes 443
Carthaginians attack Himera, Sicily 409
Dionysius I, tyrant of Syracuse, makes peace with Carthage 405

Gauls sack Rome c. 387
Office of Consul, chief magistrate, open to plebeians 367
Rome swallows up Latin neighbors 338
Appian Way begun 312

300

ROMAN

WHAT'S NEW IN FASHION? *Diana, Roman goddess of the hunt, models a "Jazz Age" tunic on a 2d-century* A.D. *relief in the Sparta Museum. Lady gymnast wears a 1,600-year-old bikini in a mosaic from a Sicilian villa. Lustrous cityscape (opposite) creates an illusion of space and depth. The fresco brought a "view" to a bedroom wall in a villa built about 50* B.C. *at Boscoreale, near Pompeii; Metropolitan Museum of Art.*

With column and arch, master builders created wonders of Greece and Rome

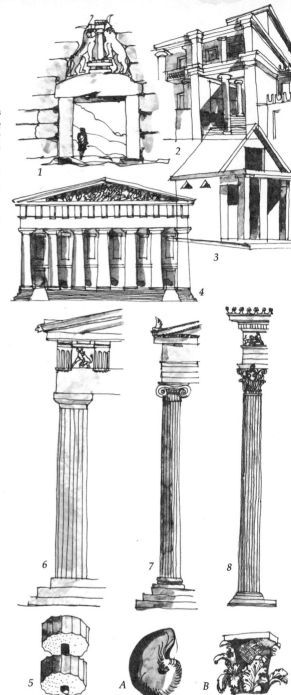

WE BUILD our homes and our cities from blueprints still etched by the vision of the Greeks and the boldness of the Romans. Greek grandeur grew from the simplicity of the post and lintel, which Bronze Age Mycenaeans fashioned when they hoisted a cyclopean stone slab across two massive uprights to form the Lion Gate (1). The same theme reverberates through the sprawling, flat-roofed Minoan palace at Knossos (2), built and rebuilt between the 20th and 15th centuries B.C. Ninth-century B.C. Greeks emerging from their Dark Ages housed images of their gods in tiny temples (3) whose post-and-lintel porticoes sheltered worshipers from rain and sun; pitched roofs were probably thatched.

Greek architects ("master builders") gave splendor to simplicity, transforming humble huts of worship into magnificent temples like that of Zeus (4) at Agrigentum in Sicily. Now the portico surrounds the inner sanctum. The lintel has become a stark architrave crowned by richly embellished frieze and cornice. Posts have evolved into columns, stacks of man-size marble drums (5) held by metal pins. Simplest of the three column styles was the Doric order (6), reaching its high point in the Parthenon (pages 40, 147). Slimmer Ionic (7) thrusts toward a capital with volutes curled like a ram's horn or seashell (A). Callimachus, 5th-century B.C. bronzesmith inspired, the story goes, by acanthus leaves (B) growing rank around a basket on a maiden's grave, designed the ornate Corinthian column (8), named for her town.

Etruscans fostered use of the keystone arch (9) that could carry more and span farther than post and lintel. With the arch, audacious Romans engineered marvels, bridging rivers in one leap (10), or in many (11; page 430). For heroes they raised triumphal arches like that of Titus (12) in Rome. Their barrel vaults (13) crossed to breed the groined vault (14). Tiered vaults of concrete —volcanic sand, stones, and water—ribbed the matchless Colosseum (15; pages 20, 352). A circular sweep of arches domes the Pantheon (16; page 22).

Arch-borne aqueducts defied river (17) and gorge (19), where water dipped, then siphoned back uphill. Mountain tunnels with repair shafts (18) maintained the flow. Pipelines in open terrain (20) tempted tappers.

Scorning detours, Roman road builders bored mountains, filled valleys, stretched causeways over marshes. While engineers with cross-staff and stakes checked level and course, men tamped the bed and fitted blocks on a roadway cambered for drainage (21). Building up stone and concrete in layers—the *strata* that gave us street —they laid enduring roads (page 420), some of which have outlived the empire that built them by 15 centuries.

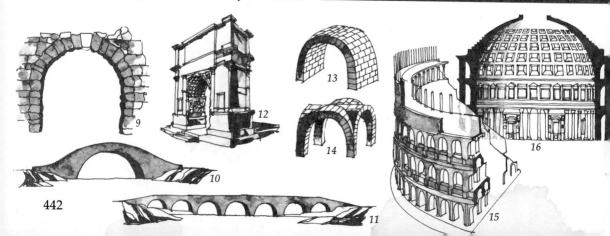

DRAWINGS BY PAUL SALMON

21

18

17

19

20

"Man is the measure of all things"
Protagoras

Cycladic idol, 2000 B.C.;
National Museum, Athens

Minoan terracotta,
1800 B.C.;
Herakleion Museum

Greek kouros (youth),
600 B.C.; Metropolitan
Museum of Art

Discus Thrower, copy
of 450 B.C. Greek bronze;
Terme Museum, Rome

Winged Victory of Samothrace,
Hellenistic, 200 B.C.; the Louvre

Dates are approximations

Etruscan warrior, 480 B.C. terracotta
from Veii; Villa Giulia, Rome

A RTISTS OF GREECE's Golden Age sculptured man with a naturalism that set a standard for 2,400 years. Yet handsome athletes and nymphs of the 5th and 4th centuries B.C. mark but one phase of an art ranging from stylized to realistic.

Geometric idol (upper left) from the Cyclades and rounded, supple statuette from Crete both depict a female figure with folded arms. Helmeted Etruscan with "archaic" smile really may have looked like the Roman below, yet artists portrayed them worlds apart. Greeks adopted Egypt's monumental statuary, but the kouros steps free of encasing stone, tense and alive despite a rigid, archaic pose.

Myron's classically proportioned Discus Thrower evokes effort without strain. Greek sculptors idealized athletes like this and the Charioteer of Delphi (page 167) while humanizing gods and goddesses (pages 24, 106, 141). Soon after Alexander's day an energetic naturalism became the fashion. Masterwork of this Hellenistic style, the Winged Victory lands on a ship's prow with a swirl of clinging drapery. Depictions of beggars and boxers led to Roman realism (pages 372, 432).

The artist, immortalizing his vision of life, shaped our concept of his age. We picture Pericleans as noble (many were not), Etruscans as exotic (from lack of knowledge we cannot deny this), Romans as down-to-earth (which they were).

Caracalla (Roman emperor A.D. 211-17); National Museum, Naples

445

Composition by National Geographic's
Phototypographic Services

Color Separations by Beck Engraving
Company, Philadelphia, Pa., Graphic
Color Plate, Inc., Stamford, Conn.,
The Lanman Company, Alexandria, Va.,
Progressive Color Corporation,
Rockville, Md., Stevenson Photo Color
Company, Cincinnati, Ohio, and R. R.
Donnelley & Sons Co., Chicago, Ill.
Printed and bound by Kingsport Press,
Kingsport, Tenn. Paper by Westvaco
Corporation, New York.

Endsheets crafted by E. N. Crain,
Master Bookbinder, Colonial
Williamsburg Foundation

Acknowledgments and Reference Guide

T HE EDITORS are grateful to many individuals and organizations for the wealth of information they provided. We especially thank Celestine Bruchetti of the Etruscan Academy in Cortona, Italy; Prof. Joël Le Gall, University of Dijon, France; Prof. John F. Latimer of The George Washington University and Prof. Bernard M. Peebles of The Catholic University of America, Washington, D. C.; Richard M. Haywood, Professor of Classics, New York University, and Cornelius C. Vermeule III, Curator of Classical Art, Boston Museum of Fine Arts, for checking paintings; and James A. Cox, who helped write picture captions.

We compared many translations of ancient sources; Lattimore's *The Odyssey of Homer* (Copyright © 1965, 1967 by Richmond Lattimore, published by Harper and Row) proved notably helpful, as did The Loeb Classical Library volumes, Harvard University Press, standard in their fields. Other reliable companions included Lattimore's *The Iliad of Homer*, Ernest Brehaut's *Cato the Censor on Farming*, E. P. Dutton's *Caesar's War Commentaries* by John Warrington, and Penguin Classics' *Livy: The War with Hannibal* by Aubrey de Sélincourt. We regularly turned to *The Oxford Classical Dictionary; The Praeger Encyclopedia of Ancient Greek Civilization; The New Century Classical Handbook; A Companion to Homer* edited by Alan J. B. Wace and Frank H. Stubbings; and *A Companion to Latin Studies* edited by Sir John Sandys.

Books of general scope often consulted were: *A History of the Ancient World* by Chester G. Starr, *An Introduction to the Greek World* by Peter D. Arnott, *A History of Greece* by J. B. Bury, *The Civilization of Rome* by Pierre Grimal, *The World of Rome* by Michael Grant, and *The History of Rome* by Theodor Mommsen. *The Life of Greece* and *Caesar and Christ* by Will Durant, *The Will of Zeus* by Stringfellow Barr, and *Greek Realities* by Finley Hooper made zestful reading.

These volumes furnished more specific glimpses of history: *Greece in the Bronze Age* by Emily Vermeule, *Crete and Mycenae* by Spyridon Marinatos and Max Hirmer, *The World of Odysseus* by M. I. Finley, *Daily Life in the Time of Homer* by Emile Mireaux, *Ulysses Found* by Ernle Bradford, *The Voyages of Ulysses* by Erich Lessing, *The Greeks Overseas* by John Boardman, *Persia and the Greeks* by Andrew Robert Burn, *The World of Herodotus* by Aubrey de Sélincourt, *Ancient Greeks at Work* by Gustave Glotz, *Alexander the Great* and *Hellenistic Civilization* by W. W. Tarn, *The Etruscans* by Raymond Bloch, *The Etruscan Cities and Rome* by H. H. Scullard, *Alps and Elephants* by Sir Gavin de Beer, *Carthage* by Gilbert Charles-Picard, *The Phoenicians* by Donald Harden, *The Legacy of Hannibal* by Arnold Toynbee, *Carthage* by B. H. Warmington, *In Search of Ancient Italy* by Pierre Grimal, *Pom-*

peii and Herculaneum by Marcel Brion, *Daily Life in Ancient Rome* by Jérôme Carcopino, *Everyday Life in Ancient Rome* and *Cicero and the Roman Republic* by F. R. Cowell, *The Celtic Realms* by Miles Dillon and Nora Chadwick, and *Caesar* by J. F. C. Fuller.

We savored the adventure of rediscovery in the early giants of archeology: *Mycenae* and *Troy and Its Remains* by Heinrich Schliemann, and *The Palace of Minos at Knossos* by Sir Arthur Evans. We studied more recent accounts: *Troy and the Trojans* by Carl W. Blegen, *Archaeology Under Water* by George F. Bass, *Pompeii* by Amedeo Maiuri, and Paul L. MacKendrick's surveys of Greek and Roman archeology, *The Mute Stones Speak* and *The Greek Stones Speak*. We also dipped with pleasure into these popular accounts: *The March of Archeology* by C. W. Ceram, *The Bull of Minos* and *Realms of Gold* by Leonard Cottrell, *The Gold of Troy* by Robert Payne, and *From the Silent Earth* by Joseph W. Alsop.

In the field of art we studied *Greek Art* by John Boardman, *The Birth of Greek Art* by Pierre Demarge, *A History of Architecture on the Comparative Method* by Sir Banister Fletcher, *The Art of Roman Gaul* by Marcel Pobé, *Art of the Etruscans* by Massimo Pallottino, and *The Etruscans: Their Art and Civilization* by Emeline Richardson.

Specialized volumes referred to included: *A History of the Greek and Roman Theater* by Margarete Bieber, *The Ancient Engineers* by L. Sprague de Camp, *Coins of the World* by R. A. G. Carson, *The Ancient Explorers* by M. Cary and E. H. Warmington, *The Decipherment of Linear B* by John Chadwick, *Writing* by David Diringer, *The Greek Myths* by Robert Graves, *Mythology* by Edith Hamilton, *Poets in a Landscape* by Gilbert Highet, and *The Ancient Olympic Games* by Heinz Schöbel.

POMPEIAN GIRL *ponders thoughts her* stilus *will record on wax* tabellae; *National Museum, Naples*

An earlier National Geographic book, *Everyday Life in Ancient Times*, contains much on the Greek and Roman periods. The Blue and the Hachette guides furnish detailed information on antiquities of classical lands.

Our editors studied art works and everyday objects from ancient Greece and Rome in the Metropolitan Museum of Art, New York; The Louvre, Paris; the British Museum, London; the Museum of Fine Arts, Boston; the Museum of National Antiquities, Saint-Germain-en-Laye, France; the National Museum, Naples; Villa Giulia, Rome; the National Archeological Museum, Athens; the Carlsberg Glyptothek, Copenhagen; the German Archeological Institute, Rome; the Royal Museum of Art and History, Brussels; the State Museum of Antiquities, Munich; the Staatliche Museen, Berlin; the Vatican Museum, Rome; the Archeological Museum, Florence; the Archeological Museum, Dijon; and the Ashmolean Museum, Oxford.

National Geographic Society staff members in many departments contributed to this book. See listing on following page. Issues of *National Geographic* contain a treasure of information, illustrations, and firsthand accounts of archeology and life in Greece and Rome. Consult the National Geographic Index.